SELF-KNOWLEDGE AND SELF-IDENTITY

CONTEMPORARY PHILOSOPHY

Induction and Hypothesis: A Study of the Logic of Confirmation. By S. F. Barker.

Perceiving: A Philosophical Study. By Roderick M. Chisholm.

The Moral Point of View: A Rational Basis of Ethics. By Kurt Baier.

Religious Belief. By C. B. Martin.

Knowledge and Belief: An Introduction to the Logic of the Two Notions. By Jaakko Hintikka.

Reference and Generality: An Examination of Some Medieval and Modern Theories. By Peter Thomas Geach.

Self-Knowledge and Self-Identity. By Sydney Shoemaker.

SELF-KNOWLEDGE
AND
SELF-IDENTITY

By *Sydney Shoemaker*

CORNELL UNIVERSITY

Cornell University Press

ITHACA, NEW YORK

This work has been brought to publication with the
assistance of a grant from the Ford Foundation.

© 1963 by Cornell University

Cornell University Press

First published 1963
Second printing 1964

Library of Congress Catalog Card Number: 63-13910

To Mollie

Preface

THE topic of this book is not nearly so lofty as its title may suggest. The term "self-knowledge" is used here, not in the Socratic sense, where it refers to something that few are able to attain, but in such a way that a person can be said to have self-knowledge whenever he knows the truth of a statement in which there is reference to himself. And the sense in which I use the term "self-identity" is not the sense in which a man with a good memory of his own past history may be said to lack, or to be struggling to achieve, a sense of his own identity. The problem of self-identity, as I have here been concerned with it, is the same as what is sometimes called the problem of personal identity. I have attempted to show that this problem arises mainly from philosophical views about, and philosophical perplexities about, the nature of self-knowledge, and that its solution consists mainly in the resolution of these perplexities and the correction of mistakes involved in these views. I have not tried to deal with all the topics that have been discussed by writers on self-identity. I have been concerned only incidentally with the notion of identity per se, and I have not at-

Preface

tempted to discuss the possibility of personal survival after death, or the relation of the notion of personal identity to the religious notions of personal immortality and bodily resurrection.

This book grew out of my doctoral dissertation, which was presented to Cornell University in 1958. A paper based on it was read at a symposium on self-identity at the meetings of the Eastern Division of the American Philosophical Association in 1959, and printed, together with Terence Penelhum's contribution to the symposium, in the *Journal of Philosophy*, LVI (October 22, 1959). Brief portions of that paper are incorporated into the present work, and I am grateful to the editors of the *Journal of Philosophy* for permission to reproduce them here. The present version was written mainly during 1960–1961, when I held the Santayana Fellowship at Harvard. I wish to express my thanks to Harvard University for this fellowship, to the Harvard Philosophy Department for their kind hospitality during my year in Cambridge, and to the Cornell Graduate School for a grant covering the cost of the final typing of the manuscript. The earliest versions of this work were read by Professor Norman Malcolm, to whom I am extremely grateful for his many valuable criticisms and for his constant encouragement. I am also grateful to other friends and colleagues who have read and criticized portions of the manuscript or discussed with me the ideas in it; special thanks are due Edmund Gettier, Carl Ginet, Norman Kretzmann, and Nelson Pike. Finally, I wish to thank Professor Max Black, editor of this series, for his encouragement and helpful advice. For whatever inadequacies and mistakes are contained in this work I am of course entirely responsible.

SYDNEY SHOEMAKER

Ithaca, New York
December 1962

Contents

SELF-KNOWLEDGE AND SELF-IDENTITY

One

Self-Knowledge and the Body

1. What we mean when we assert something to be the case cannot be different from what we know when we know that thing to be the case. If we have knowledge of things of a certain kind, and know them in a certain way, and if it is a consequence of some assertion or theory about the nature of those things that they cannot be known, or cannot be known in the ways in which we do in fact know them, then that assertion or theory must be mistaken. An important way of investigating philosophically the nature (essence, concept) of a particular kind of things is by considering how things of that sort are, or can be, known.

As we shall see, however, the epistemological approach to metaphysical questions presents special difficulties when the things under investigation are persons and therefore self-knowers. It is perhaps significant that the word "self" has been more frequently used than the word "person" in the formulation of metaphysical questions. The expressions "personal identity" and "self-identity" are often used interchangeably, and I shall so use them. But while the term "self" is commonly used by philosophers as a synonym of the word "person," the term "self-knowledge" clearly does not mean "knowledge of a person." One's knowledge of oneself is self-knowledge, but one's knowledge of other "selves" is not. The nature of the latter is of course of considerable philosophical interest, and I shall have something to say about it in later chapters. But it is primarily because of the existence and nature of *self*-knowledge, I believe, that there is a special philosophical problem, or set of problems, about the nature of persons (selves) and personal (self) identity. It is with the origin and nature of these problems, and their relation to the problem of self-knowledge, that I shall be concerned in this chapter and the one following.

Understanding a philosophical problem is partly a matter of seeing the plausibility of (which is by no means the same as accepting) the philosophical views that underlie, are presupposed by, the traditional formulations of the problem. In this chapter I often argue for, in an attempt to make plausible, views that in later chapters I argue to be in important respects mistaken. What I claim that it is natural or plausible to say, or that we are "inclined" to say, is often not what I would have us say in the end.

2. As it is normally used in discussions of personal identity, and as I shall use it here, the term "identity" implies persistence, i.e., the existence of one and the same thing at different times. There are of course identity statements, like "Tully is the same person as Cicero," that do not explicitly assert persistence in this sense, and some, like "The lightning flash you saw is the same as the one I saw," that do not even imply it. But when I speak of identity judgments, or identity statements, I shall generally be referring to judgments, or statements, that are expressible in sentences of the form "A, existing

at t_1, is the same as B, existing at t_2," where "t_1" and "t_2" refer to different times. Epistemological questions about identity can be expressed by asking how identity judgments, or identity judgments about objects of such and such a kind, are (or can be) known. Questions about the nature of identity, or about the nature of the identity of a certain kind of things (Φ's), can be expressed by asking "What is it for something (or: a Φ) existing at t_1 to be identical with something (a Φ) existing at t_2?" or "What does it mean to say that something (a Φ) existing at t_1 is the same as something (a Φ) existing at t_2?" or, as an abbreviation of such questions, "In what does identity (or the identity of Φ's) consist?"

In recent discussions the questions "How is the identity of Φ's known?" and "In what does the identity of Φ's consist?" are often reduced to the single question "What, or of what sort, are the *criteria* we use in making judgments about the identity of Φ's?" (or, more briefly, "What are the criteria of Φ-identity?"). For present purposes we may characterize the criteria for the truth of a judgment as those states of affairs that are (whose existence would be) direct and noninductive evidence in favor of the truth of the judgment.[1] A test of whether

---

[1] The sense of "criterion" introduced here and employed throughout this work is intended to be that which has become current through the influence of Wittgenstein's later writings. The sense in which I use the term "evidence," which is broader than that favored by some authors, is such that the criteria for the truth of a judgment, as well as what Wittgenstein would call "symptoms" of its truth, may be called evidence of its truth (for this distinction between criteria and symptoms, see Ludwig Wittgenstein, *The Blue and Brown Books* [Oxford, 1958], pp. 24–25). In this section I attempt only a brief and sketchy account of the notion of criterion, but I shall have more to say about it later on (especially in Chapters Five and Six). Nowhere, however, do I attempt to deal directly with the doubts and difficulties that have been raised concerning this notion in recent philosophical discussion—e.g., by Rogers Albritton in "On Wittgenstein's Use of the Term 'Criterion'" (*Journal of Philosophy*, LVI [Oct. 22, 1959], 845–857)—or to give anything like a complete analysis of it.

something is one of the criteria for the truth of judgments of a certain kind is whether it is conceivable that we might discover empirically that it is not, or has ceased to be, evidence in favor of the truth of such judgments. If it is evidence, and it is not conceivable that it could be discovered not to be (or no longer to be) evidence, then it is one of the criteria. If so and so's being the case is a criterion for the truth of a judgment of Φ-identity, the assertion that it is evidence in favor of the truth of the judgment is necessarily (logically) rather than contingently (empirically) true. We know that it is evidence, not by having observed correlations and discovered empirical generalizations, but by understanding the concept of a Φ and the meaning of statements about the identity of Φ's. It is because there is a necessary relationship between the concept of the identity of a Φ and the criteria for the identity of Φ's that in stating the criteria we can be said to be giving at least part of the answer to the question "In what does the identity of Φ's consist?" The search for the criteria for the truth of a judgment is the search for necessarily true propositions asserting that the existence of certain phenomena or states of affairs is evidence of the truth of the judgment, and the term "criteria" is sometimes used, and I shall sometimes use it, to refer to these propositions (which might be called "criterial rules" or "criterial principles") rather than to the phenomena or states of affairs to which they ascribe evidential status (the status of being "criterial evidence").

What we use as criteria of identity depends on what sort of thing it is about which we are judging.[2] In the case of ordinary "material things," e.g., tables and stones, we can speak of spatiotemporal continuity as a criterion, and as a logically neces-

---

[2] See Terence Penelhum, "Hume on Personal Identity," *Philosophical Review*, LXIV (1955), especially p. 581.

sary (and perhaps sufficient) condition, of identity.[3] But the criteria for the identity of such entities as regiments, corporations, and baseball teams are obviously of quite a different kind. To say what sort of criteria we use in making judgments about the identity of objects of a certain kind is to say something, often a great deal, about the nature (essence, concept) of that sort of objects. Thus it is that the problem of personal identity is a problem about the nature of persons.

3. The problem of self-identity is often characterized as the problem of specifying the criteria of personal identity. But why should *this* be regarded as a philosophical problem? Philosophers do not regard it as their task to investigate the nature of every distinguishable kind of things and do not recognize as many different "problems of identity" as there are different kinds of things. We need to consider why the nature of persons, and of personal identity, is regarded as posing a distinctive philosophical problem in a way in which the nature and identity of other things does not. Until we have done this, any attempt to specify the criteria of personal identity, even if it should yield correct results, is likely to be philosophically unenlightening.

People sometimes become puzzled by the notion of personal identity on being told that during any seven-year period (or so) all the molecules in a human body are replaced by different ones. Clearly, anyone who is puzzled by the notion of personal

---

[3] Roughly speaking, the identity of Φ's involves spatiotemporal continuity if and only if the positions occupied by a Φ during any interval during which it exists must form a continuous line (or, in the special case in which the Φ remains motionless, a single point). This of course does not amount to a definition of identity or persistence in terms of the notion of spatiotemporal continuity, for we presuppose the notion of persistence in speaking of the positions of an object (and therefore of one and the same object) during an interval of time.

identity for this reason should be equally puzzled by the identity of dogs and oak trees. A recent writer describes the problem of personal identity as the problem of "trying to justify a practice which seems at first sight strange, and even paradoxical. This is the practice of talking about people as single beings in spite of the fact that they are constantly changing, and over a period of time may have changed completely." [4] But this again is a problem that can just as well be raised about other things—rivers, bicycles, trees, and the like—as about persons. There is a sense in which persons are "material things." That is, one can ask how tall a person is, how much he weighs, what color he is, and where he is located in physical space. And the way in which we judge concerning the identity of persons can seem (and in most circumstances is) essentially no different from the way in which we judge concerning the identity of other things; as Thomas Reid said, "Our judgments of the identity of objects of sense seem to be formed much upon the same grounds as our judgments of the identity of other persons beside ourselves." [5] There is an equally obvious sense in which persons are a kind of organism, and, more specifically, a species of animal. So the question "What is a person?" *can* be asked in the way in which philosophers sometimes ask questions like "What is a stone?" i.e., as a way of inquiring into the concept of a material thing, and the question "In what does the identity of a person consist?" *can* be asked, like the question "In what does the identity of a dog consist?" because one is puzzled by the notions of identity and persistence, or puzzled by these notions as applied to organisms and artifacts (things which can undergo change of composition). But if, in raising such questions, we are mentioning persons simply

---

[4] Penelhum, "Hume on Personal Identity," p. 571.

[5] *Essays on the Intellectual Powers of Man,* ed. by A. D. Woozley (London, 1941), p. 205.

as examples of things that persist through time, or as examples of material objects or organisms, then we are not raising any problem about persons as such or about *personal* identity as such. And if all our philosophical questions about persons were of this sort, there would be no more reason for speaking of a problem of personal identity than there is for speaking of a problem of canine identity, and there would be no more of a philosophical problem about the nature of persons (as such) than there is about the nature of stones (as such).

While there is a sense in which persons are a species belonging to various genera (organisms, animals, mammals, and so on), this is not how they tend to be regarded in philosophical theories of personal identity. The word "person" is commonly treated, in philosophical discourse, quite differently from those expressions, like "man" and "human being," that might be supposed to be synonymous with it. Locke held that "the identity of man" differs in no essential way from the identity of animals in general. But he made it clear that by "personal identity" he did not mean "the identity of man," and his account of personal identity, unlike his account of the identity of man, is not a case, not even a very special case, of his account of the identity of animals. Some philosophers have held that the identity of persons is not only importantly different from the identity of other things but is the only *real* identity there is, or at least of which we have any knowledge. Thomas Reid said that "the identity . . . which we ascribe to bodies, whether natural or artificial, is not perfect identity; it is rather something which, for convenience of speech, we call identity." [6] Identity, he says, "has no fixed nature when applied to bodies; and questions about the identity of a body are very often questions about words." As applied to persons, however, identity "has no ambiguity and admits not of degrees. It is the founda-

---

[6] *Ibid.*, p. 206.

tion of all rights and obligations, and of all accountableness; and the notion of it is fixed and precise." Bishop Butler said that the word "same," which is used in a "loose and popular sense" when applied to such things as trees, is employed in a "strict and philosophical manner" when applied to persons.[7] If we are to understand the problem of personal identity we must find the source of the plausibility that such views as these have had for philosophers.

It is obvious enough that the existence of a special problem about the nature of persons, and the nature of personal identity, is somehow connected with the fact that persons have minds. It makes no sense to say that a mind *is* a material thing, and there is a philosophical tendency to regard minds as nonphysical entities, to identify persons with their minds, and to equate the question "In what does the identity of a person consist?" with the question "In what does the identity of a mind consist?" Although there is, of course, a sense in which persons are material things, there is often thought to be a much more important sense in which persons are not material things. But in merely pointing out that persons have minds, and that minds cannot be said to be material things, one does not sufficiently explain the plausibility of this view. One philosophical theory, in many respects a very plausible one, does not deny that persons have minds, and does not assert that a mind is a material thing, but nevertheless regards persons as essentially just one of the many kinds of material objects. According to philosophical behaviorism, for something to "have a mind" is simply for it to be a material object that behaves, or is disposed to behave, in certain complicated ways. And if one regards the question "What is a person?" as simply calling for a specification of the criteria for the truth of statements about persons, and takes as

[7] Joseph Butler, "Of Personal Identity," *The Works of Bishop Butler*, ed. by J. H. Bernard (London, 1900), II, 281.

8

one's paradigms of statements about persons those expressed by sentences in which the word "person," or one of its synonyms, is used to designate the subject of discourse (sentences having as grammatical subjects expressions like "that man" and "the person who . . ."), one's account is likely to be that of the behaviorist. Anyone who proceeds in this way is likely to be left wondering why persons have been thought to be radically different in kind from other objects, and why there has been thought to be a special philosophical problem about the nature of persons and personal identity.

4. As indicated in Section 1, I think that it is primarily the way in which first-person statements are made and known, not the way in which third-person statements are made and known, that gives rise to a special problem about the nature of persons and personal identity. It is a striking fact about this problem that, although it concerns the nature of persons, it is often raised by a question that does not contain the word "person" or any synonym of it, namely the question "What am I?" Before considering how the way in which first-person statements are made gives rise to problems about the nature of persons, I must say something about the legitimacy of regarding first-person statements as statements about persons, and of regarding the question "What am I?" as raising a problem about the nature of persons.

If, with Descartes, I ask "What am I?" I clearly assume that I am *something* (that the word "I," when I use it, refers to something). Descartes tells us that he "noticed that while I was trying to think everything false, it must be that I, who was thinking this, was something." [8] It is clear that he regarded it as self-evident that if the statement "I am thinking" is true

---

[8] "Discourse on the Method," *Philosophical Writings*, ed. by G. E. M. Anscombe and P. T. Geach (Edinburgh, 1954), p. 31.

there must be something that is thinking, and that the word "I" must refer to that something. But the self-evidence of this has not always been granted. Lichtenberg remarked that Descartes had no right to say "I think," and was entitled only to say "It thinks," and it is not unreasonable to ask why the "I" in "I am thinking" should not be regarded as like the "it" in "It is raining" and "It is snowing." [9] If this were the correct way of regarding it, of course, then the inference from "I am thinking" to "Something is thinking" (or to "I exist") would be as absurd as the inference from "It is raining" to "Something is raining" (or to "It exists").

At least one valid point can be read into Lichtenberg's remark; namely, the fact that "I" is used as a grammatical subject does not *by itself* justify the idea that this word stands for something, and so is not sufficient to give sense to the question "What am I?" But there is undoubtedly more behind the remark than this. It can easily seem that in the actual making of first-person statements, or at any rate of first-person "experience" or "psychological" statements, the notion that the word "I" refers to something plays no part at all; for me to be entitled to say "I see that it is raining" it seems no more necessary that I should observe, or be able to identify, something designated by the word "I" than that I should observe, or be able to identify, something designated by the word "it." [10] Leibniz remarks that "as I conceive that other beings may also

---

[9] G. E. Moore, in "Wittgenstein's Lectures in 1930–33," reports that Wittgenstein "quoted, with apparent approval, Lichtenberg's saying 'Instead of "I think" we ought to say "It thinks" ' ('it' being used, as he said, as 'Es' is used in 'Es blitzet')" (Moore, *Philosophical Papers* [London, 1959], p. 309). And Bertrand Russell remarks that the grammatical form of "I think" is misleading, and that "It would be better to say 'it thinks in me,' like 'it rains here' " (*The Analysis of Mind* [London, 1921], p. 18).

[10] I shall have a good deal more to say about this later on, especially in Chapter Three.

have the right to say *I*, or that it could be said for them, it is through this that I conceive what is called *substance* in general." [11] But if one is struck by the apparent lack of reference of the word "I" in one's own first-person statements, and ignores, or is not equally struck by, the fact that there are first-person statements that are not one's own, i.e., that other beings say "I" (or "have the right" to say it), it can easily seem that the word "I" does function like the "it" in "It is raining."

This is connected with the problem of solipsism. If one explicitly denies, rather than ignores, the possibility that there are other beings who say "I" in the way one says it oneself, one is maintaining a variety of solipsism. Now as solipsism is often characterized, the solipsist asserts that he is, as a matter of necessity, the only person; he asserts that there is necessarily only one being of a certain kind, and that he (what he calls "I") is that being. But in holding this the solipsist appears to be holding that it is logically impossible for there to be any thinking that is not *his* thinking, any pain that is not *his* pain, and similarly for other psychological states. And it would seem to be a consequence of this that for the solipsist the statement "I am thinking" is logically equivalent to some such statement as "Thinking is going on," the statement "I have a pain" is equivalent to "There exists a pain," and so on. So if solipsism were true, the "I" in the solipsist's statements would seem to be dispensable, or to have a function (or lack of function) rather like the "it" in "It is raining." Russell once suggested that instead of "I think" we should say "It thinks in me" or "There is a thought in me." [12] For the solipsist, however, the "in me" in these statements would seem to add nothing. Solipsism seems to be in a peculiar sense self-defeating, for, if it

---

[11] *Selections*, ed. by P. Wiener (New York, 1951), p. 358.

[12] *Analysis of Mind*, p. 18.

were true, the solipsist's "I" would not refer to the only object of a certain kind, and would not refer at all; the question "What am I?" would be like the question "What is the *it* that rains and snows?" and certainly would not raise the question "What is a person?"

My purpose here is not to refute solipsism. It is rather to indicate what must be the case if one is to use the question "What am I?" to raise a problem about the nature of persons. Unlike the behaviorist, one must be struck with the way in which first-person statements are made, but, unlike the solipsist, one must also be struck with the fact, or at any rate with the possibility, that there are first-person statements that are not one's own. Once one recognizes that "other beings may also have the right to say *I*," one immediately notices that there is what may be called a "logical correspondence" between first-person and third-person statements. The statement "Jones is thinking," said by someone other than Jones, is true when and only when Jones could truly say "I am thinking." Moreover, if asked how we know that Jones is thinking we might very well reply "He says that he is." So when someone says "Jones is thinking," and Jones says "I am thinking," both appear to be saying the same thing, namely that Jones is thinking. But there is no doubt that the word "Jones," in "Jones is thinking," refers to something. It refers to Jones. Since this is so, and since the statement "I am thinking," said by Jones, says the same thing, states the same fact, as the statement "Jones is thinking," said about him, it appears that the word "I," as used by Jones, must also refer to something; like the name "Jones," it must refer to Jones. Questions we can answer by saying "It is Jones" —i.e., questions of the form "Who is it that . . . ?"—Jones can answer by saying "It is I."

The idea that the word "I" stands for or refers to something —an idea that is presupposed by the question "What am I?"

—has its basis, not primarily in the fact that the word "I" functions gramatically as a subject, but in the fact that corresponding to any first-person statement there are third-person statements that are in a certain sense equivalent to it and are certainly "about something." Obviously these third-person statements are about persons. So first-person statements must also be about persons. The word "I" in my first-person statements refers to a person. More briefly, I am a person.

Of course, I am not *only* a person. I am also an American, a mammal, a vertebrate, and a male, to mention just a few of the things I can truly be said to be. But the philosopher who asks "What am I?" is not looking for an answer of the sort "Well, you are a philosopher, a taxpayer, an amateur musician, and many other things." He wants to know, not what things he happens to be, but what he is essentially. We need to consider why the question "What am I?" is commonly regarded as equivalent to the question "What is a person?" in a way in which it is not equivalent to, for example, the question "What is a vertebrate?"

If the word "person" were a classificatory term on a level with "animal," "vertebrate," "mammal," "*homo sapiens*," and the like, it should be possible for someone to understand the term "person" and yet be unaware that it is applicable to himself. Certainly someone could know the definition of the term "vertebrate" and be able to apply the criteria for determining whether something is a vertebrate without ever thinking of applying these criteria to himself. And it does not seem inconceivable that someone might discover that he is not a vertebrate. Statements like "I am a vertebrate," "I am a blond," and "I am an American" are contingent statements, which could be false. And if the term "person" were like "vertebrate," "blond," and the like, the same should be true of the statement "I am a person."

Locke discusses the possibility that there could be a "very intelligent rational parrot" which could "discourse, reason and philosophize." [13] He was anxious to deny that such a parrot, should it exist, could be called a *man*. But Locke defines "person" as meaning "a thinking intelligent being, that has reason and reflection, and can consider itself as itself, the same thinking thing, in different times and places," [14] and it follows from this definition that such a parrot would be a *person*. The parrot would speak falsely if it said "I am a man," but it would speak truly if it said "I am a person." For on Locke's definition of "person," the statement "I am a person" turns out to be necessarily self-verifying; if it is asserted, then, no matter what asserts it (be this man, beast, or god), it must be true. We distinguish between the making of an assertion and the mere uttering of the words in a sentence. A machine can produce the sounds I produce when I say "It is raining," but a machine cannot be said to have asserted that it is raining. To assert something one must understand the words one is using, and to understand anything at all one must be "a thinking intelligent being, that has reason and reflection." If something produces any sentence whatever, it is either uttering the words as a machine might, in which case it asserts nothing, and therefore nothing that is true or false, or else it is making an assertion, in which case it is, by Locke's definition, a person. So on this definition it is logically impossible for the sentence "I am a person" to be used to make a false statement. Either it makes no assertion at all, or it makes one that is true. It is necessarily the case that it is true if asserted.

Locke's definition of "person" is plausible. We do tend to regard it as a necessary truth that persons, and only persons,

[13] *An Essay concerning Human Understanding*, ed. by Fraser (Oxford, 1894), I, 446.

[14] *Ibid.*, p. 448.

are capable of thought, reason, and understanding. And this does suggest, what Locke thought, that there is a difference in meaning between "person" and "man," if the latter is taken to denote a certain biological species. If one thinks, with the behaviorist, that statements like "He understands what he is saying" are translatable into statements about behavior, one might accept this definition and nevertheless hold that the word "person" simply refers to material objects that behave in certain complicated ways, and that it does not differ in kind from classificatory terms like "vertebrate" and "member of the species *homo sapiens.*" But the argument of the preceding paragraph seems to give the word "person" a special status. While there is a sense in which what I am, what the word "I" when I use it refers to, is anything that I can truly be said to be, it now appears that the sense in which I am a person, or in which "I" stands for a person, is different from the sense in which I am, or in which "I" stands for, a mammal, an American, or a male. It is only contingently true that I am a mammal or an American. But since the word "I" refers to the being that is using it to refer, it necessarily refers to a person. So there is an urge to say that what I am essentially is a person, and that it is only *per accidens* that I am the other things that I can truly be said to be. And now it seems that if I can discover what I am, I will thereby know what sort of thing a *person* is. Locke was perhaps giving expression to this idea when he wrote "*Person,* as I take it, is the name of this self. Wherever a man finds what he calls himself, there, I think, another may say is the same person." [15]

5. As the behaviorist points out, discourse about a person, where the person is other than the speaker, necessarily involves reference to the body of that person. The subject of a state-

---

[15] *Ibid.,* pp. 466–467.

ment about a person is commonly identified by pointing toward a body, by use of physical descriptions ("the tall man with red hair"), or by use of names whose reference can be explained by pointing or by physical descriptions. Moreover, we come to know the truth of statements about other persons by observing their behavior (including, of course, their verbal behavior), and this is the behavior of a human body, a "material object."

But the case is strikingly different with many of the statements we make about ourselves. To consider first the matter of identification and reference, suppose I make the statement "I have a toothache." Someone else, not knowing who is speaking, might ask for an identification of the person with the toothache, and I might oblige by saying "I am the tall man sitting at the typewriter." But in saying this I would not be explaining what I had *meant* by the word "I" in my statement, and it is not a condition of my being able to use the word "I" that I must always be capable of providing such a description of myself in physical terms. In no sense do I use the word "I" as an abbreviation for any physical description of myself. If it should turn out that I am having an hallucination, and that the description "the tall man sitting at the typewriter" does not apply to me, I would have to withdraw or amend the statement "The tall man sitting at the typewriter has a toothache," but would not have to withdraw or amend my statement "I have a toothache."

It thus appears that reference to oneself, at least in the case of what I shall call "first-person psychological statements" (e.g., "I have a toothache," "I believe that it will rain," and the like), is not reference to one's body. But it also seems that one knows the *truth* of first-person psychological statements quite apart from knowing anything about one's body. Certainly I do not have to observe my bodily behavior in order to be entitled to say "I have a toothache," "I am thinking about this book," or "I want to go to the movies." My knowledge of the truth of these statements, and of many others, appears to be independent of whatever knowledge I have of my body. But the subject of all of these statements is the word "I," and this word necessarily refers to a person. So it appears that I can make statements that are about a person, that do not refer to any body, and whose truth I can know without referring to any body. But "other beings have also the right to say *I*"; these considerations apply to others and the statements they make in the first person as well as to me and the statements I make in the first person. And if of every person there can be knowledge (its own) that is not knowledge of a material object, it seems to follow that persons are not, or at least are not essentially, material objects.

There is an inclination to express the argument above by saying "When I am in pain I know that I am, and it doesn't matter what is true of my body, or even whether I *have* a body." Perhaps one closes one's eyes and says "For all I know for certain, my body has just vanished, yet there can be no doubt that I am in pain." Here we are getting close to Descartes's *Cogito* argument. For Descartes argued that since he could doubt the existence of bodies, but could not doubt the existence of himself, he could not be a body. At one point he considers what, before his doubt, "used to occur to me spontaneously and naturally whenever I was considering the question 'what am I?'" and says: "First came the thought that I had a face, hands, arms—in fact the whole structure of limbs that is observable also in a corpse, and that I called 'the body.'" [16] But while he could not doubt the truth of statements like "I am thinking," he could doubt the existence of any such body. "I am not that set of limbs called the human body . . . but I still have the

---

[16] "Meditations on First Philosophy," *Philosophical Writings*, pp. 67–68.

assertion 'nevertheless I am something.' " [17] The question "What am I?" thus became for Descartes a question about the nature of a nonbodily "something."

Of course, first-person "psychological" statements are by no means the only sort of first-person statements. And sometimes the word "I" does seem to refer to a body, e.g., in the statement "I am over six feet tall." But it no more follows from the truth of such statements that a person *is* his body than it follows from the truth of statements like "I am out of gas" that a person *is* his automobile. It is natural to say that in the statement "I am out of gas" the word "I" is not really being used to refer to oneself, but is rather an abbreviation for the words "my car." Strictly speaking, it is not I, but rather something that belongs to me, that is out of gas, has been running on two cylinders, and needs a new coat of paint. And it can seem that the word "I" in "I am over six feet tall" is really an abbreviation for the words "my body," and that it is not really I, but rather something that in some way belongs to me, that is over six feet tall, weighs one hundred and fifty pounds, and has a certain physical and chemical composition. Of my first-person statements it is the psychological statements that seem most clearly to be statements about a person, and therefore to be really about myself rather than about something belonging to me, for they, unlike statements ascribing height, weight, and the like, are statements that could be made *only* about "a thinking intelligent being, that has reason and reflection" (Locke's definition of "person"). And it is just these statements that I can know to be true quite apart from knowing anything about my body.

6. From the view that a person (or self) is something logically distinct from a human body it may seem to follow that the identity of a person is not the same as, and does not neces-

---

[17] *Ibid.*, p. 69.

sarily involve, the identity of that person's body. On this view there would appear to be no logical reason, though there may be causal reasons, why I should not continue to exist without my body's continuing to exist, and why I should not have existed at some time in the past when it did not exist. And even if what is now my body has existed as long as I have existed, it does not seem necessary that it should always have been *my* body (just as it is not necessary that what is now my car should have been my car as long is it has existed).

But the most that follows from the argument of Section 5 is that some facts about a person are not facts about that person's body, or, as it might be expressed, that some properties of persons are nonphysical properties. Only if we take the word "body" to mean "something *all* of whose properties are physical properties" can we conclude from this argument that a person is not a body. And that something is not a body in *this* sense does not imply that it is a completely nonphysical entity, that it does not have physical properties as well as nonphysical ones, or that its identity does not involve the identity of a body. Of course, if one thinks with Descartes that one can significantly deny that there are objects having physical properties, and can significantly conjoin this denial with an affirmation of one's own existence, one can conclude that one is (and therefore that at least one person is) something that could conceivably exist without having physical properties. But even from this it does not follow that one (or a person) is a nonphysical entity. From the fact that a thing *could* exist without having physical properties it certainly does not follow that it *does* exist without having physical properties, and it therefore does not follow that the physical properties that appear to belong to the thing must really be properties of some different thing (its body) which is somehow connected with it.[18]

---

[18] Descartes was perhaps aware of this. In replying to Hobbes's objections he says that in the "Second Meditation" he did not assume (and, by im-

In any case, the argument of Section 5 is only analogous to, and not identical with, Descartes' *Cogito* argument. It does not assume that one can know one's own existence without knowing that one has a body, but assumes only that one can know some truths about oneself without knowing any facts about one's body that are relevant to these truths, and so does not lead even to the conclusion that a person could exist without having physical properties.

While the argument of Section 5 may make plausible the view that personal identity is logically independent of bodily identity, its conclusion does not entail this view. In the following sections I shall be considering an argument (or a class of related arguments) that has been thought to establish this view. Unlike the argument of Section 5, this argument rests directly on a consideration of the ways in which judgments of personal identity are known. The argument, or rather what I shall call the "third-person version" of it, is to the effect that the criteria we use in making identity judgments about persons other than ourselves are, at bottom, psychological (or "mental") criteria rather than physical criteria, i.e., that questions of personal identity are most definitively settled by reference to the psychological rather than the physical features of persons.

7. Our identity judgments about persons other than ourselves are most commonly based on similarity of bodily appearance. Normally I need only look at a person in order to know whether he is the friend with whom I spent the previous day. Of course, similarity of appearance cannot be the sole criterion of personal identity, and perhaps cannot be said to be a *criterion* at all. Two different persons can look exactly alike

---

plication, did not prove) that what is conscious is not something "corporeal," but "left it quite undecided until the sixth Meditation, where it is proved" (*Philosophical Writings*, p. 130).

(as with "identical" twins), and the appearance of one and the same person at different times may be totally different (the infant becomes a man, and the hunted criminal disguises himself or undergoes plastic surgery). But even when we cannot use similarity of appearance as our evidence, or as our sole evidence, of personal identity, we can often make judgments of personal identity on the basis of purely physical considerations. If I have before me a pair of identical twins, quite indistinguishable in appearance, I may know that it was this one, and not the other, who made a certain remark this morning, for I may have been with him ever since without ever having lost sight of him. The man who is unrecognizable to those who have not seen him since his childhood may be perfectly recognizable to me, for I may have grown up with him and observed his gradual change. And I may be able to identify the disguised criminal, not through any defect in his disguise, but because I happened to be looking on while he was disguising himself. The grounds I would have for my identity judgments in these cases would be like those I might have for an identity judgment about any "material object"; roughly, my judgments would be based on observed continuity of change and, most important, observed spatiotemporal continuity.

But there is no doubt that our grounds for making identity judgments about other persons sometimes involve psychological considerations. I might know that this twin is John, not Tom, because he is lively and good humored. Better still, I might know that this is John because he remembers, is able to describe in detail, events that happened yesterday while John was present and Tom was not. Similarly in the case of the disguised criminal. Detective-story writers are fond of the device of having a criminal "give himself away," either by revealing his "true character" in some remark or action or by inadvertently revealing knowledge of something, e.g., the time at which the crime was committed, that no innocent person could be in a position to know.

That we sometimes use psychological facts about persons as grounds for identity judgments about them, however, in no way implies that our criteria of personal identity are even partly, let alone wholly, psychological. It is certainly a fact that the personality, character, and interests of a person can generally be counted on to remain relatively unchanged for long periods of time. It is also a fact that only someone who was present when an event occurred, who witnessed it or knew of it in some equally direct way (e.g., knew of it because it was his own voluntary action) at the time of its happening, will later on be able, without inferring inductively from later observations and without relying on the testimony of others, to give correct and detailed descriptions of the event. But so far we have found no reason for thinking that the facts just mentioned are not purely contingent facts that have been discovered empirically by the use of bodily identity as the criterion of personal identity. We have found no reason to suppose that these facts are in any way involved in the meaning of "same person."

8. There is, however, an argument of considerable plausibility, which I shall call the "change-of-body argument," that purports to show that at least some of our criteria of personal identity are psychological criteria. Locke remarks that "should the soul of a prince, carrying with it the consciousness of the prince's past life, enter and inform the body of a cobbler, as soon deserted of his own soul, every one sees that he would be the same *person* with the prince, accountable only for the prince's actions." [19] Locke had the idea that a person might cease to have the body that had been "his" in the past and come to have a different body. The change-of-body argu-

---

[19] *Essay*, I, 457.

ment tries to give sense to precisely this idea by describing conceivable circumstances in which, it is said, we would be forced (or at least would find it natural) to say that such a change of body (or bodily transfer) had occurred. I shall now consider one such ostensible case of bodily transfer.

It is now possible to transplant certain organs, e.g., eyes and lungs, from one body to another in such a way that the organ continues to function in its new setting. Physiologists may have grounds for thinking that this cannot be done with human brains, but it is at least conceivable (logically possible) that a human body could continue to function normally if its brain were replaced by one taken from another human body. So let us imagine the following. First, suppose that medical science has developed a technique whereby a surgeon can completely remove a person's brain from his head, examine or operate on it, and then put it back in his skull (regrafting the nerves, blood-vessels, and so forth) without causing death or permanent injury; we are to imagine that this technique of "brain extraction" has come to be widely practiced in the treatment of brain tumors and other disorders of the brain. One day, to begin our story, a surgeon discovers that an assistant has made a horrible mistake. Two men, a Mr. Brown and a Mr. Robinson, had been operated on for brain tumors, and brain extractions had been performed on both of them. At the end of the operations, however, the assistant inadvertently put Brown's brain in Robinson's head, and Robinson's brain in Brown's head. One of these men immediately dies, but the other, the one with Robinson's body and Brown's brain, eventually regains consciousness. Let us call the latter "Brownson." Upon regaining consciousness Brownson exhibits great shock and surprise at the appearance of his body. Then, upon seeing Brown's body, he exclaims incredulously "That's me lying there!" Pointing to himself he says "This isn't my body; the one over there is!" When asked his name he automatically replies "Brown." He recognizes Brown's wife and family (whom Robinson had never met), and is able to describe in detail events in Brown's life, always describing them as events in his own life. Of Robinson's past life he evidences no knowledge at all. Over a period of time he is observed to display all of the personality traits, mannerisms, interests, likes and dislikes, and so on that had previously characterized Brown, and to act and talk in ways completely alien to the old Robinson.

What would we say if such a thing happened? There is little question that many of us would be inclined, and rather strongly inclined, to say that while Brownson has Robinson's body he is actually Brown. But if we did say this we certainly would not be using bodily identity as our criterion of personal identity. To be sure, we are supposing Brownson to have *part* of Brown's body, namely his brain. But it would be absurd to suggest that brain identity is our criterion of personal identity. For if the outcome of the brain transfer were different than I have imagined, and if upon regaining consciousness Brownson were to act and talk just as Robinson had always done in the past, surely no one would say that this man, who looks, acts, and talks just like Robinson, and has what has always been Robinson's body, must really be Brown rather than Robinson because he has Brown's brain. Here we would conclude simply that there is not the close causal relationship we had supposed there to be between the state of man's brain and his psychological features, i.e., his personality and his ability to report events in his past history. If we did not think there to be such a causal relationship we should not think that having the same brain has anything more to do with being the same person than, say, having the same liver. But whatever relationship there is between the state of one's brain and the state of one's mind (i.e., one's psychological features) is surely causal and contingent, not logically necessary. Brownson's possession of Brown's brain makes his psychological affinity to the old Brown (in my original case) causally intelligible, rules out the possibility of a hoax (e.g., the possibility that Robinson has been "primed" with information about Brown's past and is merely pretending to be Brown), and disinclines us to say (as we might be inclined to say of other alleged cases of bodily transfer imagined by philosophers) that the psychological affinity is merely "coincidental." But it cannot itself be our grounds for saying, or being inclined to say, that Brownson is Brown. If we say the latter, as there is certainly an inclination to do, it seems that we must be using psychological criteria of personal identity and allowing these to override the fact of bodily nonidentity.

9. The sort of argument just presented I shall call the "third-person version" of the change-of-body argument. This argument tries to persuade us that personal identity does not involve, or at least does not entail, bodily identity, and that our criteria of personal identity are, at least in part, psychological criteria. It tries to do this by forcing us to reflect on the weight we give to psychological considerations in making judgments about the identity of other persons. Having tried to make this argument as plausible as possible, I shall now argue that it is, in a certain sense, inconclusive. I do not mean that it fails to show that change of body is possible or that some of our criteria of personal identity are psychological; whether this is so I shall not attempt to decide here.[20] What it fails to do, taken by itself, is to provide any for support the Cartesian conception of a person as an essentially nonphysical entity, or for the view that personal identity is different, in a philosophically significant way, from the identity of other things.

To begin with, the immediate conclusion of the change-

---

[20] I return to this question in Chapter Six, Section 8.

of-body argument, namely that change of body is logically possible and that our criteria of personal identity include psychological criteria, is perfectly compatible with philosophical behaviorism. The behaviorist, since he holds that all psychological statements are reducible to statements about behavior, can regard psychological features as simply a special, no doubt very complicated, sort of physical feature. So he might say that my brain-transfer case, while it does show that some of the criteria of personal identity are psychological criteria, is far from showing that these are not physical criteria. After all, he could point out, it is the *behavior* of Brownson that inclines us to say that he must be Brown. The behaviorist could admit that the identity of persons differs from the identity of human bodies, if the criterion for the latter is spatiotemporal continuity, but he could maintain at the same time, without contradicting the conclusion of the change-of-body argument, that all the properties of persons can be regarded as physical properties (behavioral dispositions and so forth) and that there is therefore an important sense in which persons are material objects. It is compatible with behaviorism, indeed with the crudest forms of materialism, to think of human minds as sets of behavioral dispositions, and one need not accept anything like the Cartesian conception of the soul in order to employ criteria of identity that would permit one and the same set of dispositions to exist in different bodies at different times.

My second point is that reflection on the third-person version of the change-of-body argument, even if it leads one to accept its immediate conclusion, can easily lead one away from rather than toward the view that there is a philosophically important difference between the identity of persons and the identity of other things. It can lead to the view that what Reid said about the identity of bodies (intending to contrast this with personal identity), namely that it is simply "something which, for convenience of speech, we call identity" and that questions about it are "very often questions about words," is equally true of personal identity.

There are two different senses, I think, in which questions of identity can be "questions about words." First, it seems to be sometimes a matter of linguistic convention that one thing rather than another is the criterion for the identity of objects of a certain kind. I can refer to something as the bicycle I bought ten years ago even though most, perhaps even all, of its original parts have long since been replaced. If someone finds this puzzling, I might say that this is simply how we use the word "same" as applied to bicycles, and that while we *could have* adopted a convention whereby a bicycle existing at t_2 is called the same as one that existed at t_1 only if it has the very same parts as the earlier one, this is not the convention we have in fact adopted. It is not a matter of linguistic convention, of course, that the bicycle I have now is related as it is to the bicycle I bought ten years ago, e.g., that while they have few parts in common they both have a large number of parts in common with a bicycle that existed five years ago. But it does seem to be in some sense a matter of linguistic convention that if a present bicycle is empirically related in certain ways to a past one it can be said to be the same as the past one. Now the third-person version of the change-of-body argument gives us no reason for thinking that questions about the identity of persons are not "questions about words" in this sense. And much of the sting of the argument, its appearance of showing that persons are a very peculiar sort of object, seems to be removed if one says "If the behavior of a person existing at t_2 is related in such and such ways to the behavior of a person existing at t_1 (e.g., as Brownson's behavior is related to Brown's in my example), then the person existing at t_2 is the same as the person existing at t_1, for this is just what we *call* 'being the same' in the case of persons." In the words of a recent writer, "Questions about the nature of personal identity are questions about the meaning of the phrase 'personal identity.' And these questions can be decided in one way only, namely, by ascertaining the way in which the phrase is used by English-speaking people. When we have ascertained the conventional usage, we have done all we can." [21] If one thinks in this way, the alleged fact that a person can change bodies can seem no more remarkable than the fact that a bicycle can "remain the same" despite the replacement of some, perhaps all, of its parts. We are not inclined to say that the identity of a bicycle consists in something "inner" and nonphysical, so why should we say this of persons?

But questions about identity can sometimes be said to be "questions about words" in the more ordinary sense of being "verbal questions," i.e., questions that, though sounding like questions about matters of fact, cannot be answered by an appeal to facts and already accepted criteria or conventions, and can be "settled" only by a decision, or agreement, as to how certain words are to be used. Most questions about identity can be settled by the discovery of empirical facts. If I want to know whether this is my coat, I look to see whether there is a coffee stain on the sleeve, whether the lining is torn, and so on. But sometimes questions of identity arise even when all the relevant facts are known. In 1944 the Germans destroyed the four-century-old bridge of Santa Trinita in Florence. Six years later it was decided that it (?) should be rebuilt. On the original site there now stands a bridge of a design exactly like that of the original, constructed by Renaissance techniques, and built in part with the original stones (each standing in its original place), in part with new stones taken from the original quarry. The facts are all clear, but how are we to answer the question

---

[21] D. J. O'Connor, *John Locke* (London, 1952), p. 121.

Self-Knowledge and the Body

"Is the present bridge of Santa Trinita the very bridge that spanned the Arno four hundred years ago?" One can imagine one person saying "This is a modern copy of a Renaissance bridge that once stood here," and another, equally cognizant of the facts, saying "This bridge has been the pride of Florence for four centuries." Suppose that these two persons were to get into a dispute as to whether the present bridge is "the same as" the original one. Clearly no factual considerations could settle the issue between them. And a third person might say, not unreasonably, "You are just disputing about words. You are agreed about the facts, so it doesn't matter whether you call it the same bridge or not. Or, if you must call it one or the other, why don't you adopt a definition of 'same bridge' that will settle the issue?"

Verbal disputes are not always idle disputes. If one has an attitude of reverence or awe toward ancient structures, one might, not unreasonably, resist accepting a criterion of sameness that would oblige one to say that something recently "restored" is hundreds of years old. Even when questions about identity are verbal, they are not always settled by *arbitrary* decisions; reasons can be given for settling them in one way rather than in another. But since such questions arise because the cases in question are borderline cases, not clearly decidable by the usual criteria of identity, the giving of reasons will consist, not in citing evidence or stating what the criteria are, but in arguing for the adoption of new or modified criteria. And in a dispute about what criteria we should adopt, or how our present criteria should be modified, there is little to appeal to except pragmatic considerations. If tradition or the law should prescribe that for twenty years after a new bridge is built it must be a toll bridge, the authorities might have to lay down criteria that distinguish sharply between the building of a new bridge (perhaps on the site of an old one) and the restoring

29

of an old bridge. And in deciding what criteria to adopt they would probably take into account such factors as, on the one hand, the need of the state for new revenue, and, on the other, the ability and willingness of the users of the bridge to pay the toll.

Returning to my brain-transfer case, I think that most people will be somewhat uncertain how the question "Is Brownson the same person as Brown?" should be answered. Now someone could be uncertain about this because he has not been told how Brownson behaves in certain situations and answers certain questions, whether Robinson knew Brown well prior to the brain transfer, and so on. But I do not think that our uncertainty is of this kind. If it were, we could easily eliminate it by including the required information, about Brownson's behavior and the attendant circumstances, in our description of the case. But if, given all the relevant facts, we continue to raise the question "Is Brownson the same person as Brown?" and to be uncertain as to how it should be answered, our question would seem to be a "question about words" in the second sense described above, in which case our present criteria of personal identity do not clearly decide the question and the case described is a "borderline case" of personal identity. So it might appear that here, as in the case of the bridge, "we can say what we like so long as we are clear about the facts." And if we feel that we must decide the question in one way or the other, it would seem that in doing so we would be adopting a new criterion, or modifying our old criteria, and that our decision would be arbitrary or made on pragmatic grounds. One can easily think of pragmatic considerations that would be relevant. On the one hand, it would clearly be easier for us to talk to Brownson, and easier for him to talk to us, if we regard him as Brown rather than as Robinson. On the other hand, if we say that he is Brown, and thus assert personal identity in the absence of bodily identity, we would create a precedent that could conceivably give rise to legal difficulties, for example, by making it difficult to prove that someone is an impostor, and thus not entitled to an inheritance, or that someone is guilty of a crime he apparently has no memory of committing.

But when Reid said that questions of identity are often questions about words, he did not mean this to apply to questions about the identity of persons. He was talking about the identity of "bodies," which he says is not "perfect identity" but rather "something which, for convenience of speech, we call identity." And he goes on to contrast the identity of bodies with the identity of persons, saying "But identity, when applied to persons, has no ambiguity and admits not of degrees, or of more or less." When identity is ascribed to persons, he says, "the notion of it is fixed and precise." [22] Since one of the effects of the third-person version of the change-of-body argument is to raise doubts whether the notion of personal identity is "fixed and precise," this argument can hardly be said to support the idea to which Reid here gives expression. I think that Reid, in common with many other philosophers, thought that questions of personal identity are not "questions about words" in either of the senses I have described. To find the source of this view, as well as of the view that the criteria of personal identity are nonphysical, we must look beyond the third-person version of the change-of-body argument.

10. There would appear to be at least one person who could not regard the question whether Brownson is Brown as a "question about words" in either of the senses discussed above. Brownson himself, it would seem, could hardly regard this question as one to be settled in the ways discussed in the preceding section. Brownson says that he is Brown, but if asked

[22] *Essays*, p. 206.

why he says this *he* would hardly reply, as someone else might, "Well, this (exhibiting behavior that is related in such and such ways to the behavior of someone existing in the past) is what we *call* 'being the same' in the case of persons, or at any rate it is what, for pragmatic reasons, we ought to call 'being the same' in cases like this one."

We might try to regard Brownson's remarks as just part of the behavior ("the verbal behavior") that we have to take into account in making our judgment about him. No one, however, can regard his own remarks as "mere behavior." And I think that the change-of-body argument is most persuasive, not when we consider the behavior of Brownson as it is observed by other persons, but when we "put ourselves" in Brownson's place. We can most easily bring out what I think to be the real force of this argument by expressing it in the first person.

It seems to me that I can imagine being in the position of the Brownson of my example. I can imagine waking up after an operation and being surprised by the appearance of my body (e.g., as seen in a mirror). I can imagine seeing another body, which I recognize (or seem to recognize) as my body of the previous day, and being told that the brain from that body had been placed in the skull of my present one. And I can imagine being told that the things I claim to have done in the past were done, not by the person whose body was the one I have now, but by the person whose body I seem to recognize as the one I had in the past. How, if this happened, would *I* react to the questions that others would raise concerning my identity?

Let us imagine that I have found myself in the position just described, and that I am listening to a debate whether I am S. S., the person who did certain things in the past, things which, as a matter of fact, I have a clear memory of doing. It is agreed by all concerned that the body of S. S. (or at any rate the body S. S. had in the past) is now a corpse, and that my present body is the body (or at any rate the former body) of someone of whose past history I have no knowledge at all. It is also agreed that my memory claims correspond to facts about the past history of S. S., that my interests, tastes, mannerisms, personality traits, and the like closely resemble those of S. S., and so on. Naturally I agree with those who say that I am S. S. But their reasons for saying that I am S. S. can hardly be my reasons for saying this. I say that I am S. S., not because I claim to remember doing the things that S. S. did, but because I do remember doing those things. The fact that I have S. S.'s brain, and the known facts concerning the causal relations between brain states and psychological states, would perhaps carry a good deal of weight with others, but they would carry little weight with me; there is no need of something to convince me, though there might well be a need of something to convince others, that I am not trying to perpetrate a hoax. And if I clearly remember doing something, I have no choice but to believe that I did do that thing, whether or not I can think of something that explains my ability to remember doing it. Other persons may be convinced that I am S. S., not simply because I display knowledge of S. S.'s past history, but also because my interests, mannerisms, and so on are like those exhibited by S. S. in the past. But the latter fact, again, would carry little weight with me, for if I were to remember doing a certain thing, and were to remember having at the time a set of interests, mannerisms, and so on quite unlike those I have now, I would still have to say that I am the person who did that thing. And while I would doubtless agree that there are "pragmatic reasons" for regarding me as S. S., I might well admit that there are equally strong, perhaps stronger, pragmatic reasons for not regarding me as S. S. But I do not express my memory of eating eggs for breakfast by saying "I had eggs for breakfast" because I think that it is convenient, or advisable, that such memories be expressed in this way; I do so because my memory is, precisely, a memory that *I* had eggs for breakfast.

In Section 5 we saw that one appears to know certain statements about oneself, statements like "I have a toothache," quite independently of knowing anything about one's body. We might express the point of the "first-person version" of the change-of-body argument by saying that a similar thing is true of another class of statements about oneself, namely memory statements about one's own past history. It would be absurd to suppose that a person must observe his body or behavior before he can be entitled to say "I have a toothache," and I dramatized this point in Section 5 by saying that when I know I have a toothache I don't even have to know whether, and it doesn't seem to matter whether, I have a body. The change-of-body argument, or rather the first-person version of it, dramatizes the point about memory statements in a similar way. One's statements about one's own past, when made on the basis of memory, are not grounded on bodily identity, or spatiotemporal continuity, as a criterion of personal identity; they are not grounded on the knowledge of *any* physical relationship between one's present body and a past one. Nor does one rely on one's memories of one's past because one has discovered, using physical criteria of identity, that such memories are usually accurate; on the contrary, one could not discover the truth of any judgment of bodily identity, or apply any physical criterion of identity, without already relying on one's memories. It would be absurd to suggest that in order to be entitled to say "I remember taking a walk last night" I must first examine my body and satisfy myself that it is the same as some particular body that existed last night. From my point of view it seems unessential that the body I have now be the body I had when I took the walk; if I remember going for a walk then I did go for a walk, no matter what my present body was doing at the time.

11. If one raises the problem of personal (self) identity by asking "In what does *my* identity consist?" it will be natural for one to conclude that personal identity cannot consist in or essentially involve the identity of a human body, and that the sorts of bodily and behavioral evidence which in everyday life we accept as establishing the truth of judgments of personal identity cannot constitute *criteria*, though they may well constitute good inductive evidence, for the truth of those judgments. If there are any criteria of personal identity, one supposes, these must be criteria that one uses in making identity judgments about oneself. But the identity judgments about oneself of which one seems to have the most direct and certain knowledge are those grounded directly on one's memory of one's past history, and these are not grounded on the kinds of bodily and behavioral evidence we use in making identity judgments about persons other than ourselves.

One natural conclusion, if one is thinking along these lines, is that the "real" criteria of personal identity are psychological rather than physical, and that only first-person identity judgments can be directly grounded on these criteria. Thus it has been held, for example, that personal identity is somehow definable in terms of memory, and that my remembering something consists, not in any fact about my body or behavior (for it is not on the basis of such facts that I say that I remember), but in some nonphysical fact to which only I have direct access. Considerable attention will be devoted to such theories later on.

But it is not at all obvious that a person uses any criteria of identity at all when he says on the basis of memory that he did (is the same as someone who did) a certain action in the past. If someone thinks that such memory judgments are not grounded on criteria of identity, but thinks also that such judgments express the most direct sort of knowledge of personal identity there is, so that *if* there are criteria of personal identity these must be criteria that are used in the making of such judgments, he will be led to the conclusion that there *are no* criteria of personal identity.

Stating the criteria for the application of a concept is obviously akin to, and is often equated with, what traditionally has been called defining or analyzing the concept.[23] Some philosophers, most notably Reid and Butler, have held that the concept of identity is indefinable,[24] and I think that the position held by these philosophers might fairly be described as the view that there are no criteria for the identity of Φ's if the identity of Φ's is real (or genuine, or "perfect") identity. This is not to say that they would deny that we have criteria on the basis of which we make identity judgments about such things as ships and trees and regiments. Indeed, I think that it is

---

[23] If in specifying the criteria for the application of a concept we are able to specify logically necessary and sufficient conditions for the application of the concept on the basis of observable phenomena, then in specifying the criteria we can be said to be giving a definition or analysis of the concept in terms of observable phenomena. There is of course a difficult question, which cannot be gone into here, as to what are to count as "observable phenomena." But I think that on any plausible conception of what is "observable" we shall have to say that there are many concepts for which such a reductive analysis cannot be given but for whose application there nevertheless are criteria. Certainly it is wrong to think that if such a reductive analysis cannot be given for a concept then the concept is "simple and unanalyzable" and such that statements involving it can be known, if at all, only by some sort of "nonsensuous intuition." If, as I believe, it is not possible to translate statements of personal identity into "observation statements" that are not identity statements, it does not follow that nothing at all of a conceptual nature can be said in answer to the question "In what does the identity of a person consist?"

[24] See Reid, *Essays*, p. 202, and Butler, "Of Personal Identity," p. 279.

largely because we apparently do have such criteria that philosophers are often inclined to say that the identity of these things, or what in everyday life is counted as the identity of them, is (in Reid's words) "not perfect identity" but rather "something which, for convenience of speech, we call identity," i.e., is what Hume calls "fictitious" identity.[25] I think that at least part of what philosophers like Reid and Butler are denying in saying that identity (real or "perfect" identity) is indefinable is the possibility of a definition that would permit us to analyze or translate a genuine identity statement into a set of statements (perhaps statements describing the phenomena that we would accept as verifying the identity statement) that are not themselves identity statements. And certainly there is a common inclination to say that if the persistence of a Φ through time can be regarded as consisting simply in the occurrence of a temporal succession of momentary states or events that are empirically related to one another in certain ways (by resemblance, spatiotemporal contiguity, and so on), or in the successive existence of momentarily existing things (e.g., Hume's "perceptions"), so that what is expressed by a statement of Φ-identity could be expressed without the notion of Φ-identity being used at all (by a statement reporting the existence of the momentary things and describing their interrelations), then what is called the persistence of a Φ is not really the persistence of anything. Where persistence can be so regarded, one is inclined to say, the unity attributed to those sequences that are regarded as histories of persisting things does not derive from anything intrinsic to the sequences themselves, but is somehow imposed on them by the conventions of language. In such cases it seems to be only our need to have economical ways of talking about the world that leads

---

[25] David Hume, *A Treatise of Human Nature*, ed. by L. A. Selby-Bigge (Oxford, 1888), p. 259.

us to describe any sequences at all as histories of persisting things, and only our practical or theoretical interest in certain kinds of sequences that leads us to single out these, and not sequences of other kinds, to be described in this way. Now if someone thinks that the persistence of some things is of this sort, and that the persistence of other things is not, then it will be natural for him to mark this distinction by saying that only the latter is *real* persistence involving *real* identity. And if one thinks that the existence of criteria of identity amounts to the definability of identity in the reductive sense indicated above, then one will naturally hold that the identity of Φ's is real identity only if there are no criteria for the identity of Φ's.

When Reid and Butler held that personal identity (and perhaps only personal identity) is "perfect" identity, or identity in the "strict and philosophical" sense of the word, I believe they held this because they thought that personal identity is not definable in the way in which they supposed the identity of other things to be, and that there are no criteria of personal identity. But it can hardly have been a consideration of the way in which we know identity judgments about other persons that led them to think this. Reid explicitly says that the identity judgments we make about other persons and those we make about material objects ("bodies") are made on essentially the same kinds of grounds, yet he disparages the reality of the identity of bodies while affirming the reality of personal identity. I think that this view about personal identity has its source in two beliefs, first, that the knowledge of one's own identity expressed in memory judgments cannot be grounded on criteria of identity, and, second, that this knowledge would have to be so grounded if there were criteria of personal identity.

Despite the obvious differences between them, there are important similarities between the view that the criteria of personal identity are psychological and nonphysical and the view that there are no criteria of personal identity at all. Both views make the identity of a person logically distinct from the identity of a human body and logically independent of physical facts in general. Both stem from the idea that a person has a privileged access to the fact, or facts, in which his identity (the truth of identity statements about him) consists. Proponents of both will tend to regard the identity of a person as the identity of a *mind*, the difference being that whereas the proponents of the one view believe that we can give a nontrivial answer to the question "In what does the identity of a mind consist?"— an analysis of the notion of the identity of minds in terms of inner phenomena from which, it is supposed, minds know identity judgment about themselves—the proponents of the other hold that the identity of a mind is *sui generis* and unanalyzable. We might, I think, regard the latter view as a special and limiting case of the former. On this view one knows the truth of identity judgments about oneself simply by being "conscious of," or "intuiting," one's identity with a past self. And we might say that on this view personal identity is a psychological fact which is its *own* criterion. What "shows" a person that he is identical with someone who existed in the past is not, on this view, his consciousness of some fact, or set of facts, that is criterial evidence of his identity with that person; it is his consciousness of that identity itself.

12. Descartes remarked that he could not help thinking

that corporeal objects, whose images are formed in consciousness, and which the senses actually examine, are known more clearly than this "I," this "something I know not what," which does not fall under the imagination. It is indeed surprising that I should comprehend more distinctly things that I can tell are doubtful, unknown, foreign to me, than what is real, what I am aware of—my very self." [26]

Descartes goes on to argue, of course, that in fact we don't understand "corporeal objects" better than we understand our own nature. But his confession that he could not help thinking otherwise is revealing. Most of us have the feeling, which Descartes had but resisted, that we do not really understand the nature of a thing unless we can imagine or picture it. The ordinary way of picturing a person is by picturing the human face or the human body. And Wittgenstein remarked that "the human body is the best picture of the human soul." [27] But once one has the idea that a person is something logically distinct from his body, this way of picturing a person no longer seems to do. It is, among other things, the apparent lack of a philosophically suitable way of picturing a person that makes persons seem a mysterious sort of objects. One way in which a consideration of the nature of self-knowledge gives rise to problems about the nature of persons is by making persons seem mysterious in this way. As we shall see, there are others.

---

[26] "Meditations," p. 71.

[27] Ludwig Wittgenstein, *Philosophical Investigations* (Oxford, 1953), p. 178.

Two

Are Selves Substances?

1. Philosophical discussion of the nature of persons or selves has often centered on the question "Is the self a substance?" What appears to be the same question is sometimes expressed by asking whether the self is (or, to improve on the traditional formulation, whether *a* self is) a "pure ego" or a "subject." This question can be divided into two parts, the question whether at each point in a person's life history there is a substance to which his states at that time belong, and the question whether the identity of a self through time consists in the identity of a single substance. The term "subject" is most frequently used in formulations of the first of these questions, but it is sometimes used in formulations of the second, and I believe that in discussions of the self the expressions "substance," "pure ego," and "subject" can generally be regarded as synonymous.

It is not easy to make sense of the controversy to which this question has given rise. The statement "The self is a substance

(pure ego, subject)" can easily seem, and I think has been regarded by many of its defenders as being, an obvious truism.
Yet its truth has often been disputed. Part of this chapter will
be devoted to showing that no clear sense has been given to
the denial that selves are substances. But it is not enough to
show this; if we are to understand many of the questions that
have been raised about the nature of the self, and many of the
theories that have been advanced, we must show how the denial that selves are substances has *seemed* to acquire a sense,
and how philosophers have been led to make it. To show this
is the primary aim of this chapter.

2. In his "Second Meditation" Descartes concludes that he
is not "that set of limbs called a human body" and goes on to
ask what he *is:* "What then am I? A conscious being. What is
that? A being that doubts, understands, asserts, is willing, is
unwilling; further, that has sense and imagination." [1] Thomas
Reid raises a similar question and gives a similar answer. Speaking of himself he says "Whatever this self may be, it is something which thinks, and deliberates, and resolves, and acts,
and suffers." [2] These remarks by Descartes and Reid exemplify
what is surely the most natural way of expressing the conclusion of the line of argument presented in the preceding chapter. The considerations that lead us to the conclusion that a
person is *not* a body seem to indicate, in a very general way,
what a person *is*. We are led to the conclusion that a person
is something distinct from a body by taking as paradigms of
statements about persons, and statements expressing knowledge
of persons, what I have called "first-person psychological statements." One might say that we know at least one thing about
what a person is, namely that it is the sort of thing that sort
of statement is about. Since typical first-person psychologi-

---

[1] "Meditations," p. 70.   [2] *Essays*, p. 203.

cal statements are "I have a headache," "I am thinking about this book," and "I want to go home," it is natural to say, as Descartes or Reid would say, that what a person is, essentially, is something that experiences (has experiences), thinks (has thoughts), desires things (has desires), and so on. This can be expressed by saying that a person is something whose features (attributes, properties) are psychological features.

If one says that a person is *essentially* something that thinks, experiences, and so on, or that a person is something that thinks, experiences, and so on, *and* is distinct from a body, or that a person is something *all* of whose features are psychological features (and not physical features), one is certainly not asserting a mere truism. What one is asserting, whether true or not, is not *obviously* true, and is philosophically controversial. But it would seem that at least part of what one is saying *is* an obvious truism, namely that a person is *at least* something that thinks and experiences, something that has "psychological features." For what is this but to say that persons think, have pains, desire things, and so forth? What should be regarded as controversial, it would seem, is not the assertion that persons have psychological features, but the assertion that what has these features is something distinct from a body, something that does not have physical features as well.

Both Descartes and Reid say that persons (selves) are substances. But in saying this, I think, they did not regard themselves as adding anything to the assertion that a person is something, a "being," that doubts, thinks, understands, deliberates, and so forth. The claim that a person is a substance is sometimes expressed by saying that a person is a subject of thought and experience. It is difficult to see what can be meant by the expression "subject of thought and experience" if it does not mean "something that thinks and experiences (has experiences)." But if it means this, and if persons think and have experiences, it follows that a person is a subject of thought and experience, and therefore a substance. To say that a person is a substance in this sense is but another way of expressing the truism mentioned above. We might distinguish this assertion from the view of which I have said that it is controversial and not a truism, the view that seems to follow from the line of argument presented in the preceding chapter, by describing the latter, in traditional terminology, as the view that a person is a *mental* substance, a *spiritual* substance, or an *immaterial* substance.

Now the latter view has typically been regarded by philosophers as but one of several "theories" about the nature of the the self, and has been held by many philosophers to be only possibly true, or to be false, or to be absurd, or to be utterly unintelligible. The view that these philosophers have questioned, or denied outright, is certainly questionable. Oddly enough, however, the part of it that is questioned has commonly been just the view of which I have said that it seems to be an obvious truism. What is challenged is the view that a person is a substance, not the view that a person is something mental or immaterial. Critics of the substance theory have often agreed with their opponents in identifying the problem of personal identity with what Broad called the problem of "the unity of the mind." [3] Hume, the most famous of these critics, held that a person is "nothing but a bundle or collection of different perceptions," [4] and on Hume's view the perceptions that constitute me are *my* perceptions, i.e., what would normally be regarded as contents of my mind. The question arises whether these critics, in denying that a self is a substance, meant to be denying that a person is something

---

[3] C. D. Broad, *The Mind and Its Place in Nature* (London, 1925), pp. 556 ff.

[4] *Treatise*, p. 252.

that thinks, perceives, feels pain, and so on. Reid apparently thought that they did. He says: "I am not thought, I am not action, I am not feeling; I am something that thinks, and acts, and suffers." [5] One can imagine Reid saying against Hume: "I am not perceptions; I am something that perceives, or something that *has* perceptions."

One is inclined to say that if there is a sense of "subject" and "substance" in which it is a truism to say that a person is a subject or substance, this merely shows that those who have denied that a person is a subject or substance must have been using these words in some other sense. Whether this is so, however, can only be decided by an examination of how the philosophers in question have used, and explained the meanings of, these terms.

3. The first important philosopher to question the view that a self is a substance was Locke. He did not question this view because he doubted the existence of "immaterial substances." Throughout his discussion of personal identity Locke implies that when a person thinks there is always a substance that does the thinking. And he thought it "probable" that a person's consciousness "is annexed to, and the affection of, one individual immaterial substance," i.e., that when one and the same person thinks on two different occasions it is one and the same substance that does the thinking. But his opinion seems to have been that if a person's consciousness is always "annexed to" one individual substance, this is so only as a matter of contingent fact, not as a matter of logical necessity. Personal identity, while it may be correlated with identity of substance, does not consist in this, and it "matters not at all," so far as the nature of personal identity is concerned, "whether it be the same identical substance, which always thinks in the

---

[5] *Essays*, p. 203.

same person." It is conceivable, Locke thought, that personal identity can be "preserved in the change of immaterial substance, or variety of immaterial substances." [6]

But what, in advancing this view, did Locke mean by "substance"? He remarks at one point that "doubts are raised as to whether we are the same thinking things, i.e., the same *substance,* or no," and his wording here would suggest that a thinking thing *is* a substance.[7] And Locke repeatedly speaks of immaterial substances as entities that think "in" persons. But if Locke allows that to be a thinking thing is to be a substance, he is clearly in difficulty, as Reid pointed out.[8] For Locke defines "person" as meaning "a thinking intelligent being, that has reason and reflection, and can consider itself as itself, the same thinking being." [9] If persons are thinking things, and thinking things are substances, then persons are substances. And if it follows from the definition of "person" that a person is a substance, it is surely self-contradictory to say that the identity of a person does not involve the identity of a substance.

A similar contradiction occurs in Russell's *The Problems of Philosophy.* The "real self," Russell says at one point, "is as hard to arrive at as the real table, and does not seem to have that absolute convincing certainty that belongs to particular experiences." [10] When I see a brown color, "what is quite certain is not 'I am seeing a brown colour,' but rather, 'a brown colour is being seen.'" The latter "involves something (or somebody) which (or who) sees the brown colour; but it does not of itself involve that more or less permanent person whom we call 'I.'" And it may be, "so far as immediate certainty goes," that "the something which sees the brown colour is

---

[6] *Essay,* I, 465, 450, 453.   [7] *Ibid.,* p. 450.
[8] See Reid, *Essays,* pp. 212–213.   [9] *Essay,* I, 448.
[10] Bertrand Russell, *The Problems of Philosophy* (London, 1950), p. 19.

quite momentary, and not the same as the something which has some different experience the next moment." Here Russell says that what we call "I" is a "more or less permanent person," not the something (which may exist only momentarily) that sees brown colors and has other experiences. Later on, however, Russell says: "We know the truth 'I am acquainted with this sense-datum.' It is hard to see how we could know this truth, or even understand what is meant by it, unless we were acquainted with something which we call 'I.' " [11] And he goes on to say that "it does not seem necessary to suppose that we are acquainted with a more or less permanent person, the same today as yesterday, but it does seem as though we must be acquainted with that thing, whatever its nature, which sees the sun and has acquaintance with sense-data." Here, as in the earlier passage, Russell distinguishes between the "more or less permanent person," with which he thinks we need not be acquainted, and something else, the entity which is acquainted with sense-data (including, presumably, the "brown colours" of the previous passage), with which he thinks we must be acquainted. But whereas he had previously said that the word "I" refers to the "more or less permanent person," here he says that it refers to this something else.

Though Russell does not use the term "substance," his position is clearly similar to Locke's. Both distinguish between persons, which can be said to exist or persist for relatively long periods of time (as long, presumably, as persons are said to live), and entities of another sort. To the latter, which Locke calls "immaterial substances" and Russell elsewhere calls "subjects," they ascribe mental states and activities. It is these that are said to think and experience, and it is presumably to these, therefore, that the word "I" in psychological statements refers (as Russell at one point says). It is held by both Locke

---

[11] *Ibid.*, p. 51.

and Russell that the identity of a person does not necessarily involve the identity of an entity of this other sort; as Russell said in a later work, "nothing is to be assumed as to the identity of the subjects of different experiences belonging to the same person." [12] From this it would seem to follow that persons cannot be identified with substances or subjects. The contradiction I have attributed to Locke consists of a conjunction of this view with the commonplace assertion that persons think (this being part of his definition of "person"), and that attributed to Russell consists of a conjunction of this view with the equally commonplace assertion that it is to persons that the word "I" refers.

That Locke and Russell both contradict themselves in expounding this view is not in itself sufficient grounds for rejecting the view as inherently self-contradictory. But, as I shall try to show, this Lockian view (as I shall call it) can escape the charge of inconsistency only at the cost of becoming unintelligible.

4. Many philosophers have held the Lockian view to be true or possibly true. C. D. Broad suggests, as a possible view concerning the nature of the unity of minds, that "there is a different Pure Ego for each different total state of the same mind, and that two successive total states are assigned to the same mind because of certain characteristic relations which they have to each other and which they do not have to other total states which would not be assigned to this mind." [13] This view he contrasts with that sort of "Pure Ego theory" which holds that the different "total states" of the same mind belong to one and the same pure ego, which persists as long

---

[12] Bertrand Russell, "On the Nature of Acquaintance," *Logic and Knowledge: Essays, 1901–1950*, ed. R. C. Marsh (London, 1956), p. 163.

[13] *Mind and Its Place*, p. 561.

as the mind persists. The same contrast is made by G. E. Moore. It *may* be, said Moore, that

the relation which unites all those acts of direct apprehension which are mine, and which is what we mean to say they have to one another when we say that they are all mine, really does consist in the fact that one and the same entity is *what* directly apprehends in each of them: in which case this entity could properly be called "me," and it *would* be true to say that, when I see this black mark, *I* directly apprehend it.[14]

But it is also possible, he says, that

the entity which directly apprehends, in those acts of direct apprehension which are mine, is numerically different in every different act; and that what I mean by calling all these different acts *mine* is either merely that they have some kind of relation to *one another* or that they all have a common relation to some other entity, external to them, which may or may not be something which deserves to be called "me."

Now what have these philosophers meant by the terms "substance," "subject," and "pure ego"? Moore, of course, did not use any of these terms; he simply uses the expression "entity which directly apprehends," and says that it is possible that the entity that directly apprehends one of my sense-data is not the same as the entity that directly apprehends another of my sense-data. But his "entity which directly apprehends" is pretty clearly the same as Russell's "subject," for Russell at one point defined "subject" as meaning "any entity which is acquainted with something." [15] Russell's subject is *that which* is acquainted with things (e.g., sees brown colors), just as Locke's substance is *that which* thinks. And this is *all* that we

---

[14] "The Status of Sense-Data," *Philosophical Studies* (London: Routledge & Kegan Paul, Ltd., 1922), pp. 174–75.
[15] "On the Nature of Acquaintance," p. 162.

are told about these entities. Broad defines "pure ego" as meaning "a particular existent which is of a different kind from any event; it owns events but is not itself an event." But in what sense does a pure ego "own" a mental event? All that Broad tells us about this "ownership" is that it is "a peculiar asymmetric relation," and this is to tell us practically nothing.[16] If Broad thought that his definition of "pure ego" was satisfactory, he must have thought that everyone is already familiar with the relevant sense of "own." And he can have thought this, I believe, only if he assumed that "own" would be taken as a synonym of "have," and was thinking of the use of "have" in such sentences as "I have a toothache" and "He just had an idea." If this is so, a pure ego, as Broad defines the term, is simply something that has thoughts, feelings, desires, and so on.

Thus it would appear that we are to understand the terms "substance," "subject," and "pure ego" as meaning: whatever is designated by the grammatical subject of a psychological statement, i.e., anything to which psychological attributes belong, e.g., anything that thinks, has experiences, or directly apprehends (is acquainted with) objects. That this is the intended meaning of these terms is indicated also by the sorts of things that have been counted as grounds for thinking that there are such entities. Broad classifies pure ego theories as "central theories" concerning the unity of the mind, and says:

The *prima facie* presumption in favor of Central theories and against Non-Central theories is the common usage of language, which strongly suggests the existence of a Centre. We say: "I am thinking of this book, and wanting my tea, and feeling tired, and remembering the tie that my friend wore yesterday." This certainly suggests that "I" is the proper name of a certain existent

---

[16] *Mind and Its Place*, pp. 558, 562.

which stands in a common asymmetric relation to all those contemporary mental events.[17]

Russell, after he had given up the view that there are subjects, gave a similar account of why it is thought (mistakenly, according to him) that there are such things. "We say: 'I think so-and-so,' and this word 'I' suggests that thinking is the act of a person." [18] What gives rise to the belief in subjects or pure egos, according to Broad and Russell, is the use of the word "I" as a grammatical subject in psychological statements, which "suggests" that there is something to which this word refers, something that is the subject of mental acts and states.

5. The accounts given by Broad and Russell, as to why it is thought that there are subjects or pure egos, seem essentially correct. There is surely a sense in which Reid is appealing to "the common usage of language" when he says "I am not thought, I am not action, I am not feeling; I am something that thinks, and acts, and suffers." [19] Reid apparently regards the statement "I am something that thinks" as following necessarily from those statements, like "I am thinking of this book," which according to Broad and Russell "suggest" its truth.

But Broad and Russell, unlike Reid, are among those who have held that the subject of thought, if there is such a thing, may have only a momentary existence and may not be identical with a "more or less permanent person." And their account of the grounds for the belief in subjects renders this view incoherent. If, as Russell says, the "I" in "I think so-and-so" suggests that thinking is the act of a person, it surely does not suggest that thinking is the act of an entity which is not, or may not be, a person. Broad says that the statement "I

---

[17] *Ibid.*, p. 584.   [18] *Analysis of Mind*, p. 18.   [19] *Essays*, p. 203.

am thinking of this book, and wanting my tea, and feeling tired, and remembering the tie that my friend wore yesterday" suggests that "I" is "the proper name of a certain existent which stands in a common asymmetric relation to all those contemporary mental events." But if this is so, the statement "I am thinking about this book now and was thinking about it yesterday" must surely suggest that "I" is the name of a *persisting* existent, one which stands, at different times, in a "common asymmetric relation" to noncontemporary mental events. Suppose that Jones now says "I thought about this book yesterday," and that, as a matter of fact, Jones did think about the book yesterday. Surely the "common usage of language" dictates that in this case Jones's statement would be true. But if the "I" in Jones's statement were the name of a momentarily existing entity, something that did not exist yesterday and hence cannot be identified with the "permanent person" Jones, then his statement would be false.

The reference of the word "I" poses a serious difficulty for anyone who wishes to defend the plausibility of the Lockian view. If one is to be able to appeal to the common usage of language in support of the view that there is a subject of thought and experience, one must hold that the word "I," indeed, any expression that occurs as the subject in a psychological statement, refers to a subject. But one cannot hold this if one thinks that subjects are not, or may not be, persons, for it seems clear that the word "I" does refer to a person. Thus we find inconsistencies like that in Russell's *Problems of Philosophy*.

Let me now put in a different way the difficulties that seem to me inherent in any version of the Lockian view. The reasons that have been given for holding that there are "subjects," "pure egos," or "immaterial substances," as well as the definitions that have been given for these terms, indicate that these expressions are intended to refer to entities corresponding to the grammatical subjects of psychological statements. Taking the word "subject," then, let us assume that it can be defined as meaning "something that has psychological attributes, e.g., something that thinks and feels." It would seem, offhand, that if we understand the expressions "think" and "feel" we should have no difficulty in understanding such a definition. And of course we do understand these expressions as they are ordinarily used. The difficulty is that, as they are ordinarily used, what can be said to think or feel is a *person*. Now, anyone who holds that there are subjects and that subjects cannot be identified with persons must be holding one of the following positions: (1) Strictly speaking, persons do not think or feel at all; only a subject can be said to think or feel. (2) Both subjects and persons think and feel, and the sense of "think" and "feel" in which persons think and feel is the same as that in which subjects think and feel. (3) There is one sense of "think" and "feel" in which persons think and feel, and there is a different sense of these words in which subjects think and feel. Let us consider these positions in order.

It is clear that (1) is altogether untenable. To hold it is to hold that any statement that says of a person that he thinks or feels something is senseless or necessarily false. But we all make such statements, and it is senseless to say that everyone misuses the words "think" and "feel"; if everyone is taught to use an expression in a certain way, and everyone does use it in that way, then that is *a* correct way of using it. The ordinary sense of "think" must be one in which a person can be said to think. Perhaps it will be said that while a statement like "That person is thinking" may be true, what it *really means* is not that a person is thinking but that a subject, which is in some way related to a certain person, is thinking. But unless the words are being used figuratively (as normally they are not) such statements cannot fail to mean that a person is thinking; they mean what they say. Of course, it might be said that any such statement can be analyzed into a statement in which a subject is said to think in a sense of "think" in which persons cannot be said to think. But this is to assert position (3), not position (1).

According to (2), subjects think and feel, and persons think and feel, and both think and feel in exactly the same sense of the words "think" and "feel." On this view a person would necessarily be a subject, and it would be a flat contradiction to say that a person may persist when no subject persists. So if one holds (2), and holds also that every thought and experience must have a subject that is not a person, one can avoid self-contradiction only at the cost of holding that every thought and experience must have at least two subjects, both of them subjects in exactly the same sense of the word "subject"; each thought and experience will have one subject that is a person and another that is not a person, and it will belong to both of these subjects in exactly the same way. I am confident that nobody would want to hold this.

So we are left with (3). About this I shall make only two remarks. First, if one holds this position one cannot cite the fact that we all understand the expressions "think" and "feel" as grounds for saying that the definition of "subject" we are considering is perfectly intelligible. For according to (3), the familiar sense of "think," the sense in which persons can be said to think, is not the sense in which subjects think. Anyone who holds (3) owes us an explanation of the sense in which he is using these terms as applied to subjects, and to my knowledge no such explanation has ever been given. Because of the way in which philosophers have supported the claim that there is a subject of thought and experience, I think that they have taken it for granted that the sense in which they have used terms like "think" and "feel" is the ordinary sense and therefore requires no explanation. But, and this is my second point, if one holds (3) one cannot support the claim that there are subjects in the way in which this claim has most commonly been supported. One cannot, that is, appeal to what Broad calls "the common usage of language." A statement like "I am thinking of this book" may suggest, or even entail, that there is something that thinks *in the ordinary sense of "thinks"*; it certainly does not suggest, let alone entail, that there is something that thinks in a sense of "thinks" that is not the ordinary sense and not the sense in which "thinking" is being used in that sentence.

6. The Lockian view, while it denies that a person *is* a subject (substance, pure ego), i.e., that the identity of a person necessarily involves the identity of a subject or substance, does not deny that there are subjects of thought and experience. I turn now to a consideration of a more radical view, one that makes just that denial. Those who have held this view have commonly held one version or another of what Broad has termed the "bundle theory" of the self, a theory that takes its name from Hume's famous remark that a person is "nothing but a bundle or collection of different perceptions." [20] The existence of a "perception," Hume apparently held, does not involve the existence of anything that perceives or has the perception. Pains and images are examples of what Hume calls perceptions, and he appears to have held that to say that a particular person has a pain is not to say that a pain belongs to a certain subject or substance, but is only to say that a pain is included in a certain "bundle," or is a member of a certain "collection," of perceptions.

---

[20] *Treatise*, p. 252.

The bundle theory of the self has also been called the "serial theory," the "associationalist theory," and the "logical construction theory," and has been widely held among empiricist philosophers. Russell held a version of it at one time. In his essay "On Propositions" Russell wrote that "the theory which analyses a presentation into act and object no longer satisfies me. The act, or subject, is schematically convenient, but not empirically discoverable."[21] This is developed at greater length in *The Analysis of Mind:*

Empirically, I cannot discover anything corresponding to the supposed act; and theoretically I cannot see that it is indispensable. We say: "*I* think so-and-so," and this word "I" suggests that thinking is the act of a person. Meinong's "act" is the ghost of the subject, or what was once the full-blooded soul. It is supposed that thoughts cannot just come and go, but need a person to think them. Now, of course it is true that thoughts can be collected into bundles, so that one bundle is my thoughts, another is your thoughts, and a third is the thoughts of Mr. Jones. But I think that the person is not an ingredient in the single thought: he is rather constituted by relations of the thoughts to each other and to the body. . . . The grammatical forms "I think," "you think," and "Mr. Jones thinks," are misleading if regarded as indicating an analysis of a single thought. It would be better to say "it thinks in me," like "it rains here"; or better still, "there is a thought in me." This is simply on the ground that what Meinong calls the act in thinking is not empirically discoverable, or logically deducible from what we can observe.[22]

The implication here is that a person, or at least the mind of a person, is simply a "bundle" of thoughts (and, presumably, other mental events or objects). In "The Philosophy of

[21] *Logic and Knowledge*, p. 305.
[22] London, 1921, pp. 17–18. Reprinted with permission of George Allen & Unwin, Ltd., and the Macmillan Company of New York.

Logical Atomism" Russell says that a person is "a certain series of experiences." [23]

My arguments in Section 5 against the Lockian view might be summarized by saying that the terms "subject," "substance," and "pure ego," as used in discussions of the self, are either synonyms of the word "person" or without meaning, and that it is therefore either self-contradictory or meaningless to say that the identity of a person does not involve the identity of a subject. If that argument is correct, it would appear that the denial that there are subjects (substances, pure egos) is either unintelligible or else amounts to a denial that there are persons. But the bundle theory is commonly put forward, not as a denial that there are persons, but as a theory concerning the nature of persons. It would seem, then, that this theory, if it has any meaning at all, implies both that there are persons (for it tries to say what persons really are) and that there are not (for it denies the existence of subjects), and is therefore incoherent. Before accepting this verdict, however, we must take a closer look at what bundle theorists have said. For there is what seems at first sight a way of making the theory intelligible and consistent.

7. Russell said that "the grammatical forms 'I think,' 'you think,' and 'Mr. Jones thinks,' are misleading if regarded as indicating an analysis of a single thought." In the same passage he says that the fact that we say "I think so and so" suggests that thinking is the act of a person, and he implies that what this suggests is false. But it appears that he does not mean that whenever one makes a statement of the form "I think so and so" one is saying something false. It is one thing, apparently, for a sentence, or the grammatical form of a sentence, to be "misleading," for it to "suggest" something that is false,

[23] *Logic and Knowledge*, p. 277.

and another for the sentence itself (or the statement expressed by it) to be false. Russell seems willing to admit that
there is a sense in which thoughts can be said to "belong" to
persons, for he tries to say what this belonging consists in:
"Thoughts can be collected into bundles, so that one bundle
is my thoughts, another is your thoughts, and a third is the
thoughts of Mr. Jones." But he thinks that the form of our
psychological statements (first person and third person alike)
misleads us by suggesting that thoughts belong to persons in
some *other* sense.

It is not clear, however, what is meant by saying that the
form of a sentence suggests something other than what that
sentence says, nor is it clear what, according to Russell, the
grammatical form of "I think" suggests. It obviously does not
help to say that what is falsely suggested is the existence of a
subject of thought and experience, for what is in question is
precisely the intelligibility of saying that this "suggestion" is
false. One thing that Russell believes to be suggested by such
grammatical forms, and is concerned to deny, is that thinking
is an "act." But this gets us no farther. What is it that thinking is not? With what is it being contrasted when it is denied
that it is an act? The grammatical form "I think" could hardly
be said to suggest that thinking is a physical act, like kicking
or hitting; what Russell must be denying is that thinking is a
mental act. But he neglects to tell us what it is (or would be)
for something to be a mental act. If we were to compare the
verb "think" with other psychological verbs, we might find
reasons for saying that it, unlike some of the others, is not
used to report the occurrence of discrete acts. If, for example,
we take *saying something to oneself* as our paradigm of a
mental act, we will doubtless conclude that *thinking that* so
and so is the case (i.e., believing) is not a mental act, and we
may also conclude that *thinking about* something is not an

act and cannot be resolved into a series of acts. But Russell was not thinking along such lines as these. It is clear that he held that there are no mental acts at all, and not merely that there is no mental act of thinking. He could not have explained the sense in which he was using the word "act" by giving us an example of what he would count as a mental act. What seems likely is that he denied that thinking is an act because he supposed, reasonably enough, that an act requires an agent, and because he wanted to deny the existence of an agent in thought, i.e., of something that thinks. But, again, it is precisely the intelligibility of the latter denial that is in question, especially since Russell apparently does not wish to deny that statements like "Jones is thinking" are often true.

But I have been ignoring an important phrase in the passage quoted from Russell. He says that the grammatical form "I think" is misleading *if regarded as indicating an analysis of a single thought.* Perhaps his view—and that of bundle theorists in general—is really a thesis about how psychological statements are to be *analyzed,* and perhaps the denial that there is a subject of thought and experience is not essential to it. Such, at first sight, seems to be the nature of the view advanced by A. J. Ayer in *Language Truth and Logic:*

We do not deny, indeed, that a given sense-content can legitimately be said to be experienced by a particular subject; but we shall see that this relation of being experienced by a particular subject is to be analysed in terms of the relationship of sense-contents to one another, and not in terms of a substantival ego and its mysterious acts.[24]

Ayer seems to be saying that it is the *meaning* of the statement "There is a subject of experience," not its *truth,* that is at issue. This is encouraging, for we have seen that the truth of

---

[24] London, 1946, p. 122.

that statement seems beyond question. But what, then, are we to make of Ayer's phrase "not in terms of a substantival ego and its mysterious acts"? What does he mean by "substantival ego"? Ayer also speaks of "the substance which is supposed to perform the so-called act of sensing," saying that it is impossible to verify the existence of such an entity, and it is pretty clear that he uses that phrase to mean the same as "substantival ego." [25] So Ayer seems to be saying that while there are *subjects* which experience sense-contents, it is false (or senseless to suppose) that there are *substances* which sense these sense-contents. And this sounds, on the face of it, like a self-contradiction.

But we must pursue further the suggestion that the bundle theory, with its seemingly paradoxical denial that selves are substances, is really a theory concerning the correct analysis of statements about persons or selves. A sophisticated bundle theorist (or logical construction theorist) might state the matter as follows: There is a sense of "A self is a substance" in which what it expresses is an incontrovertible truism. For this sentence may mean simply that statements like "I am thinking about this book," "Jones has a backache," and "The person who has a severe headache now is the same as the person who had a pain in his foot yesterday" are significant and sometimes true. When it means this, the bundle theorist has (or should have) no quarrel with it. But the sentence "A self is a substance" has another possible meaning. It might be used to mean that such psychological statements, in addition to being significant and sometimes true, are, in the forms in which they are ordinarily expressed, unanalyzable (or "fully analyzed"). This the bundle theorist does deny, and this he can deny without being open to the charge of having denied an obvious truism. The bundle theorist holds that the correct analysis of

---

[25] *Ibid.*

a proposition about a person will always result in a sentence radically different in form from the sentences by which the proposition would ordinarily be expressed. In denying that a self is a *persisting* substance he is maintaining that the final analysis of a proposition that would ordinarily be expressed in a sentence of the form "The person who had Φ at t_1 is the same as the person who had Ψ at t_2" will always result in a sentence that does not have the form of an identity statement (here he is contradicting the view of those substance theorists, like Reid and Butler, who have held that personal identity is "indefinable"). And in denying that there is a subject of experience he is maintaining that the final analysis of a proposition that would ordinarily be expressed in the form "A is Φ" (where "A" is an expression referring to a person, and "Φ" is a psychological predicate), will always turn out to be a sentence in which expressions that would ordinarily be said to refer to persons ("I," "Jones," "the person who . . . ," and so on) do not occur, and one for whose subject expressions and individual variables these "person-referring expressions" could not significantly be substituted. The analysis of "I see an image," for example, would yield a sentence that does not contain "I" or any other person-referring expression, and does not contain any verb or predicate which, like "see," requires a person-referring expression as its grammatical subject.[26]

This account, of course, can be no clearer than the notion of analysis and the distinction between statements that are "analyzable" and statements that are "fully analyzed." In fact, I believe, this notion is far from clear, but I shall not argue the point here. It is worth noting, however, that some explanations given of this notion make the account given above circular, namely those that invoke a correspondence

---

[26] See H. P. Grice, "Personal Identity," *Mind*, L (1941), 334, where essentially this account is given.

theory of meaning and explain the phrase "fully analyzed sentence" by saying that a fully analyzed sentence is one whose elements ("simple symbols") stand for "elements of reality." For what then turns out to be meant by the claim that ordinary psychological sentences are analyzable is that person-referring expressions do not stand for, are not "logically proper names of," real particulars. But to say that person-referring expressions do not stand for real particulars, i.e., that persons are not real particulars, seems to be just another way of expressing the very claim whose meaning is to be explained, the claim that persons are not subjects or substances, and seems no less paradoxical than the original claim. The statement "Persons are particulars" seems at least as much a truism as the statement "Selves are substances." And if we try to distinguish two senses of the former sentence (as was done earlier with the latter one), and try to specify a nontruistic sense of it by using the notion of analysis, then we shall find ourselves either moving in a circle or involved in an infinite regress—unless, of course, we introduce another way of explaining the notion of analysis.

But whatever (if anything) turns out to be meant by the claim that psychological statements are analyzable, it is clear that those who have denied that selves are substances, or that there is a subject of thought and experience, did not first become persuaded that psychological statements are analyzable and then assert, on the basis of this, that selves are not substances. Rather, I think, they first became convinced that there is no subject (are no substances), and then tried to defend the intelligibility of this view by interpreting it as the view that psychological statements are analyzable. What these philosophers typically say is not "These statements are analyzable, for here is an analysis of one," but rather "There is no subject for the word 'I' to refer to, so these sentences (since they are obviously significant) *must* be analyzable (though I don't know just what the analysis of any of them is)." What needs to be explained is how, prior to its interpretation in terms of the notion of analysis, the denial that selves are substances has seemed to philosophers to make sense and why many philosophers have thought it to be true. This I shall try to explain in the following sections. I shall try to show that our language, together with certain philosophical conceptions, seems to force on us certain pictures as representations of psychological facts and facts about the identity of persons, and that if one reflects on these pictures, and on the question of how persons can have knowledge of themselves, one can easily be led to deny that selves are substances.

8. It is a common philosophical view that every contingent fact a person knows he either knows directly on the basis of what he is presently observing or remembers having observed in the past, or else knows "inferentially" on the basis of his present and past observations. And it has generally been supposed that what I have called "first-person psychological statements" are such that a person who makes such a statement can be said to know it to be true. It is supposed, indeed, that when a person makes such a statement, and is not lying, he knows it to be true with the highest degree of certainty. But these statements are certainly contingent; it is contingently true that I now have a backache, that I am thinking about this book, and that I wonder when it will stop snowing. It is therefore plausible to suppose that if a person knows such a statement to be true he knows this is one of the ways just mentioned. But for anything to be known in any of these ways there must be *some* things that can be known solely on the basis of what the knower observes at the time at which he knows. And it is natural to suppose that the sort of fact that can be known in this way is precisely the sort of fact that is

expressed in a first-person psychological statement. My knowledge that I have a backache seems absolutely certain, and it certainly does not seem that in saying that I have a backache I am relying on my memory or making any sort of inference. But now it appears that when one knows the truth of a psychological statement about oneself, one must be in some sense observing or perceiving something. One need not, of course, be observing any material object. But involved in the view I am describing is the idea that *some* sort of perception, or something *like* perception, occurs whenever a person says (truthfully) that he thinks something, or feels something, or wants something. To this sort of perception philosophers have given a variety of names. They have called it "awareness," "consciousness," "immediate apprehension," "direct perception," and "acquaintance." [27]

If knowing that I am in pain involves some sort of perception or observation, it must involve that I perceive or observe *something*. Perception requires an *object*. There seems, offhand, to be no difficulty here. It is natural to say that when I know I am in pain what I perceive is the *pain*, and that when I know I have an image what I perceive is the *image*. There is not an equally natural answer to the question "What do I perceive when I know that I am thinking about this book?" but if this is also a case of empirical knowledge, as it is plausible to regard it, then it seems that here too there must be something that I perceive.

But it is also the case that nothing can be perceived or ob-

---

[27] Since I think the notion that philosophers intend to express by these terms is modeled upon the notion of perception or observation, I shall allow myself, in this and the two following chapters, to use the terms "perceive" and "observe" to express it. Eventually I shall argue, in Chapter Six, that it is senseless to say that we perceive or observe our pains, images, and the like, and that our so-called "awareness" of, or "acquaintance with," mental contents cannot be regarded as like observation at all and cannot be said to explain our knowledge of first-person psychological statements.

served unless something observes or perceives it. Perception requires a *subject* as well as an object. So if my knowledge that I am in pain is based on some sort of observation or perception of a pain, there must be something that observes or perceives the pain. And since it is *I* that knows that I am in pain, it must be *I* that observes or perceives the pain.

Russell defined the term "subject" as meaning "any entity which is acquainted with something." Now persons are said to be subjects of other things besides acquaintance (or what I am calling perception); for instance, they are said to be subjects of thought and desire. But I want to suggest that the philosophical notion of a person as a subject has often been the notion of a person as primarily the subject of *perception* (acquaintance, awareness) and as only secondarily the subject of other things. This notion goes naturally with the views about knowledge described above. I am the subject of desire, for example, only when I desire something, which is not always. But on the view being considered, no matter what first-person statement I make, whether it be "I have a headache," "I want to sleep," or "I think it will rain," I must be observing or perceiving something. This is so, on that view, because when I make such a statement I know it to be true, and because I can only know it to be true on the basis of some sort of perception or awareness. Hume, it may be noted, remarks that "To hate, to love, to think, to feel, to see; all this is nothing but to perceive." [28]

In representing pictorially what is expressed by a statement of the form "S perceives O," it is natural to use a diagram like that in Figure 1. The concept of perception lends itself to

$$S \longrightarrow (\text{ perception }) \longrightarrow O$$

Figure 1

---

[28] *Treatise*, p. 67.

pictorial representation in a way in which other psychological concepts do not. If one were asked to draw a picture of a man thinking about philosophy, one might draw any number of different things; one might draw a man with a furrowed brow, a man scratching his head, a man staring at the floor, and so on. If asked to draw a picture of a man having a severe pain one might draw a man grimacing or a man with his body "doubled up." These pictures would not reflect the grammar of the sentences used to describe the states of affairs they represent (the sentences "He is thinking about philosophy" and "He has a severe pain"); there would not be in any of them a distinct thing representing what is designated by the grammatical object of the corresponding sentence, and there would therefore be nothing in the formal structure of the pictures to indicate the relational or quasi-relational character of these sentences. But if one were to draw a picture of a man perceiving something, e.g., a man seeing a tree, one would be likely to produce a picture similar in form to Figure 1. The picture would probably contain both a picture-man and a picture-tree; the grammatical subject and the grammatical object of the sentence "He sees a tree" would be represented in the picture by distinct things, and the relation of seeing would be represented by the spatial relationship between the two.

Of course, the objects of the sort of "perception" I have been talking about (which is essentially Russell's "acquaintance") are not material objects like trees; they are "mental objects" like images and pains. Nor is the subject what would be represented as subject in the picture of a man seeing a tree, namely a human body or a pair of human eyes. Nevertheless, I think that our tendency to represent the perception of these "mental objects" as in Figure 1 is to be accounted for by the fact that we take as our paradigm of perception the case of visual perception, or seeing, and that the sort of "seeing" we are likely to be thinking of is not, initially, the seeing of such things as afterimages, but is rather the seeing of material objects. We might say that the picture we use to represent the perception (awareness) of mental objects is modeled upon the sort of picture we would draw if asked to draw a man seeing a material object.

On the conception I am discussing, a person is a subject, and a subject is essentially a perceiver of various kinds of mental objects. All the images, sensations, thoughts, and the like that a person is said to "have" at a given time are, according to this conception, related to a common subject by what Russell calls "acquaintance" and what I have been calling simply "perception." This may be represented as in Figure 2. The S represents the subject, and each O represents some mental object,

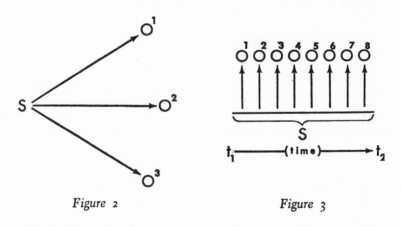

Figure 2   Figure 3

e.g., a pain, thought, or image, of which the person is aware at a given time. The arrows represent the relation of acquaintance or perception by which the subject is related to the objects. But since it is part of this conception that the subject *is* the person, the same subject must persist throughout the person's history. This can be represented as in Figure 3. The persistence of a single subject from t_1 to t_2 is represented by an unbroken line, and the fact that at different times during

67

that interval a number of different objects are perceived by that subject is represented by the fact that different O's are connected to that line by arrows.

I shall now try to show how such pictures as Figure 2 and Figure 3 can seem to give sense to, and grounds for, the doubts that philosophers have raised concerning the assertion that a person is a subject. I shall consider first the Lockian doubt whether the same subject persists throughout the history of a person.

9. Figure 3 is supposed to represent the history, we might say the mental history, of a person. But does it represent the history of a person as that person himself knows it, i.e., as he remembers it? Consider the following analogy. Imagine that we have before us a number of glass beads strung on cords, and that we wish to determine whether two of the beads are strung on one and the same cord. Since both the beads and the cords are visible, we can start with one of our beads, follow along the cord on which it is strung, and see if we come eventually to the other bead. But what if our vision is obstructed and part of a strand of beads is hidden from us? Then we may see bead A, and the section of cord on which it is strung, and bead B, and the section of cord on which it is strung, and yet be unable to see whether A and B are strung on one and the same cord. Now let us compare seeing a bead and the section of cord on which it is strung with remembering a mental object, say an image, and the subject to which it belonged. To say that two different beads are on one and the same cord will correspond to saying that two different objects (say an image and a pain), occurring at different times, belong to one and the same subject. What will then correspond to having an unobstructed view of the strand of beads, presumably, will be having an uninterrupted memory, i.e., being able to remember every moment of a certain interval of time.

If a person had such a memory of his past history, it would seem that we could use Figure 3 to represent, not merely his past history, but the past history that he remembers. And then, it appears, there would be no difficulty about his know- ing of two remembered mental objects that they belonged to one and the same subject; it would be like the case where one has an unobstructed view of a strand of beads, and can thus see that two different beads are on one and the same cord. But in fact our memories are full of gaps. One does not re- member the intervals in one's past during which one was asleep, and much of one's past is simply forgotten. So the history a person actually remembers cannot be represented by Figure 3; it must be represented by something like Figure 4. But now one seems to be in a position, with regard to one's own past history, of the person who has an obstructed view of a strand of beads. It may be that S_1, S_2, S_3, and S_4 are all one subject (or segments of the history of one subject), but how can one know that they are if one has no memory of the intervals indicated by the gaps? One's memory, it appears, cannot tell one (except in the rare case in which one has an uninterrupted memory) whether a pain occurring at one time and an image occurring at another, e.g., a pain one remembers and an image one sees, belong to one and the same subject. And now one seems to be faced with the alternative of either admitting that one normally has no good grounds for ascrib- ing any past mental object to oneself, even when one has a clear memory of it, or else denying that in order to know that a past mental object (for instance, a pain) was one's own one must know that it's subject is the same as the subject of one's present mental objects.

In his general discussion of the notion of substance Locke speaks as if substances are in principle unobservable. It would therefore seem that for Locke even Figure 4 cannot represent the history that a person remembers. Yet Locke sometimes seems to argue along the lines indicated in the paragraph above. He says that no one would have had any reason to doubt that it is always the same substance that thinks in a person if our "perceptions, with their consciousness, always

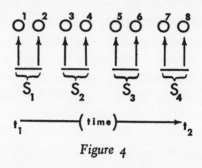

Figure 4

remained present in the mind, whereby the same thinking being would always be consciously present, and, as would be thought, evidently the same to itself." [29] But in fact, he says,

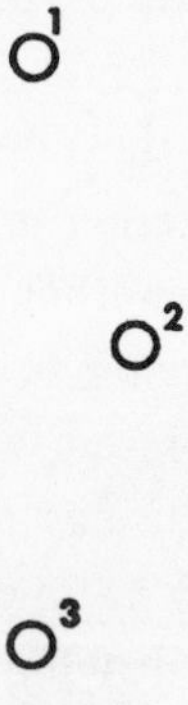

$$O^1$$

$$O^2$$

$$O^3$$

Figure 5

we never have "the whole train of all our past actions before our eyes in one view." Therefore, "our consciousness being interrupted, and we *losing sight of our past selves*, doubts are raised whether we are the same thinking being, i.e., the same

[29] *Essay*, I, 450.

substance, or no." [30] But the fact that our consciousness is interrupted, Locke thinks, is no reason for supposing that one cannot be sure that one is the same as the *person* one remembers doing a certain action, or having a certain thought, in the past. The very fact that one has the "same consciousness" of a past action as one has of one's present actions, i.e., remembers doing it, assures one that one is the person who did it. But since one can know with certainty that one is the person who did a certain action (or had a certain thought or experience), and cannot know with certainty that the substance that was the subject of that past action (thought, experience) is the subject of one's present actions and thoughts, it cannot be the case that one bases statements about one's own identity on facts about the identity of a substance, and it cannot be the case that the identity of a person *is* (consists in) the identity of a substance.

Locke's language is revealing. He speaks of our "losing sight of our past selves," and this suggests that he was thinking in terms of a visual analogy, such as my string-of-beads example or the diagrams in Figure 3 and Figure 4. But it is likely that he was also thinking in terms of an analogy of the following sort. Suppose that I have been given the job of following a certain person and recording his actions. And suppose first that I have followed him all day long and have never "lost sight" of him (have never "let him out of my sight," or "taken my eyes off him"). If now, at the end of the day, I remember having followed him all day, never letting him out of my sight, I can be sure that the person I see now is the same as the person I started following this morning. But suppose that just once during the day I let him out of my sight. Then the most that I can remember now is that I followed *a* person of a certain description until I lost sight of him, and that later on (perhaps only a minute or two later) I found *a* person of

---

[30] *Ibid.,* first italics mine.

the same description and have been following him ever since. That I remember all of this does not exclude the possibility that I have followed two different persons; it just might be the case that the man I see now is not the man I started following this morning, but is instead his identical twin. Similarly, I think that Locke is arguing that the most that I can remember, normally, is that *a* substance was the subject of certain actions or perceptions, and that later on *a* substance, perhaps exactly *like* the first one (if this has any meaning) was the subject of other actions or perceptions. If my memory is interrupted, or if I was not conscious throughout the period in question, there is nothing in what I remember that tells me whether or not these were one and the same substance.

All of this implies, of course, that if my memory were *not* interrupted then if one mental substance had been replaced by another just like it I would know that this had occurred; i.e., I would have detected the change when it occurred and would remember it now. Locke does not tell us what it would be like to observe, or remember, such a substitution of one substance for another. And as we saw in Section 5, if one inquires into the meaning of the terms "substance" and "subject," the idea that the subject of my present actions, thoughts, and so on may not be the subject of my actions and thoughts of yesterday seems either self-contradictory or unintelligible. All that I am saying now is that if one thinks in terms of certain pictures and analogies, which seem initially to be appropriate ones, this view does not seem at all absurd.

10. If, as Locke says, we frequently "lose sight" of our past selves, then at least we have something to lose. If the past history that a person remembers is represented by Figure 4 rather than Figure 3, then at any rate what a person perceives (is aware of) at a given time is *sometimes* what is represented

in Figure 2, for surely one cannot remember a subject existing at *t* if one was not aware of that subject at *t*.

But *can* Figure 2 represent what a person is aware of at a given time? What a person perceives are only the *objects* of perception (a tautology), so apparently the picture that represents what one perceives at a given time is not Figure 2 but Figure 5. But in that case *no one* ever perceives what is represented in Figure 2. If the person is myself, I do not perceive what corresponds to the *S*, and certainly no one else ever perceives a mental subject that is perceiving *my* pains, images, and thoughts. Yet, in a sense, Figure 2 suggests that the subject ought to be perceivable. For we perceive it *in the picture*. Figure 2 is an elaboration of Figure 1, and I have suggested that Figure 1 is modeled on the sort of picture we would draw if asked to depict a person seeing a material object. In pictures of the latter sort, however, what is represented as the subject of perception is in itself as capable of being perceived (though not by itself) as the object of perception. So we feel that the subject in Figure 1 and Figure 2 ought likewise to be perceivable by someone, and that if it is never perceived it must have the status of mermaids and unicorns, i.e., of things whose existence is doubtful because they are never perceived.

Hume, in a well-known passage, reports: "For my part, when I enter most intimately into what I call *myself* I always stumble on some particular perception or other, of heat or cold, light or shade, love or hatred, pain or pleasure. I never can catch *myself* at any time without a perception, and never can observe anything but the perception." [31] In *The Problems of Philosophy* Russell held that we are sometimes acquainted with the subject of our own experience. Yet he remarks that this, while he thinks that it must be the case, does not *seem* to be the case, for "When we try to look into ourselves we

---

[31] *Treatise*, p. 252.

always seem to come upon some particular thought or feeling, and not upon the 'I' which has the thought or feeling." [32] Later on, as we have seen, Russell gave up the view that there are subjects on the grounds that the subject "is not empirically discoverable." [33] According to Ayer, the substantival ego is "an entirely unobservable entity" and "not revealed in self-consciousness." [34] And G. E. Moore remarks, in "The Refutation of Idealism," that "when we try to introspect the sensation of blue, all that we can see is the blue: the other element is as if it were diaphanous." [35] Moore is talking about the act of apprehension or sensation, not the subject of this act, but I think that he would say the same thing of the subject.

The remarks quoted above, with the possible exception of Ayer's, are offered as introspective reports. These philosophers claim that they have looked for something and failed to find it, and according to some of them this failure is grounds for saying that there are no entities of the sort they claim to have been looking for. But these claims must be treated with skepticism. If I am seen looking under tables and rummaging through wastepaper baskets, it will naturally be supposed that I am looking for something. But unless I have some conception of what the thing I claim to be looking for would look like, or of what it would be like to find it, my "looking" is mere show; whatever I may think I am doing, I am not looking for something. Likewise, a philosopher may close his eyes, furrow his brow, and "attend" ever so closely to the contents of his mind, but he cannot be said to be looking for the "I" (the subject of his experience) unless he knows what it would be like to find it, i.e., could identify a subject as such if he found one. None of the philosophers I have quoted, however, offers any account

---

[32] Page 50. [33] "On Propositions," p. 305.
[34] *Language Truth and Logic*, p. 126.
[35] *Philosophical Studies* (London, 1951), p. 25.

of what it would be like to be aware of a subject (or act of awareness), or of how he would know that he had found one, and it seems pretty certain that none of them has such an account to offer. Why, then, do they think that they have failed to find a subject by introspection? I think that this is because it seems to them, even before they "look" into themselves (if, indeed, they bother to make a show of looking), that *whatever* they find will inevitably be something other than the subject of awareness. And this is precisely what Figure 2 suggests. This picture is based on the distinction between the perceiver and the perceived, is indeed simply a graphic representation of that distinction, and the perceiver and what it perceives are represented in the picture by distinct things. So as the picture is set up, the perceiver is automatically excluded from what is perceived.

Now in a sense those philosophers who have attacked the notion of a subject and advocated some form of the bundle theory have been attacking the picture of the self given by Figure 2 and Figure 3. Yet they have not *completely* repudiated this picture. It is what they start from. What they have done is to cut off, as it were, the part of the picture that represents the subject of perception or acquaintance, keeping the part that represents the objects of acquaintance. And what remains becomes their picture of a person or self. A person at a particular time becomes, on this picture, simply a collection of objects (i.e., the collection consisting of those feelings, thoughts, images, and so on which the person is said to "have" at that time), and the history of a person becomes just a series of such collections.

Paradoxically, the original picture, even though *it* represents the person as a subject which perceives these objects, seems in the end to suggest that the person is the aggregate of the objects themselves. For the conception that originally suggests

75

this picture is based on the idea that a person knows the truth of his first-person psychological statements and must know this *from* what he perceives. But these statements, having as their subject the word "I," are regarded as statements about a *person*, namely the person who asserts them. And if they are based *solely* on what is immediately perceived and are known with perfect certainty, it would seem that they must be statements *about* what is immediately perceived. And from this it would follow that they are statements about the objects of perception, not about any subject. If so, then if they are statements about a person, a person cannot be a subject. The view that seems to follow from this picture is the view that to make a statement about a person is simply to make a statement about "mental objects" (feelings, thoughts, images, and so on) and their relations to one another. And this makes it plausible to say that in some sense a person *is* that collection of thoughts, images, and so on that he is said to "have."

The view that a person is a subject seems paradoxical when it is represented as in Figure 2, for this picture seems to suggest that statements about a person (here one is thinking only of first-person statements) are not statements about a subject, from which it seems to follow that a person is not a subject. But the bundle theory is equally paradoxical, and in a similar way. For the picture it gives of a person, the picture that results when we eliminate the subject in Figure 2 and Figure 3, is derived from Figure 1 and Figure 2 and seems to presuppose the very thing that is eliminated from them. The virtue of the bundle theory is supposed to be that it sticks to what is empirically given and does not posit unobservable entities. By constructing the self out of images, thoughts, "perceptions," and so on, the bundle theorist claims to make intelligible the fact that a person *can* have self-knowledge. For the things out of which he constructs the self are, it seems, just the sort of things that can be observed. As Ayer put it,

"The considerations which make it necessary, as Berkeley saw, to give a phenomenalist account of material things, make it necessary also, as Berkeley did not see, to give a phenomenalist account of the self." [36] The paradox appears when one reminds oneself that in order for there to be something that is observed there must be something that observes. If pains, images, and so on are *not* observed then the bundle theory is no more "empirical" than the view that a person is a "substantival ego," and is completely without a point. If they *are* observed then surely there must be something that observes them, and what can that be if not the subject which the bundle theory wants to reject?

Prima facie, then, both the view that there is a subject and the denial of this view are paradoxical. But ways of avoiding both paradoxes have been proposed. Those who say that a self is a subject have sometimes sought to avoid the paradox by maintaining that, contrary to what is represented in Figure 2, the subject of acquaintance is itself an object of acquaintance. What they have done, in effect, is to transform Figure 2 into Figure 6, and Figure 5 into Figure 7. It seems most unlikely that Figure 6 would be the first picture someone would produce if asked to give a schematic representation of what is hap-

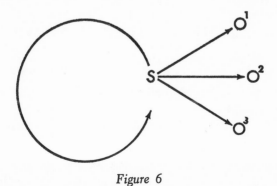

Figure 6

---

[36] *Language Truth and Logic*, p. 126.

pening in the mind of a person who (for example) has a pain, sees an image, and feels warmth, or that Figure 7 would be the first picture someone would produce if asked to represent what such a person would be aware of. For one thing, the analogy

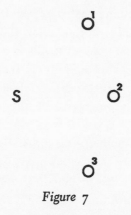

Figure 7

between the awareness of mental objects and visual perception, which makes Figure 2 seem appropriate, breaks down if we represent the subject of awareness as being itself an object of awareness. One cannot see one's eyes (except in a mirror) if one is seeing with them; the place *from* which one sees is necessarily excluded from one's field of vision. The perception of the subject by itself, as represented in Figure 6, is introduced only as a later sophistication, to take care of the difficulties raised above.

The bundle theory, in its more sophisticated forms, adopts a rather different way of avoiding the paradoxical consequences apparently implicit in it. This theory holds that all first-person statements, such as "I have a pain," are statements about "objects" and are not about any "subject." The objection was raised that in order to be an object in the required sense something must be an object *of* perception (awareness, acquaintance), and that if something is an object of perception, i.e., is perceived, there must be something that perceives it. Instead of denying this (as Hume was perhaps inclined to do) the sophisticated bundle theorist resorts to the notion of analysis. Even the statement that something is perceived, he says, is a statement solely about objects. Although the ordinary forms of expression suggest that perception, or acquaintance, is a two-term relationship, any sentence in which the word "perceive," or a synonym of it, occurs must be analyzable into a sentence in which no such expression occurs and one that is different in form from the original sentence. The assertion that a person perceives a certain object, on this view, will turn out, when analyzed, to be either a statement solely about the "perceived" object itself, to the effect that it exists or has a certain property, or a statement about it and other objects, to the effect that it is related to those objects in a certain way.

On this view, person-referring expressions will disappear in the analysis of psychological statements. And it is a consequence of this view, I think, that it is necessarily false or senseless, rather than contingently false, to say that we are acquainted with the referent of the word "I," or with a subject of experience. For to say this, if the logical construction theory is true, is to misunderstand the use of the word "I"; it is, in Russellian terms, to suppose that "I" is a "logically proper name," when in fact it is an "incomplete symbol." If this is so, however, anyone who "looks into himself" in an attempt to find a referent for the word "I" is rather in the position of someone who looks in his bureau drawer in search of Platonic Forms; he cannot properly be said to be looking for something at all. It follows that the bundle theorist cannot intelligibly claim that his denial that we are acquainted with a subject is based on introspection. This denial, if it is to be used to support the bundle theory, must be based on a priori rather than empirical grounds. I think that there is a conclusive a priori argument against the possibility of self-acquaintance (if this is regarded as a perception of the "I" that entitles one to make first-person statements). But, as I shall argue in the following chapter, this argument can be directed with equal force against the bundle theory and its account of the nature of self-knowledge.

Three

The Self and the Contents
of Consciousness

1. "Why do we regard our present and past experiences as all parts of *one* experience, namely the experience we call 'ours'?" [1] This question of Russell's is both a question about the nature of self-knowledge and a question about the nature of selves. There is the question of how I *know* of my present and past experiences that they are mine (and therefore the experiences of a single person), and there is the question of what *makes* a set of experiences mine (or the experiences of a single person). The second of these questions might also be expressed by asking what it *means* to say that certain experiences are mine (or are the experiences of a single person). Dividing Russell's question in another way, there is the question of how I know, and of what it means to say, that certain *past* experiences are mine (are the experiences of a single person), and

---

[1] Russell, "On the Nature of Acquaintance," p. 131.

the question of how I know, and of what it means to say, that certain *present* experiences are mine (are the experiences of a single person). The first of these two questions concerns what Broad calls the "longitudinal unity of the mind" [2] and what Hume calls "the principles, that unite our successive perceptions in our thought or consciousness." [3] It is, for example, the question of what distinguishes those series of experiences or mental events that constitute the mental history of a single person (e.g., the set of all the experiences I have ever had) from those that do not (e.g., the series consisting of the experiences I had before 1950 together with those that my wife has had since 1950). This question will be discussed, in connection with the problem of personal identity, in Chapter Four. It is with the second question, about present experiences, that I shall be concerned in the present chapter. This is, if generalized, a question about the nature of what Broad calls the "transverse unity of a cross section of the history of a mind." [4] The experiences or mental events occurring at a given time can be divided into classes in an indefinitely large number of different ways. What is it, then, that distinguishes those classes of contemporary experiences that constitute the experiences of a single person at a certain time, or constitute the "total temporary state" of a person's mind, from those that do not?

There would seem to be an intimate relationship between the question of how I know of a set of present experiences that they are mine (and therefore the experiences of a single person) and the question of what it means to say that an experience is mine, or that a set of experiences are "co-personal." What I mean when I say "I have a headache" must be what I know when I know that I have a headache. And if what I mean is that an experience belongs to a certain person (my-

---

[2] *Mind and Its Place*, p. 560.   [3] *Treatise*, p. 636.
[4] *Mind and Its Place*, p. 560.

self), this must be what I know, and it must be explained how I can know this. If belonging to a certain person is being related in a certain way to a particular subject or substance, then when I say "I have a headache" I presumably must mean and know that a headache is related in that way to a particular subject or substance. If, on the other hand, belonging to a certain person is being related in such and such ways to certain other experiences, is being a member of a certain "bundle" or "collection" of experiences, then I must mean and know that a headache stands in a certain relationship (of "co-personality") to certain other experiences. Any theory of the self, if it holds that every such "first-person psychological statement" is a statement about a person and can be known by that person to be true, must explain how, given its account of what these statements assert, such statements can be known to be true.

2. Let us now develop further one of the problems about self-knowledge that was introduced in Chapter Two. And let us consider, to begin with, the question "How do I know that I see a tree?" The statement "I see a tree" seems clearly to be an empirical statement, so if one knows it to be true one apparently must know this on the basis of what one perceives or observes. So the question "How do I know that I see a tree?" gives rise to the further question "What must I observe if I am to know on the basis of what I observe that I see a tree?" The answer to this question seems obvious. I must of course observe a tree, and it seems obvious that a tree is *all* that I need observe—assuming that my view of the tree is sufficiently good to enable me to identify it as a tree. If I see a tree, and know that it is a tree, surely I am entitled to say "I see a tree."

But the statement "I see a tree" has the person-referring expression "I" as its subject, and is thus apparently a statement about the person who asserts it. From this it can appear that in order to know this statement to be true one must observe something more than just a tree. Consider, for the moment, the statement "Jones sees a tree." This is clearly a statement about two things, Jones and a tree. And it is quite obvious that if I am to know the truth of this statement on the basis of what I observe, I must observe more than just a tree. There is no observable feature of any tree that could tell me that it is seen by Jones. If I observe that Jones sees a tree, part of what I observe will be that Jones's eyes are open and directed toward a tree. Jones, as much as the tree, will be among the objects I observe. Now it is natural to say that when Jones says "I see a tree" he is reporting the very same fact that we report when we say "Jones sees a tree." For his statement is true if and only if ours is. And since our statement about Jones is a statement about two things, the same would seem to be true of Jones's statement about himself. But if Jones's statement is a statement about two things, himself and a tree, how could he possibly know it to be true if he were only observing one thing? Trees are no different when Jones sees them than when he does not, so if Jones sees only a tree then what he sees does not entitle him to say that he sees a tree; otherwise we could see the same thing (a tree) and thereby be entitled to say that Jones sees a tree, and this is obviously not the case.

So we seem to be involved in a dilemma. On the one hand it seems absurd to suppose that in order to know that I see a tree I must observe more than a tree. On the other hand it seems impossible that I could know a statement asserting a contingent relationship between two things, myself and a tree, solely on the basis of an observation of one thing, a tree.

Now let us turn from the observation of material things, like trees, to the observation, or awareness, of "mental objects," like afterimages and pains. It is obvious that not everything that

I have said about the statements "Jones sees a tree" and "I see a tree" remains true if we substitute the word "image" for the word "tree" in these statements. We do not establish that Jones sees an image by observing a relationship between Jones and an image. Nevertheless, if the statement "I see an image" is a statement about a person (the person who makes it), the same dilemma seems to arise. On the one hand it seems obvious that in order to be entitled to say "I see an image" I need observe, or be aware of, only an image. But if this statement is a statement about myself, and if I know it to be true, it seems that I must observe or be aware of something in addition to an image, something that entitles me to say, not simply that there exists an image, but that *I see* an image.

Although it can seem obvious that one need observe only an image in order to be entitled to say "I see an image," to hold this seems to involve one in solipsism. The dilemma I have posed would not arise for a solipsist. The statement "I see an image," according to the solipsist, is entailed by the statement "An image exists," and the latter statement, it seems, is such that one can know it to be true if one perceives an image and nothing else. But unless one accepts solipsism one cannot allow that any such entailment holds, for one must allow that there may be images, namely those perceived by other persons, that one does not perceive. If solipsism is false, it seems, one must observe more than the mere existence of an image if one is to be entitled to say, on the basis of observation, that one sees an image.

3. "When I am acquainted with 'my seeing the sun,'" says Russell in *The Problems of Philosophy*, "it seems plain that I am acquainted with two different things in relation to each other. On the one hand there is the sense-datum which represents the sun to me, on the other hand there is that which sees

this sense-datum." [5] Russell seems to think that while I may perhaps see something without perceiving myself seeing it, I cannot *know* that I see something unless I perceive (am acquainted with) the subject that perceives it. He goes on to say "we know the truth 'I am acquainted with this sense-datum.' It is hard to see how we could know this truth, or even understand what is meant by it, unless we were acquainted with something which we call 'I' " [6] McTaggart makes a similar remark. Though admitting that, "if we merely inspect our experience, the fact that we are aware of the 'I' by perception is far from obvious," he contends that "it is impossible to know the 'I' except by acquaintance." [7]

The account suggested by these remarks of Russell and McTaggart would seem to be the simplest and most straightforward theory of self-knowledge. If one must observe something more than an image in order to know that one sees an image, it would seem that this "something more" should be that which sees the image, i.e., oneself. When I know that I see an image, on this view, I actually observe a self or subject seeing an image, and when I say "I see an image" I am simply reporting what I thus observe. This view goes together with the idea that the word "I" is a logically proper name in Russell's sense, i.e., a word that directly designates an object with which the speaker is "acquainted." Following Broad and others I shall refer to this as the "proper name theory of the self." [8]

Russell's theory of language provides a convenient way of classifying the theories concerning the nature of self-knowledge that I wish to consider in this chapter, for these theories can be regarded, and have sometimes been advanced, as theories

---

[5] Page 50.   [6] Page 51.

[7] J. M. E. McTaggart, *The Nature of Existence* (Cambridge, 1927), II, 76.

[8] C. D. Broad, *Examination of McTaggart's Philosophy* (Cambridge, 1938), II, Pt. 1, 174.

concerning the meaning of the word "I." As is well known, Russell held that many expressions that function grammatically like names—i.e., are substantives, "singular terms," or "singular referring expressions"—are not genuine names. These he calls "incomplete symbols." Since it is essential to Russell's conception of naming that only objects of acquaintance can be named, it is clear that anyone who holds that there is no such thing as self-acquaintance, or acquaintance with a subject of experience, must hold that "I" is not a genuine name. If the proper name theory is false then, assuming the adequacy of Russell's theory of language, only two alternatives remain. The word "I" may be an abbreviation for a definite description denoting a particular that is known "by description" rather than "by acquaintance." If this is so, it should be possible to replace the word "I" in each of its occurrences by a descriptive phrase of the form "the self (or the thing) having such and such properties." One's knowledge of the statement "I see an image" would be explained on this view by saying that what one perceives provides one with evidence that a self having the appropriate description sees an image. This view has been termed (by Broad) the "disguised description theory of the self." Alternatively, the word "I" may denote no actual individual at all, neither one that is observed nor one whose existence can be inferred from what is observed. On this view, what Broad calls the "logical construction theory" and what we are familiar with as the bundle theory, statements "about persons," i.e., statements containing person-referring expressions, are analyzable in such a way that no person-referring expressions occur in their final analyses. This view, toward which Russell inclined in some of his writings (most notably in *The Analysis of Mind*), avoids the supposition that we are directly acquainted with anything that can strictly be called a self or subject, but it allows, as the disguised description theory apparently does not, that first-person psychological statements can be direct reports of what the speaker directly perceives, as opposed to being inferences concerning unobserved, and perhaps unobservable, entities.

All three of these theories have been held by writers on the self; in fact, all have been held, at different times, by Russell. I shall try to show that none of these theories is coherent. Russell's theory of language, with the standard empiricist epistemology implicit in it, breaks down when applied to the problem of the self.

4. I shall begin by considering the proper name theory, or the view (of which the proper name theory is perhaps only one version) that one knows that one is aware of something, or that one is having a certain experience, because one observes oneself (or the subject of one's experience) being aware of it or having it.

This view gives rise to the question: Supposing that I observe *a* self (subject) perceiving an image, how do I know that this self is *my*self? Surely I must know this if I am to be entitled to say, on the basis of my observation that this self perceives an image, that *I* perceive an image. So if I know this, how do I know it? To put the question in another way: How do I identify an object of awareness as something, or as the thing, that I am entitled to call "I"?

It will perhaps be said that if I am aware of a self then it *must* be myself, since my own self is the only self that can ever be an object of direct awareness for me. But how, when I perceive a self, am I supposed to know that I *do* perceive it? This question seems no less legitimate than the question that the proper name theory attempts to answer, namely "When I perceive an image, how do I know that I perceive it?" But the proper name theory's answer to the latter question, namely that I know that I perceive an image because I observe myself perceiving it, obviously cannot be given to the question of how I know that I perceive a self. If the self that I perceive is in fact myself, as it presumably must be if I directly perceive it, then for me to observe myself perceiving it would be for me to perceive it perceiving itself. But the fact that it perceives itself would not tell me that *I* perceive it unless I *already* knew the very thing in question, namely that it is myself.

It would appear that if I can identify a perceived self as myself I must identify it by the properties (relational and non-relational) that I perceive it to have. Now if I can identify a self as myself by a certain set of properties, and if it is only a contingent fact that my self has (that I have) these identifying properties, then it must be explained how I have come to know this fact, i.e., how I discovered that the possession of these properties by a self is evidence that it is myself. Presumably I could not have discovered such a fact unless I already had a way of identifying a self as myself, a way that does not involve identifying it as myself by the possession of those contingent properties. And if this other way consists in using another set of contingent properties as an identifying set, it must be explained how I discovered that *those* properties uniquely characterize myself. And so on. To avoid an infinite regress, it seems, we must suppose that there are identifying properties the possession of which *makes* a self myself, and that what I *mean* in calling a self myself is that it has these properties.

Most properties, and most sets of properties, are capable in principle of characterizing more than one thing. To be sure, there are properties, e.g., the property of being the mother of John Kennedy, that it is logically impossible for more than one thing to possess. But I think that all properties that are uniquely predicable in this way are relational properties of a certain kind. We can distinguish two kinds of relational properties.

Being a mother of John Kennedy is an example of one of these kinds; having this property consists in standing in a certain relation to a particular specified thing. Being a mother is an example of a relational property of the second kind; having this property consists in standing in a certain relation, not to some specified thing, but to *something or other* of a certain kind. Relational properties of the second kind, like nonrelational properties, are capable of belonging to more than one thing. Only of relational properties of the first kind can it be said that they are incapable of belonging to more than one thing, nor can this be said of all such properties (it can be said of the property "being a mother of John Kennedy," but not of the property "being a child of John Kennedy"). So if one wishes to say that there is a set of identifying properties the possession of which makes a self myself (i.e., that the assertion that something has certain properties entails that it is myself), and wishes to avoid the absurdity of holding that there could be several selves each of which is myself, one must hold that at least some of the properties in this identifying set are relational properties of the first kind. It follows from this, however, that knowing that a self is myself involves knowing that it stands in a certain relation to some specified individual (and not simply to an individual of a certain kind). But supposing that I have established that a self stands in the appropriate relation to something of the appropriate kind, how am I to know that the thing to which it is so related is *the* particular thing to which a self must be so related in order to be myself? If to be myself something must stand in the relation R to a particular thing *a*, the question of how I am to identify a self as myself gives rise to another question of the same kind, namely the question of how I am to identify something as *a*. And if we try to answer the second question in the way in which it was proposed that we answer the first one, i.e., if we say that

I identify something as *a* by its possession of certain properties, we shall be on our way to a vicious infinite regress.

It will perhaps be said that the proper name theory avoids these difficulties, and avoids having to answer the question raised at the beginning of this section, by holding that "I" is a logically proper name. If "I" is a logically proper name in Russell's sense, it has no descriptive content, and in that case there can be no question of applying it, or refusing to apply it, on the grounds that something satisfies, or fails to satisfy, a certain identifying description. If "I" is a logically proper name, it may be said, it refers directly like the word "this," and it is senseless to ask what entitles one to call something "this."

But there are obvious differences between the use of the word "I" and that of words like "this" and "that." The possible referents of the word "this" form a heterogeneous class, whereas the word "I" can be used, as a first-person pronoun, to refer to objects of only one kind, namely persons or selves. And while I can use the word "this" to refer to different things on different occasions, the word "I," when used by me as a first-person pronoun, must always refer to the same thing, and must refer to the very thing (myself) that is using it to refer. This suggests that the word "I" could be *mis*applied in ways in which the word "this" cannot be and raises the question of how a person knows that he is applying it correctly, i.e., to the right thing. If it is part of the notion of a logically proper name that such a word has no descriptive content, i.e., that in correctly using the word to refer to an object one implies nothing at all about the nature of the object, then the word "I," since it can refer only to persons, is not a logically proper name.

It might be held, however, that the word "I" can be regarded as an abbreviation for the words "this self" or "this subject." Assuming that it is logically impossible for a person to be directly acquainted with any self or subject that is not his own self or subject, then, since the words "this self" will always refer to a self with which the speaker is acquainted (if "this" is used as a logically proper name), these words, as used by any given person, will always refer to the same thing, and will always refer to the very thing (the speaker) that is using them to refer. Hence, it might be held that to regard the word "I" as synonymous with the words "this self" is to give it just the reference that it ought to have. Yet in using "I" (so defined) to refer to a self one would not have to *establish* that that self is the one he had referred to as "I" in the past and would not have to *establish* that it is the very self that is doing the referring. As long as one uses "this" as a logically proper name, and does not mistake a nonself for a self, one will never have an opportunity to misapply the words "this self" or the word "I." On this account the question "Is this self my self?" will be, as the proper name theorist presumably wants it to be, a senseless question.

In subsequent discussions of the proper name theory I shall assume the modification of it just suggested, i.e., I shall take the theory as holding, not that the word "I" is itself a logically proper name, but that it is equivalent to some phrase, like "this self," which refers to a self by use of a logically proper name and indicates further that the thing referred to is a self. It should be noted that on this theory a question that initially seems to require an answer—namely "When I perceive a self, how do I know that it is myself?"—cannot be significantly raised. We shall have to consider whether the same is not true of the very question that the proper name theory attempts to answer, namely "When I am aware of something, how do I know that I am aware of it?"

5. On the proper name theory I know that I perceive an image in essentially the way in which I can know by observa-

tion that Jones sees a tree, i.e., by observing two things and perceiving that one of them perceives the other. So let us consider more closely the case in which I know by observation that Jones sees a tree.

The relation that I can observe to hold between Jones and a tree is one that holds contingently. Otherwise it would make no sense to say that I can observe that it holds, i.e., know empirically that it holds. And I *could* observe that this relation does *not* hold between Jones and a tree; I could see Jones and a tree, and observe that Jones does not see that tree. Notice that in the last sentence I say ". . . Jones does not see *that* tree," not ". . . Jones does not see *a* tree." What I would know in this case would not be that Jones does not see a tree, i.e., that there is no tree that he sees, but that he does not see some particular tree, i.e., that a certain tree is not seen by him. And when I observe that the relation does hold, what I observe is that Jones sees a particular tree, or that a certain tree is seen by Jones. Roughly speaking, what I perceive is what might be expressed by saying "Jones sees this tree," the denial of which is "Jones does not see this tree." The statement "Jones sees this tree" entails the statement "Jones sees a tree," but the denial of the former statement, namely "Jones does not see this tree," does not entail the denial of the latter, namely "Jones does not see a tree." Now to say that I perceive that a certain tree is perceived by Jones, or that I am entitled on the basis of observation to say "Jones sees this tree," implies that I can identify the tree that Jones sees in such a way as to leave it an open question, one to be settled empirically, whether Jones sees it. And of course I can do this. For example, I might identify the tree as the tree *I* see, and this leaves it an open question whether *Jones* sees it.

In the light of this it certainly cannot be said that my knowledge that I perceive an image is essentially like the observational knowledge I can have that Jones sees a tree. For if we rewrite the preceding paragraph by substituting "my self" for "Jones," "image" for "tree," and "perceive" for "see," we almost immediately get a self-contradiction, and we eventually get a number of statements that are self-contradictory or conceptually false.

To begin with, we get the self-contradiction "I could perceive my self and an image, and observe that my self does not perceive that image." And self-contradictoriness of this seems to me to be sufficient reason for rejecting the proper name theory as absurd. The relation "perceives" (or "is perceived by"), if I can observe it holding between two things, must be an empirical relationship, and hence a contingent one. This being so, it seems apparent that if I can perceive a self and an image, and observe that the self perceives that image, then it ought to be possible for me to perceive a self and an image and observe that the self does *not* perceive that image. But clearly this is not possible. On the proper name theory selves are conceived as mental subjects, immaterial entities that are distinct from human bodies, so presumably I cannot perceive selves other than my own self at all (and of course, if it is claimed that one could perceive more than one self, the problem of how I identify a self as *my* self rears its head again). And it is self-contradictory to suppose that I could perceive an image and perceive, as a fact about it, that I do not perceive it. So the relation "perceives" (or "is perceived by"), if regarded as a relation holding between mental subjects and mental objects, cannot itself be a perceivable relationship. Being seen by Jones (in the ordinary sense of "see") is a relational property something can be observed to have, and it goes with this that it is a property something can be observed to lack. I can look to see whether a thing I observe has this property, and I can find that it does not have it. The statement "Jones sees this," if "this" has a definite reference, is falsifiable by experience. But the "relational property" of being perceived by me is not one that I could conceivably observe something to lack, and for just this reason it cannot be a property that I can perceive something to have. "I perceive this," if "this" is used demonstratively to refer to an object of experience, is not falsifiable by experience, and is not verifiable by experience; it does not even express a significant statement.[9]

It will perhaps be objected that in order for the property of being perceived by me to be an observable property it need not be possible for *me* to observe something lacking this property. All that is necessary, it might be said, is that it be possible for *someone* to observe that something lacks this property. But can anyone *at all* observe something and observe that it lacks the property of being observed by me? I cannot do this. And since my self is presumably something that only I can observe, no other person could observe my self and an image and observe that the one does not perceive the other. Can it perhaps be said that someone is entitled to assert that I do not perceive an image if he observes the image and does not observe my self perceiving it, and that this counts as observing that the image lacks the property of being perceived by me? If so, then if *I* perceive an image and do not perceive myself per-

---

[9] In 5.6331 of his *Tractatus Logico-Philosophicus* (trans. by D. F. Pears and B. F. McGuiness [London, 1961]) Wittgenstein says: "Really you do *not* see the eye. And nothing *in the visual field* allows you to infer that it is seen with an eye." From the context it is clear that what Wittgenstein here says of the eye he means also to apply to the "I." In 5.634 he goes on to say: "This is connected with the fact that no part of our experience is at the same time *a priori*. Whatever we see could be other than it is." It was these remarks of Wittgenstein's that originally suggested to me the line of argument developed in this section and the three sections following. See also Moore's "Wittgenstein's Lectures in 1930–33," pp. 306–310, and Wittgenstein's *Investigations*, pp. 123–124.

ceiving it, then *I* am entitled to say that I do not perceive it
—which is of course absurd.

Russell says that "we know the truth 'I am acquainted
with this sense-datum,'" and offers the proper name theory
as an explanation of how this "truth" is known. Now the
negation of "I am acquainted with this sense-datum" is "I
am not acquainted with this sense-datum." But the latter,
on Russell's own theory, denies itself a sense. For Russell
regards "this" as a logically proper name and holds that a
logically proper name has meaning only if it refers to something with which the speaker is acquainted. So if "I am not
acquainted with this sense-datum" were true the word "this"
in it would be meaningless, since it would not refer to an object of acquaintance, and the sentence would itself be meaningless (and therefore, of course, *not* true). As Russell himself
once said, "we can never point to an object and say: '*This* lies
outside of my present experience.'" [10] So Russell is trying to
explain how we can know empirically the truth of a statement
("I am acquainted with this sense-datum") which, on his own
theory, has a meaningless negation and hence cannot itself be
meaningful. Perhaps it will be said that "I am acquainted with
this sense-datum" is tautologous rather than meaningless. But
whether it is meaningless or tautologous, clearly it cannot be
known empirically, as Russell's account supposes it to be.

The paragraph above, as it stands, is simply an *ad hominem*
refutation of Russell. But it brings out an important point.
The reason why the proper name theory leads to absurdities is
that it is an attempt to answer a senseless question. The same,
as we shall see later in this chapter, is true of other theories
concerning the nature of the self and self-knowledge. We begin with a question like "When I see an image, how do I know
that I do?" But it is supposed that this question is equivalent

---

[10] "On the Nature of Acquaintance," p. 134.

to, or essentially involves, the question "When I perceive an image, how do I know that I perceive *it?*" and it is questions of the latter sort that theories like the proper name theory attempt to answer. They try to explain how I can know of a certain mental object (an afterimage, a pain, or the like) that I perceive *it* (am aware of it, am acquainted with it), or that it is *my* experience (my afterimage, my pain). But when do I know of a particular mental object that I perceive it, or of a particular experience that it is mine? I am not denying (or affirming) that statements like "I see an afterimage" and "I have a headache" can legitimately be said to be known to be true by the person who asserts them. What I do wish to deny is that such statements assert, or express knowledge, that some particular afterimage is perceived by the speaker or that some particular headache belongs to the speaker. How could I identify a particular image or pain so as to be able to say of it that I perceive it or that it is mine? If I wish to identify a tree and say that Jones sees it I might identify it as the tree *I* see. But if I were to identify an image as "the afterimage I see" and then go on to say that I see it, I would not be reporting any fact that I have discovered about the object thus identified; I would simply be repeating part of my identifying description. Can I refer to an image as "this afterimage" and go on to say that I see it, or that it is mine? It is questionable, first of all, whether the word "this" can be used, as a demonstrative pronoun, to refer to mental objects like afterimages, since such entities cannot be pointed to. But let us suppose, for the sake of argument, that "attending to" a mental object can take the place of pointing. I can point to a material object that I do not see, so there are circumstances in which it would make sense to say "I don't see this tree," and therefore circumstances in which it would make sense to say "I see this tree." What Russell says about logically proper names, namely that they can significantly be used to refer to an object only when the speaker is acquainted with that object, does not apply to "this" when it is used demonstratively to refer to material objects. But surely it does apply to "this" when (supposing this to be possible) this word is used demonstratively to refer to mental objects. For it is logically impossible, surely, to attend to an object with which one is not acquainted. So when the act of attending plays the role, in giving "this" reference, that is ordinarily played by pointing, the sentence "I am not aware of this" is surely senseless (or, if we regard "this" in such contexts as equivalent to the description "that to which I am attending," self-contradictory). And in such cases "I am acquainted with this" is either senseless or tautologous and cannot be a statement whose truth can be known empirically.

It now appears that the question quoted from Russell at the beginning of this chapter, namely "Why do we regard our present and past experiences as all parts of one experience, namely the experience we call 'ours'?" rests on a confusion, at least in so far as it concerns present experiences. Russell seems to be asking the question "What does it mean to say, and how is it known, that certain present experiences are mine?" But by whom is it ever said, and by whom is it ever known, that certain present experiences are mine? My wife knows that I have a headache, and (if we can speak of knowledge here) so do I. But neither of us knows of any particular headache that it is mine. My headache can, of course, be identified or referred to. I can refer to it as "my headache," and my wife can refer to it as "my husband's headache." But there is no way of referring to it that permits us to raise concerning it a question of the sort that the proper name theory (along with others) tries to answer. There is, to be sure, such a thing as coming to know that a certain headache is my headache. If Jones overhears Smith saying "His headache is growing worse," he might wonder whether it is my headache that Smith is talking about (whether a certain headache, the one Smith is talking about, is mine). He could find out whether it is by asking Smith to whom he was referring. In a similar case *I* could wonder, and try to find out, whether a certain headache is mine. But this would simply be a matter of wondering, and trying to find out, whether it is about me that someone is talking, and to the verification procedure for this such theories as the proper name theory have no relevance at all.

6. The arguments in the preceding section were directed primarily against the proper name theory and its contention that we have self-knowledge by being directly acquainted with a self or subject of experience. It will perhaps be thought that the other theories described in Section 3, the disguised description theory and the logical construction theory, avoid the difficulties I have raised by their denial that there is direct acquaintance with selves. I shall now try to show, however, that the grounds for rejecting the proper name theory are also grounds for rejecting the disguised description theory and the logical construction theory.

First let us consider the disguised description theory. According to this theory, the word "I" is an abbreviation for a definite description, not a proper name, and the object it refers to is known "by description" rather than "by acquaintance." Characterizations and criticisms of this theory are to be found in both McTaggart and Broad, but neither of these writers mentions any philosophical work in which this view is actually propounded. The only such work that I have been able to find is Russell's essay "On the Nature of Acquaintance," and it is his version of the theory that I shall discuss.

Russell claimed that "we may define the word 'I' as the subject of the present experience." [11] In this definition, he said, the phrase "the present experience," or whatever phrase is used in its stead, must be functioning as a logically proper name. And Russell's theory is most simply expressed by saying that the word "I" can always be regarded as an abbreviation for the description "the self that is acquainted with this," where "this" functions as a logically proper name of an object of acquaintance.

The subject attending to "this" is called "I," and the time of the things which have to "I" the relation of presence is called the present time. "This" is the point from which the whole process starts, and "this" itself is not defined, but simply given. The confusions and difficulties arise from regarding "this" as *defined by the fact of being given,* rather than simply as given.[12]

Russell apparently thought that in order to know that I am aware of a given object, say an afterimage, I need not be acquainted with any object other than the afterimage. *Part* of what I know when I know that I see an afterimage is what might be expressed by the sentence "This is an afterimage." Now it would seem that if I know the truth of the statement "This is an afterimage," and define "I" as meaning "that which is acquainted with this," where "this" refers to the afterimage, there is still one more thing that I must know before I can be entitled to make the statement "I am acquainted with an afterimage": I must know that there is something that satisfies the description "that which is acquainted with this." But according to Russell I can know this. For he held that when one is acquainted with an object one can, without being acquainted with a subject or with any other object, be acquainted with the *fact* that something is acquainted with that object. "Our

---

[11] *Ibid.,* p. 165.   [12] *Ibid.,* p. 168.

theory maintains that the datum when we are aware of an object O is the fact 'something is acquainted with O.' " [13] Being acquainted with this fact I know that something is acquainted with the object, and I simply use the word "I" to refer to this something.

Russell did not explain how one can be acquainted with the fact "something is acquainted with O" when the only object with which one is acquainted is O. Perhaps he held a view like one suggested by Broad. If we hold that we have "non-intuitive but non-inferential knowledge of a Pure Ego," according to Broad, we shall have to suppose that "each particular mental event which we become acquainted with in an introspective situation manifests in that situation the relational property 'being owned by something.' " [14] It is possible that Russell held that whatever is an object of acquaintance has an observable (introspectable) property that is the property of "being perceived by something." This view, however, is clearly open to objections of the sort raised against the proper name theory in Section 5. For if there were such an observable property, then, since this would have to be a contingent property, it ought to make sense to suppose that one might observe something and observe that it lacks this property. And of course it does not make sense to suppose that something could be observed to lack the property of being perceived. To put the difficulty in another way, if I can know by acquaintance with a certain thing that it is an object of acquaintance, I ought to be able to express what I know in the statement "Something is acquainted with this," where "this" refers to the object of acquaintance. And since this statement, being known by acquaintance, would be a contingent statement, its negation would have to be meaningful and contingent. But the negation of "Something is acquainted with this" is "Nothing is acquainted with this,"

---

[13] *Ibid.*, p. 164.   [14] *Mind and Its Place*, p. 281.

and the latter statement, on Russell's own conception of meaning, cannot be meaningful.

There is another difficulty in Russell's theory, which I can best bring out by first considering an argument raised against the disguised description theory by McTaggart.[15] Broad has given a formulation of the argument which is somewhat clearer than McTaggart's, and it is essentially his version that I shall present.[16]

The argument is this. The first thing that is required if "I" is to stand for a definite description is a description such that there must be one and only one thing that satisfies it. We may grant, for the sake of argument, that this requirement is satisfied by any description of the form "the subject that is acquainted with this," where "this" is the logically proper name of an object of acquaintance. (We can perhaps improve on Russell's theory, though possibly not with his approval, by maintaining that it is a logical truth, rather than a truth known by experience, that any such description is uniquely satisfied.) If "I" is defined as "the subject that is acquainted with this," and "this" is the logically proper name of an afterimage, there seems to be no difficulty about how the speaker can know the proposition "I am acquainted with an afterimage"; if I know that *this* is an afterimage, and define "I" as meaning "that which is acquainted with *this*," I can easily deduce the statement "I am acquainted with an afterimage." [17] But suppose that I am acquainted with *two* things, e.g., an afterimage and a headache. How in this case am I to know the truth of the statement "I am acquainted with an afterimage *and* a headache"? Supposing "this" and "that" to designate, respectively,

---

[15] See McTaggart, *Nature of Existence*, II, 63 ff.

[16] See Broad, *Examination of McTaggart*, II, Pt. 1, especially pp. 197–199.

[17] Assuming that the two italicized tokens of "this" have the same reference.

the afterimage and the headache, we can assume that the descriptions "the subject acquainted with this" and "the subject acquainted with that" both refer uniquely, i.e., that each of these descriptions picks out one and only one subject. But how am I to know that both descriptions pick out *one and the same subject?* There is nothing in either of them that tells me this. No matter which of these descriptions I use as my definition of "I," I am faced with the question "How do I know that I am acquainted with *both* an afterimage and a headache?" I am faced either with the question "How do I know that the subject acquainted with this is also acquainted with that?" or with the question "How do I know that the subject acquainted with that is also acquainted with this?" Perhaps it will be said that here I can define "I" as meaning "the subject acquainted with *both* this afterimage *and* that headache." But how do I know whether there is anything that satisfies this description? It would seem to be a necessary truth that any experience or mental object has one and only one subject that is acquainted with it (though it is not clear that Russell regards this as a necessary truth). But it is certainly not a necessary truth that any *two* experiences or mental objects have the *same* subject. It would seem that on the disguised description theory I must, if I am to know the truth of such a statement as "I have a headache and see an afterimage," have some way of knowing that two experiences have the same subject. McTaggart maintains that if I know myself (the subject of my experiences) only by description, and never by acquaintance, I could never know this. I must, he concludes, be acquainted with myself; only by observing concerning two objects that both are perceived by this self can I know that both are perceived by me.

As it happens, Russell's essay, with which McTaggart may not have been familiar, contains an answer to the question that McTaggart believes the disguised description theory to be incapable of answering. Russell says:

We shall have to say . . . that "being experienced together" is a relation between experienced things, *which can itself be experienced*, for example when we become aware of two things which we are seeing together, or of a thing seen and a thing heard simultaneously. Having come to know in this way what is meant by "being experienced together" we can define "my present contents of experience" as "everything experienced together with *this*," where *this* is any experienced thing selected by attention.[18]

According to Russell, then, when I experience both an afterimage and a headache, I know that they are both experienced by the same subject because I observe, or experience, that they are related by the relation "being experienced together."

Russell's answer, while perhaps no worse than McTaggart's, is also no better, despite the fact that it does not posit acquaintance with a subject. For as I have said before, it is not intelligible to hold that a given relation can be experienced as holding (observed to hold) between two things unless one allows that one *could* experience two things and experience (observe) that this relation did not hold between them. But what should I say if I were to experience an afterimage and a headache and observe that the relation "being experienced together" did not hold between them? I should have to say that one or the other of them was not experienced by me! But as Russell himself says, "we can never point to an object and say: 'This lies outside my present experience.'"[19]

Since Russell defines "I" as meaning "that which is acquainted with this," it might seem that his theory has the virtue of making the question "How do I know that I am ac-

[18] "On the Nature of Acquaintance," p. 131. First italics mine.
[19] *Ibid.*, p. 134.

104

quainted with this?" a senseless question. But in fact Russell does not regard this question as senseless. Adopting his definition, and replacing the second "I" in the question by its *definiens*, the question becomes "How do I know that the subject that is acquainted with this is acquainted with this?" Either the word "this" has the same reference in both its occurrences in this question or it does not. If it does not, e.g., if it refers in one place to an afterimage and in the other to a headache, then Russell would certainly regard the question as significant, for it is just the sort of question he is trying to answer in the account criticized in the preceding paragraph. Suppose, however, that the word "this" has the same reference in both its occurrences. Then, though the question looks senseless, it is equivalent on Russell's theory of descriptions to the question "How do I know that there is one and only one subject that is acquainted with this and that this subject is acquainted with this?"—which reduces, when we eliminate its redundancy, to the question "How do I know that there is one and only one subject that is acquainted with this?" And Russell clearly thinks that the latter question is a sensible one, for he is trying to answer it (or at least give a partial answer to it) when he says that when I am acquainted with an object O I am acquainted with the fact "something is acquainted with O."

I have not challenged, and am not concerned to challenge, the adequacy of Russell's definition of "I." If we suppose that "this" can be used demonstratively to refer to mental objects or contents (images, pains, and the like), it is clear that if the "this" in the description "the self that is acquainted with this" refers demonstratively to a mental content then the description will refer to the speaker and therefore to what the speaker refers to as "I." But assuming that Russell has shown that "I" can be regarded as an abbreviation of a definite description, he has not shown, and could not have shown, that one knows oneself "by description." Using Russell's definition of "I," to say that I know myself by description would be to say that I am entitled to use the word "I" in a statement by the fact that I have empirical evidence that there exists something that satisfies the description "the self that is acquainted with this." But nothing could be empirical evidence of this; if this description has the required sense, i.e., if the "this" in it refers demonstratively to a mental content, then it is senseless to suppose that the description might not be satisfied.

7. I turn now to the logical construction theory, or what I have sometimes called the bundle theory. If both the proper name theory and the disguised description theory must be rejected, only the logical construction theory seems to remain as a possible theory concerning the nature of the self and self-knowledge. But this theory, as we shall see, is no more satisfactory than the others.

Advocates of the logical construction theory, though they reject the notion of a subject, do not deny that statements like "I see an image" are in some sense statements about persons. Russell came to hold that the grammatical form of "I think" is misleading because it suggests that there is a subject. But he held that the form of "Jones thinks" is misleading for the same reason, and he can hardly have been denying that a sentence like "Jones thinks that it will rain" can express a statement about a person. If one holds that first-person psychological statements are statements about persons and are known on the basis of observation, one seems to be faced with the problem raised in Section 2, even if one abandons the idea that a person is a subject or substance. If "I see an image" is a statement about a particular person, it asserts something more than is asserted by the statement "An image exists," and, it seems, something more than one is entitled to assert if one simply observes an image. So a problem seems to arise as to how this something more is known. The logical construction theory (the bundle theory) can be seen as an attempt to solve just this problem.

As I pointed out in Chapter Two, the denial that there is a subject seems paradoxical, or even self-contradictory, when it is coupled with the assertion that the "mental objects" with which first-person psychological statements deal are objects of acquaintance or perception. For surely, one wants to say, there cannot be objects of perception or acquaintance, or knowledge of objects "by acquaintance," unless there is something that perceives or is acquainted with these objects. The way in which the logical construction theory attempts to avoid this difficulty, and also (I think) to solve the problem raised in Section 2, is indicated by Ayer in a passage I have quoted before: "We do not deny, indeed, that a given sense-content can legitimately be said to be experienced by a particular subject; but we shall see that this relation of being experienced by a particular subject is to be analysed in terms of the relationship of sense-contents to one another, and not in terms of a substantival ego and its mysterious acts." [20] If this view is applied to first-person experience statements, it has the consequence that when one asserts a statement like "I see an afterimage" one is asserting that a sense-content (in this case an afterimage) is related to other sense-contents in a certain way. Ernst Mach says just this. According to Mach, "the primary fact is not the ego, but the elements (sensations). . . . The elements *constitute* the *I*." [21] And he goes on to say: "*I* have the sensation green signifies that the element green

---

[20] *Language Truth and Logic*, p. 122.
[21] *Contributions to the Analysis of Sensations*, trans. by C. M. Williams (New York, 1959), p. 23.

occurs in a given complex of other elements (sensations, memories)."

Mach and Ayer do not say, in so many words, that in order to make a statement like "I see an image" one must *observe that* a sense content (an image) is related in certain ways to certain other sense contents, or that it "occurs in a given complex of other elements." But this seems implicit in what they say. According to Ayer, "the considerations which make it necessary, as Berkeley saw, to give a phenomenalist account of material things, make it necessary also, as Berkeley did not see, to give a phenomenalist account of the self." [22] Here Ayer was anticipated by Hume, who said in the Appendix to the *Treatise* that "philosophers begin to be reconcil'd to the principle, *that we have no idea of external substance, distinct from the ideas of particular qualities.* This must pave the way for a like principle with regard to the mind, *that we have no notion of it, distinct from the particular perceptions.*" Hume's view is summed up in his statement: "When I turn my reflection on *myself*, I can never perceive this *self* without some one or more perceptions; nor can I ever perceive anything but the perceptions. 'Tis the composition of these, therefore, which forms the self." [23] And Ayer's reason for thinking we must give a "phenomenalist account" of the self is that "the substantival ego is not revealed in self-consciousness." [24] In calling his theory a phenomenalist account of the self Ayer certainly seems to be suggesting that what his theory does, or attempts to do, is to explain how we can know statements about selves by interpreting these statements as statements solely about "sense-contents." And since what led him to think such an account necessary is the fact that no "substantival ego" is revealed in self-consciousness, it would seem that he must in-

[22] *Language Truth and Logic*, p. 126.   [23] *Treatise*, pp. 635, 634.
[24] *Language Truth and Logic*, p. 126.

tend his phenomenalist account to do what, according to him, the substance (pure ego) theory cannot do, i.e., explain how one can have knowledge of one's *own* self. As I said in Chapter Two, the chief virtue that is claimed for theories of the Humean sort, of which Ayer's and Mach's are examples, is that they make the self something empirically knowable, rather than an unobservable entity such as a subject or substance is alleged to be. What such theories claim to do is to make each person's self empirically accessible *to himself*. Clearly they do not make one's self any more accessible to persons *other than* oneself than the substance theory does, for other persons cannot observe one's own sense-contents or "perceptions." If anyone observes that my image is related in certain ways to certain other sense-contents, it is I who observes this. And if the point of holding that my seeing (or being acquainted with) an afterimage consists in there being such a relationship between sense-contents is that this makes my seeing an image an empirically knowable fact, then surely anyone who holds this must maintain that I observe this relationship holding when I say "I see an image," and that it is by observing this that I know that I see an image.

Various difficulties can be raised concerning this view. We might ask, for example, how I identify certain sense-contents as *the* sense-contents to which an image must be related in the appropriate way in order to be my image. Presumably, the relationship I observe between an image and other sense-contents is a relationship of "co-personality." But even if I can observe that an image is co-personal with other sense-contents, this will not tell me that it is *my* image, or that *I* am aware of it, unless I already know that those other sense-contents are mine. And how, on this theory, do I know this?

But the main objection I wish to raise against this theory is essentially the same as that I raised against the proper name theory in Section 5. If I can observe (be acquainted with) an image and observe that it stands in a certain empirical relationship to certain other sense-contents, surely it must make sense to suppose that I might observe an image and observe that it does not stand in that relationship to those other sense-contents. But if my seeing (being acquainted with) an image consists in its standing in that relation to other sense-contents, then for me to observe an image and observe that it is not so related to the other sense-contents would be for me to observe an image and observe that I do not see it (am not acquainted with it). Like the proper name theory, this theory makes the relational property of being perceived by me an empirical property that I can observe something to have. And this is absurd, for if I could observe something to have this property I could also observe something to lack it. Again, like the proper name theory, this theory attempts to explain what it means to say of a certain sense-content that it is experienced by a given person, and how one can know of a particular sense-content that one perceives (is acquainted with) it. And this, as I argued in Section 5, is a fundamentally misguided enterprise. When I say that I see an image, I am not saying, and cannot normally be said to know, that some particular image is seen by me.

8. I want now to discuss another theory which, like the logical construction theory, rejects the notion that a self is a substance or subject. This theory has been advanced, or at any rate sympathetically entertained, by Ian Gallie and J. R. Jones.[25] While rejecting the subject, this theory holds that there is such a thing as awareness and that things can be said to be objects of awareness. What it tries to do is to analyze

---

[25] See Ian Gallie, "Mental Facts," *Proceedings of the Aristotelian Society*, N.S. XXXVII (1936–1937), 191–212, and J. R. Jones, "The Self in Sensory Cognition," *Mind*, LVII (1949). 40–61.

the notion of "being an object of awareness" into the notion of "occurring in a sense-field" and in this way, it is thought, dispense with the need for positing the existence of a subject. Each of us, it is said, "has" a sense-field corresponding to each of the external senses; we each have a visual field, an auditory field, a tactile field, and so on. In addition to these we each have a "somatic field." The somatic field plays an important role in this theory; roughly, a person *is* his somatic field in a sense in which he is not, but only has, his other sense-fields. The theory is that when I say that I am aware of something I am saying *either* (1) that something is now occurring in my somatic field, which, as Jones puts it, "I designate '*this* somatic field,' using 'this' as a logically proper name," [26] *or* (2) that something is now occurring in some other sense-field, say a visual field, which is related in a certain way to what I call "this somatic field." As Gallie puts it,

When I report that I am experiencing a certain somatic sensation —e.g., that I am feeling cold—the fact recorded by this statement is simply the fact that some region of this present somatic field is pervaded or occupied by a certain sensible quality, and . . . in general the notion of a bodily sensation being experienced by a particular subject reduces to the notion of the spatio-temporal inclusion of a somatic sense-datum within a somatic field.

There is a sense, he says, in which my visual field is spatially and temporally continuous with my somatic field. And he suggests that "the statement 'I am now seeing a red patch' simply records that 'this somatic field is partially continuous . . . with a contemporary visual field, which is pervaded in some part by a certain shade of red.' " [27]

The expressions "this somatic field" and "my somatic field" are synonymous, according to this theory, and the statement

---

[26] "The Self," p. 53.   [27] "Mental Facts," pp. 199, 202.

"This somatic field is my somatic field" is a tautology. But the expressions "this visual field" and "my visual field" are not synonymous, and the statement "This visual field is my visual field" apparently expresses a contingent truth, namely that the visual field referred to stands in an empirical relationship, some sort of spatiotemporal contiguity, to the somatic field that the speaker refers to as "this somatic field." My first objection to the theory is that this cannot be so. If "this" is used as a logically proper name to refer to sense-fields, it can refer to a sense-field only if the speaker is "acquainted with" that sense-field. Presumably, however, a person cannot be acquainted with a sense-field that is not his *own* sense-field. So the statement "This visual field is my visual field" must be as much a tautology as the statement "This somatic field is my somatic field."

But can "this" be used as a logically proper name to refer to a sense-field? According to this theory it can, for "my somatic field" is analyzed as meaning "this somatic field," where "this" is used as a logically proper name. But the notion of a logically proper name, at least as Russell introduced it, is the notion of an expression that can significantly be used to refer to something only if the speaker is acquainted with, or directly aware of, that thing. So if I use the word "this" as the logically proper name of a sense-field, I must be directly aware of the sense-field. But this theory proposes to analyze the notion of being an object of awareness into the notion of being included within a sense-field. So if I am aware of a sense-field, it must be included within a sense-field, presumably some sense-field other than itself. But the sense-field in which it is included would have to be a sense-field of mine (since it is I that am aware of the sense-field included in it), and therefore (on this theory) a sense-field that I can designate "this sense-field." So I would have to be aware of it as well, which means (again on this theory) that it would have to be included in still another sense-field. And so on ad infinitum. Clearly something has gone wrong here. Just because anything that one perceives must be included in a sense-field, a sense-field cannot itself be perceived, or be an object of awareness or acquaintance, in the sense in which its contents can. It is tautologically true that whatever I see is included in my visual field, and it is senseless to say that I see my visual field in the sense in which I see its contents. The same goes for the other senses and their sense-fields. To say that I perceive, or am aware of, a sense-field makes sense only if it is an elliptical way of saying that I perceive, or am aware of, the particular contents of a sense-field.

Because of what I have just said, the analysis of the expression "my sense-field" as meaning "this sense-field" will not do. But another point of importance emerges. Paradoxical though this may seem, sense-fields are no more observable than the subjects or substances that Gallie and Jones reject on the grounds that they are unobservable. The contents of sense-fields are observable, but that is another matter. The point is that by analyzing awareness in terms of the notion of occurrence in, or inclusion in, a sense-field, Gallie and Jones do not succeed in making the fact expressed by a statement like "I see an afterimage" any more empirically accessible than does the view that awareness consists in a certain two-term relationship holding between an object of awareness and an unobservable subject.

It is not clear whether this theory holds that I am justified in asserting the statement "I am aware of a pain" (for example) because I am aware of a pain and observe, as a fact about it, that it lies within the somatic sense-field I call "this." If it does hold this, it is certainly mistaken, for the same reasons that the proper name theory and the logical construction theory are mistaken. I have said that sense-fields cannot be perceived in the sense in which their contents are perceived. The important thing to be seen is that it makes no sense to speak of perceiving the *boundaries* of a sense-field. Gallie says that a person's somatic sense-field has a boundary, an "outer surface," which is, "in normal circumstances" coincident with the surface of the person's skin.[28] And he speaks as though one can observe that one's pains, feelings of hunger, and the like lie within this boundary. Let us suppose, for the sake of argument, that I can in some sense observe that a pain lies within the area enclosed by my skin. This implies that I *could* feel a pain and observe that it lies outside that area, i.e., that I could have a pain and locate it outside the area enclosed by my skin. And in fact, a person who has had a limb amputated will sometimes locate a pain outside his body; he will locate it in the place where his missing limb would be if he still had it. But Gallie holds that in such cases one's somatic sense-field extends beyond the area enclosed by one's skin; in such a case the circumstances are no longer "normal circumstances." It is pretty clear, indeed, that there is nothing that Gallie would count as someone's feeling a pain that lies outside the boundaries of his somatic field. As long as one thinks of one's somatic field as the area enclosed by one's skin, there is some plausibility in the view that in reporting that I have a pain I am reporting, as an observed fact about a pain, that it lies within my somatic field. For that a pain lies within the area enclosed by one's skin does seem to be something one can know by experience; it is natural to say that one can in some sense observe that one's pain is *here*, in one's arm, and not *there*, in the table. But this plausibility begins to dissolve once it becomes apparent that if I did feel a pain in the table, supposing this to be possible, this would not show that the pain was not felt by me, but would show instead that my somatic

---

[28] Page 198.

field extends beyond the area enclosed by my skin, and encompasses the area occupied by the table. It becomes apparent that I cannot locate the boundary of my somatic field and then observe that something lies within it. There is no sense in which I can establish empirically that the boundaries of my somatic field exclude a certain area. And to say that I have established empirically that the boundaries of my somatic field do not exclude a certain area is simply to say that I have felt a somatic sensation and located it in that area. It is my statement "I feel a pain there" that establishes that the place referred to lies within my somatic field. It cannot be the case, therefore, that I am entitled to say "*I* feel a pain there" on the grounds that the place in which the pain lies is part of *my* somatic field.

My main point can be expressed as follows. I could only observe that something lies within a sense-field of mine if I could observe the boundaries of that sense-field. But it makes no sense to say that I could observe the boundaries of a sense-field, for that would be to say that the boundaries themselves lie within the sense-field, i.e., that they lie within themselves. If the boundaries were in the sense-field, then part of the field would lie outside the boundaries (for a boundary must have two sides), and would therefore *not* be part of the sense-field. I cannot observe a sense-field at all if "observing a sense-field" means anything more than observing the particular contents of a sense-field, and I cannot observe that something lies within a sense-field if "observing that a sense-datum lies within a sense-field" means anything more than "observing a sense-datum."

Before leaving this theory I must make one more comment about it. Gallie and Jones propose their theory as an alternative to the view that there is a subject of experience, a view they regard as too metaphysical. It occurs to me, however, that their theory is much closer to the subject theory than they realize. There is a sense in which it is trivially true that there is a subject of acquaintance. And it is trivially true that anything one sees is included in one's visual field, and, in general, that anything of which one is aware is included in some "sense-field." Now if one sets about to represent pictorially the fact that a person is acquainted with, say, a set of visual sense-data, one may at first be inclined to think that a picture like that in Figure 8, where the visual field is represented along with the

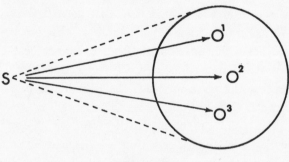

Figure 8

subject and the objects, is the best way to represent this fact. But it becomes apparent on slight reflection that there is

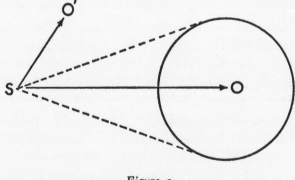

Figure 9

something wrong with this picture. It lacks the right multiplicity for representing the fact at hand. For the fact that an object is perceived by the person is represented both by the fact that the O which represents the object is connected by an arrow to the S which represents the subject, and by the fact that the O is contained in the circle which represents the boundary of the visual field. If we allow both the subject and the visual

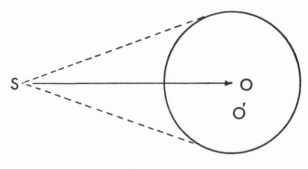

Figure 10

field to be represented in the same picture it will be possible to construct pictures that are, as it were, self-contradictory. Thus Figure 9 and Figure 10. Both these pictures represent the object O′ as being both perceived and not perceived by the person. It seems, then, that either the S, representing the subject, or the circle, representing the boundary of the field of vision, should be deleted from the picture. And it does not matter in the least which we delete. Either diagram in Figure 11 will serve to represent the fact that certain objects are perceived by a certain person. Nor does it matter what we call the element which, in addition to the elements representing the objects, we leave in the picture. We could, if we like, keep the circle in the picture, but say that it represents the subject and that the relation of acquaintance is represented in the picture by the relation of inclusion in the circle. There is no reason why in Figure 11 one diagram is not just as good a picture of the subject-object relationship as the other. So one could say that Gallie and Jones have not really rejected the subject at all, but have simply proposed a different way of picturing the subject-object relationship.

But whatever picture one uses, and whatever words one uses to describe it (i.e., whether one uses the word "subject," the words "sense-field," or what you will), the important point to be seen is this: If what is represented in the picture is the fact that a certain person is perceiving (aware of, acquainted with)

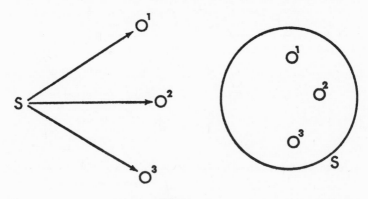

Figure 11

certain objects, it cannot be allowed that the person himself perceives anything that corresponds to the picture as a whole. If we use the circle, for example, then whether we let it represent a subject or the boundary of a visual field, we cannot allow that anything corresponding to the circle, or to the fact that something is included in this circle, is perceived by the person himself. To put this in a different way, while these pictures can be used to represent the fact that a person is aware of certain objects, they cannot be used to represent what the person is aware of when he is aware of those objects. This is just another way of putting the point that one cannot answer the question "How do I know that I see an image?"

by supposing that in addition to an image one is aware of something else which tells him that he sees the image.

9. One further point should be made concerning theories of the sort I have been considering. It is assumed by these theories that one cannot be entitled to say "I perceive an X" unless one perceives something more than an X. And this idea derives much of its plausibility from what sounds like a truism, namely that when I assert something on the basis of observation it is *what* I observe that entitles me to assert what I assert, or justifies me in asserting it. From this apparent truism it seems to follow that if I am entitled to say "I perceive an X" I must either observe that I perceive an X or observe something from which it can be inferred that I perceive an X.

Here, I think, we are led astray by careless usage. Strictly speaking, *what* I observe never entitles me to say anything. Suppose that I observe that P (e.g., that my typewriter is on my table). What I observe is that P, or that it is the case that P. But does this, the fact that P, entitle me to assert that P? Certainly not, for it can be the case that P without my being entitled to assert that P. If it is the case that P, but I am not in a position to observe that P and have no grounds for believing that P, then I am not entitled to assert that P. When I do observe that P, I am certainly entitled to assert that P. But what entitles me to assert this is not the fact that P but the fact that I observe that P. This does not mean that the latter fact is my grounds for saying that P in the sense of being evidence from which I conclude that P. It means simply that if in fact I do observe that P then I am entitled to assert that P.

What is it, then, that entitles me to say that I perceive an X, e.g., to make the statement "I see a tree"? If anything can be said to entitle me to say this, it is the fact that I perceive an X (a tree). Here the fact that "justifies" me in making my statement is the very fact that "corresponds" to the statement, i.e., the very fact that makes the statement true. In this respect the statement "I see a tree" differs from the statement "My typewriter is on my table" when the latter is made on the basis of observation; what makes the latter statement true is the fact that my typewriter is on my table, whereas what entitles me to assert the statement is the different fact that I observe that my typewriter is on my table. And this difference goes together with another one, for the statement "I see a tree," unlike the statement "My typewriter is on my table," is not a description of *what* I observe. But in one respect these cases are alike; in neither case does *what* I observe entitle me to make the statement. When I see a tree, what I observe is a tree, and it is senseless to say that a *tree* entitles me to say anything. If we are puzzled as to how I can make the statement "I see a tree" without observing the fact that entitles me to make this statement, we should also be puzzled as to how I can make the statement "My typewriter is on my table" without observing the fact that entitles me to assert it.

And this can seem puzzling. Partly, perhaps, this is because we are inclined to regard all statements of the form "The fact that Q entitles me to assert that P" as elliptical for statements of the form "My knowledge of the fact that Q entitles me to assert that P." And then it seems that if it is the fact that I observe that P that entitles me to assert that P, I must know that I observe that P before I can be entitled to assert that P. And one wants to ask how I can know this. But there is certainly a confusion here. One regards the statement "It is the fact that I observe that P that entitles me to assert that P" as being of the same kind as the statement "It is the fact that he is coughing up blood that entitles me to say that he has tuberculosis." But these are different sorts of statements; the latter gives one's evidence for something, whereas the former does not. And while the latter statement is elliptical, namely for the statement "It is my knowledge of the fact that he is coughing up blood that entitles me to say that he has tuberculosis," the former statement is not elliptical.

But to reveal this confusion is not completely to dispel the puzzle. For one is still inclined to say: "When I know that P because I observe that P, surely I cannot be *ignorant* of the fact that I observe that P. And if I am not ignorant of this fact, surely I must *know* it. So *how* do I know it?" Now it is not at all clear that it follows from my not being ignorant of a fact that I know that fact. However, let us suppose that I cannot be entitled to assert that P on the basis of observation unless I know that I observe that P. And let us further suppose, as a proper name theorist might, that the only way in which I can know that I observe that P (no matter what proposition P is) is by observing myself observing that P (or observing the "fact" that I observe that P). These suppositions clearly lead to an infinite regress. If I know that P I am certainly entitled to assert that P, and if I am not entitled to assert that P then I do not know that P. So to know that P, on the account being considered, it is not sufficient that I observe that P; I must also know that I observe that P, and to know this I must observe that I observe that P. But now we can let "P'" be the statement "I observe that P," and give the same argument again. To know that P' I must observe, not simply that P', but also that I observe that P', i.e., that I observe that I observe that P. Letting "P''" be the statement "I observe that I observe that P" (or "I observe that P'"), the same argument can be given again. And so on ad infinitum.

But how, if not by observation, can I know that I observe that P? When I am entitled to assert that P on the basis of observation, it seems that I am entitled to assert, not only that P, but also that I observe that P. So what entitles me to say that

I observe that *P?* The answer, I think, is that if anything entitles me to assert that I observe that *P* it is the very fact that entitles me to assert that *P*, namely the fact that I observe that *P*. One might even say that it is a distinguishing characteristic of first-person-experience statements (like "I see a tree," "I observe that it is raining," and "I have a headache") that it is simply their *being* true, and not the observation that they are true, or the possession of evidence that they are true, that entitles one to assert them. Of course, whereas the statement "I observe that *P*" is an answer to the question "How do you know that *P?*" it would hardly be given as an answer (except in exasperation) to the question "How do you know that you observe that *P?*" But this is because the latter question, when it makes sense at all, is not the question it may initially appear to be. It is not the question "How do you know that it is *you* (as opposed to someone else) that observes that *P?*" or the question "How do you know that you *observe* (as opposed to knowing in some other way) that *P?*" but the question "How do you know that what you observe is that *P?*" or "What justifies you in describing what you observe as the fact that *P?*" ("What justifies you in saying that you observe *that it is raining?*—Perhaps someone is sprinkling water from the roof.") Likewise, if it is asked how I know that I see a tree, what is being asked is not how I know that it is *I* that sees a tree, or that I *see* a tree, but how I know that what I see is really a *tree*.

Four

Self-Identity and the Contents of Memory

1. In Chapter One I argued that a major source of the problem of personal identity is the fact that persons make what appear to be identity statements about themselves, namely memory statements about their own past histories, without having or needing the sorts of evidence we use in making identity judgments about persons other than ourselves. Since one can make such statements about oneself, and know them to be true, without first knowing the facts that would justify an assertion about the identity of one's body, it appears that bodily identity cannot be the criterion of personal identity and is at best only contingently correlated with it. The knowledge expressed in such statements appears to be the most direct knowledge of personal identity there is, and it would seem that the fact in which the truth of such a statement consists must be directly accessible to whoever has direct knowledge of the truth of the statement. So one is easily led to

the conclusion that the real criteria of personal identity cannot be bodily or physical criteria of any sort, but must be "mental" or "psychological" criteria that a person can know to be satisfied in his own case quite apart from knowing anything about his body. The search for an empirical and nonphysical relationship of "co-personality," which links together the successive mental events in a person's history, is one form that the search for these criteria has taken.

My main object in this chapter is to show that the search for a "first-person criterion" of personal identity—and the attempt to analyze facts about the identity of a person (facts expressed by identity statements about a person) into psychological facts (e.g., the holding of certain relations between mental events) that are directly accessible to that person— rests on a mistake. I shall argue that while one does not use bodily identity as a criterion of personal identity when one says on the basis of memory that one did a certain thing in the past, this is not because one uses something else (some nonphysical fact) as a criterion, but is rather because one uses no criterion of identity at all. Where one's relevant knowledge of the past is derived solely from one's own memeory, I shall argue, it is impossible by the nature of the case for one's claim to have done or experienced something to be grounded on a criterion of identity. Such claims, i.e., first-person statements made solely on the basis of memory, are not judgments of personal identity at all, though they do imply the persistence of a person through time. I do not wish to say, of course, that we never make identity statements about ourselves, or that we never apply criteria of identity to ourselves. In Chapter Five I shall argue that there are criteria of personal identity, of which bodily identity is the most important, that we can use in making identity judgments about other persons. And I think that in certain circumstances, namely when one has no memory of one's past or does not trust the memories one has, one's knowledge of identity statements about oneself can be said to be grounded on these criteria. This will be so if, for example, one asserts one's identity with someone in the past on the basis of a similarity between one's present appearance and what one knows, on the basis of photographic records or the testimony of other persons, to have been the appearance of that person. But of course there is nothing distinctively "first-person," and nothing distinctively psychological, about the criteria one would use in such cases. The cases in which it seems that the criteria one uses can only be psychological, and such that one can apply them directly only to oneself, are those in which one's knowledge of the past is based solely on one's memory, and in which one is able to assert that one did a certain thing in the past without knowing anything about the present state of one's body. And it is in just these cases, I shall argue, that one uses no criteria of identity at all; the criteria are not physical, not because they are nonphysical, but because there are none.

2. According to William James, "there is nothing more remarkable in making a judgment of sameness in the first person than in the second or third." James goes on to say that "the sense of personal identity" is "the sense of a sameness perceived *by* thought and predicated of things *thought-about*. These things are a present self and a self of yesterday. The thought not only thinks them both, but thinks that they are identical." [1] I think that it is commonly supposed that any first-person past-tense statement, including those that are based on memory, asserts that, in James's terminology, a "present self" is identical with a "self of yesterday." How does this idea arise?

---

[1] *Principles of Psychology* (New York, 1893), I, 331, 332.

It is often said by philosophers that the time reference of the word "I" is always to the *present*. According to James Mill, "Each of the terms . . . I, Thou, He, marks a particular chain of antecedents and consequents, terminating with the I, the Thou, the He, of the present moment. The I, the Thou, the He, of the present moment, is marked by these terms, *primarily*, the preceding links are marked, *secondarily*." [2] The notion that the primary reference of the word "I" is to something present finds expression in William James's remark that the word "I," for the "passing Thought" that thinks, means "nothing but the bodily life which it momentarily feels," [3] and is implicit in both the theories of Russell that were discussed in the preceding chapter. Perhaps what lies behind this notion is the fact that while one can say "I did not exist at *t*," where *t* is some time in the past, it would be absurd for anyone to say "I do not exist now." Clearly, anyone who makes a statement containing the word "I" must exist at the time at which he makes that statement. And since such statements are about the person who makes them, it seems that any such statement, whatever its tense, must assert something about a person who exists at the time at which the statement is made. In James's terminology, any such statement says something about a "present self."

But if the word "I" always refers to something in the present, then a statement like "I went for a walk yesterday" refers both to something present and to something past. It contains the word "I," but it also refers to something that was done yesterday by someone who existed *then*. And this makes it natural to regard such a statement as asserting that a "present

---

[2] *Analysis of the Phenomena of the Human Mind* (London, 1878), II, 170.

[3] *Principles*, I, 341n.

self" (that which I call "I") is identical with a "self of yesterday" (someone who went for a walk yesterday).

In any case, it is evident that we must establish an identity in order to verify such a first-person statement. If Tom says "I broke the front window yesterday," and we wish to establish whether what he says is true, we must discover whether the front window was broken yesterday, and, if it was, whether Tom is (is the same as) the person who broke it. This being so, it is plausible to regard Tom's statement as itself being, or at least containing, a judgment of personal identity.

But it clearly will not do to say that "I broke the front window yesterday" simply *is* an identity judgment asserting that a certain "present self" is identical with a certain "self of yesterday." If it were, then its denial would be the denial of an identity, i.e., would be the assertion that a certain present self is not identical with a certain self of yesterday. In the case at hand, the self of yesterday would presumably be the person who broke the front window yesterday, and the denial of the statement could be expressed in the statement "I am not the person who broke the front window yesterday." But this will not do. "I am not the person who broke the front window yesterday" implies that someone did break the front window yesterday, but the denial of the original statement is simply "I did not break the front window yesterday," and this carries no such implication. To say "I am not the person who did X" is *a* way of denying the claim that I did X, but it is not *the* denial of that claim, for another, and incompatible, way of denying it is by saying "X was not done at all."

So if one wants to say that the statement "I broke the front window yesterday" asserts an identity, one cannot maintain that this is *all* that it asserts. One must say, I think, that it asserts two things, (1) that someone broke the front window yesterday, and (2) that that person was oneself. If this is so, the question "Did I break the front window yesterday?" resolves into two questions, one of which is prior to the other. The first of these is not a question of identity at all, but is simply the question of whether a certain thing was done in the past, i.e., whether the front window was broken yesterday by someone or other. Only if this question is answered in the affirmative can there arise a question of identity, the question whether the person who did a certain thing in the past was oneself.

3. Assuming that first-person past-tense statements do in some sense express judgments of personal identity, let us try to see why it is supposed that these statements, when known to be true by the person asserting them, must be grounded on criteria of personal identity.

It cannot be said in general that in order to know the truth of an identity statement one must employ criteria of identity. Looking at my desk, I might say (in an appropriate context) "The typewriter on my desk and the largest object on my desk are one and the same thing." In making this statement I would not have to make use of criteria of identity; to know its truth I need only observe that there is exactly one typewriter on my desk, and that it is larger than any other object on my desk. Here the verification of an "identity statement" consists simply in the observation that something simultaneously fits two different identifying descriptions. There are similar cases in which identity judgments be said to be based solely on memory. If asked how I know that the typewriter on my desk at noon yesterday was (was the same as) the largest object on my desk then, I might reply simply "I remember that it was," or, if required to be more specific, "I remember that at noon yesterday there was exactly one typewriter on my desk, and that it was larger than any other object then on my desk." Here again, no criterion of identity is employed, and none is needed.

But as Hume remarked, "my memory, indeed, informs me of the existence of many objects; but then this information extends not past their past existence, nor do either my senses or memory give any testimony to the continuance of their being." [4] I can simply observe that the typewriter on my desk now is the largest object on my desk now, and I can simply remember that the typewriter on my desk yesterday was the largest object on my desk then, but I cannot, in the same way, either observe or remember that the typewriter *now* on my desk *was* the largest object on my desk yesterday, or that the typewriter on my desk yesterday was the largest object there on the day before yesterday. It is precisely where identity statements imply the persistence (or to use Hume's term, the continuance) of an object through time that they seem to go beyond what can be known directly on the basis of observation and memory. When we judge that something known to have existed at one time is the same as something known to have existed at another time, it may indeed be observation and memory that inform us of the existence of the things judged to be identical. But the judgment that these things are identical cannot itself be an observation report or a memory report; it must, it seems, be an inference from the data of sense and memory, an inference that can be justified only in terms of criteria of identity.

We have seen that first-person past-tense statements seem to contain identity judgments, and it is apparent that such statements imply the persistence of a person through time. If such statements assert the identity of a "present self" and a "self of yesterday," they express just the sort of identity judgment that apparently cannot be known except on the basis of cri-

---

[4] *Treatise*, p. 196.

teria of identity. The question "How do you know that you broke the front window yesterday" is *in part* the question "How do you know that the window was broken yesterday?" and the answer to this question can be simply "I remember." But it also seems to involve the question "How do you know that the person who broke the window was yourself, the person here now?" And it now appears that the answer to the latter question cannot be simply "I remember." My memory can inform me of the existence of a self at t_1 and of its properties and activities at that time, of the existence of a self at t_2 and of its properties and activities at that time, and so on, but it seems that any statement that identifies a past self with a present self, or a past self existing at t_1 with a past self existing at t_2, necessarily goes beyond what can be known solely on the basis of memory. Such a statement, one is inclined to say, cannot simply describe or report *what* I remember, but must rather express a conclusion *from* what I remember, and perhaps also from other facts that I know (e.g., facts about my "present self"). And if such statements express conclusions, and if we can know them to be true, we must have some principle or criterion that entitles us to draw such conclusions from remembered facts.

The plausibility of this way of thinking is strengthened if we consider in what sense past-tense statements in the *third* person can be said to be based on memory. Suppose that I am testifying at a murder trial, and that I point to someone and say "That man shot the bank teller." If asked how I know this, I might say "I remember seeing him fire the gun." The fact that it would be natural for me to say that I remember that *this* man (someone existing now) did a certain thing in the past might initially suggest that the answer to the question of how I know the truth of an identity statement can be simply "I remember," even if that statement implies the persistence of something through time. But it might conceivably turn out that the man I identified as the murderer is the double, or the identical twin, of the actual murderer. Would this show that my memory was mistaken? Surely it would be much more natural to say that my memory was accurate enough (which is shown by the fact that the man whom I identified as the murderer looked exactly like the murderer), but that I drew a mistaken, though natural, conclusion from what I remembered. And this makes it plausible to say that the most that one can actually remember is that someone of such and such a description did something in the past, and that the assertion that *this* person (someone standing before us now) did such and such must always be, if based on memory, a conclusion from what is remembered rather than a report or description of what is actually remembered, and that it must be a conclusion that is grounded on resemblance, spatiotemporal continuity, and other such considerations. Thus Thomas Reid says that our knowledge of the identity of other persons and objects of sense is "grounded on similarity and on other circumstances which in many cases are not so decisive as to leave no room for doubt." [5] And if one thinks that a statement like "I broke the front window yesterday" says that a "present self" is identical with a "self of yesterday," it will be natural for one to hold that the same is true of our knowledge of first-person statements of this kind. Thus William James held that *"The sense of our own personal identity . . . is exactly like any one of our other perceptions of sameness among phenomena. It is a conclusion grounded on the resemblance in a fundamental respect, or on the continuity before the mind, of the phenomena compared."* [6]

---

[5] *Essays*, p. 205.

[6] *Principles*, I, 334. Italics in the original.

4. What James, in the passage just quoted, says are "exactly like" one another, Thomas Reid says are "totally of a different kind." According to Reid,

the evidence we have of our own identity, as far back as we remember, is totally of a different kind from the evidence we have of the identity of other persons or of objects of sense. The first is grounded on memory, and gives undoubted certainty. The last is grounded on similarity and on other circumstances which in many cases are not so decisive as to leave no room for doubt.[7]

Reid's remark is acute, but also misleading. He seems to be saying that the difference between first-person judgments of identity and their third-person counterparts is that the former are grounded on memory whereas the latter are grounded on similarity and "other circumstances." But of course there is a perfectly good sense in which a third-person judgment of identity may be grounded on similarity and at the same time be grounded on memory. If I say "This is the man I met yesterday," my statement may be grounded on the similarity between this man and the man I met yesterday. But since I may be aware of this similarity only because I *remember* what the man I met yesterday looked like, we can say that my statement is grounded on memory. Reid's mode of expression tends to obscure what I think to be the important point he was making, namely that the sense of "grounded on" in which my statement "This is the man I met yesterday" is grounded on memory is different from that in which my statement "I went for a walk yesterday" is grounded on memory. And he does not make clear that the sense of "grounded on" in which the former statement is grounded on similarity is different from both of these other senses of "grounded on."

We can distinguish between statements that are based on memory in the sense of being memory statements, i.e., descrip-

---

[7] *Essays*, p. 205.

tions, reports or expressions of what the speaker remembers, and statements that are based on memory in the sense of being conclusions *from* what is remembered. This distinction can be expressed roughly by saying that if a memory statement turns out to be false it follows that the person who made the statement misremembered, or had a mistaken memory (assuming that he made the statement honestly), whereas if a statement that expresses a conclusion from memory turns out to be false it does not follow that the speaker had a mistaken memory, since he might have remembered correctly but drawn a false conclusion from what he remembered. Anyone who supposes that first-person past-tense statements made on the basis of memory express identity judgments, and that they are grounded on criteria of identity, e.g., as James says, on "the resemblance in a fundamental respect, or the continuity before the mind, of the phenomena compared," must suppose that such statements are based on memory in the second of these senses. Reid, I think, believed that this is the only sense in which *third*-person past-tense statements can be grounded on memory, but held that first-person past-tense statements can be, and normally are, based on memory in the first sense, i.e., that they can be memory statements as opposed to being conclusions from what is remembered. And he saw, I think, that if a statement like "I broke the front window yesterday" is based on memory in this sense then it *cannot* be based on similarity, continuity, or any of the other considerations on which third-person statements of identity are based.

To put this more precisely, if "*P*" is a statement based on memory in the sense of being a conclusion from what is remembered, then the question "How do you know that *P*?" can be given an answer of the form "I know that *Q* and *R*, and the fact that *Q* and *R* is good evidence that *P*." Here "*P*" might be the statement "This man robbed the jewelry store," "*Q*" the statement "The man who robbed the jewelry store was blond and had a scar on his right cheek," and "R" the statement "This man is blond and has a scar on his right cheek." "Q" and "R" are grounds, or evidence, for "P" independently of *how* they are known. But it might be the case that "Q" is a memory statement, i.e., is known "on the basis of memory" in the first sense distinguished above. And then we could say that "P" is based on memory, which would mean simply that one of the grounds for "P" (namely "Q") is a memory statement. But in addition to asking from what facts "P" is inferred (answer: from the fact that Q and the fact that R), and how those facts are known (answer: the one is known on the basis of memory, the other on the basis of present observation), we can ask why those facts are grounds that P. It is in answering this question that reference to criteria will enter in. For the answer will be either (1) that the meaning of "P" is such that, or the criteria for the truth of "P" are such that, it is logically true that the fact that Q and R is good grounds that P, or (2) the criteria are something else, and it has been discovered empirically, by reference to these criteria, that when statements of the sorts "Q" and "R" are true then a corresponding statement of the sort "P" is generally true also.

By way of contrast, when "P" is a memory statement, as opposed to being a conclusion from memory, the only answer to the question "How do you know that P?" is "I remember that P." The latter statement does not express evidence or grounds that P in the sense in which "Q" and "R" expressed evidence or grounds that P in the case above. "I remember that P" entails that P, and it entails this, not because of the meaning of the particular statement "P" that is asserted (for the entailment holds no matter what statement "P" happens to be), but because of the meaning of the word "remember." If it makes any sense at all to ask why the fact that someone remembers that

P is grounds that P, this question is to be answered by explaining the meaning of the word "remember," and not by reference to criteria for the truth of the statement "P."

Now if, as Reid apparently thought and I shall try to argue in the following sections, a statement like "I broke the front window yesterday" can be based on memory in the sense of being a memory statement, then to explain how such statements are known we do not need to suppose that there are private "first-person" criteria of personal identity on the basis of which such statements are made. Indeed, that supposition could not possibly help to explain this. For to say that such a statement is a memory statement is to say that it is not a conclusion from anything, and therefore is not a conclusion grounded on criteria of identity.

Moreover, it seems to me that if such statements (first-person past-tense statements) can be memory statements then it is a mistake, or at any rate very misleading, to say that they always express identity judgments. The question whether A and B are identical can arise only if one knows, or thinks one knows, of the existence of both A and B. And a judgment of identity can be made only where a question of identity can be sensibly asked. Suppose, then, that the statement "I broke the front window yesterday" is made as a memory statement. It will not be the case that the speaker first knows that someone broke the front window yesterday and then discovers that that person was himself. If what he remembers is that *he* broke the front window, then for him the question "Am I the person who broke the front window?" cannot arise. Bishop Butler remarked that "very often a person's assurance of an action having been done, of which he is absolutely assured, arises wholly from the consciousness that he himself did it." [8] When this is so, the person cannot raise the question whether the

---

[8] "Of Personal Identity," p. 284.

past action was done by him, since he knows the past action only as an action that he himself did. For him to doubt whether he did it would be for him to doubt his memory, and therefore to doubt whether the action was done at all. In such a case, it seems to me, it would be as misleading to say that the statement "I broke the front window yesterday" expresses a judgment of identity as it would be in normal circumstances to say that the statement "That novel is lewd" expresses a judgment of identity. In certain circumstances it would be appropriate for me to say "I am the same as the person who broke the front window yesterday" even though I remember breaking the window, as opposed to having concluded that I broke it from evidence. This would be so if my hearer knew that the window was broken yesterday but not that I broke it. And there are analogous circumstances in which it would be appropriate for me to say "That is the same as the novel that is lewd," for instance, if someone had heard me talking about a lewd novel but did not know that I was talking about this particular novel. But we cannot say in general that judging that a novel is lewd is judging that it is identical with something, and neither can we say in general that judging that one did a certain thing in the past is judging that one is identical with a "past self."

The crucial question, then, is whether first-person past-tense statements can be memory statements, or whether they must always be conclusions from what is remembered, conclusions that require justification in terms of criteria of identity.

5. In the standard sense of the word "remember," it is self-contradictory to say "I remember such and such happening, though I wasn't present when it happened and was quite unaware of its occurrence at the time." [9] This is sometimes ex-

---

[9] The word "remember" is sometimes used, at least by philosophers, in

pressed by saying that it is a necessary truth, or a conceptual truth, that if a person remembers an event then he must have been a witness to the event, or must have observed its occurrence. This is not completely accurate, for one can remember one's own actions, and it is normally not the case that one observes one's actions, or in any ordinary sense witnesses them, while one is performing them. It is more accurate to say that if one remembers an event then one must have been in a position to have direct knowledge of the event at the time of its occurrence. If I remember Tom hitting Dick, or the fire on Main Street, I must have observed these events, for there is no other direct way in which I could have known of them. Of my own actions I have, while they are occurring, direct knowledge that is not observational. In the following discussion, however, I shall use the verb "witness" to mean "have direct knowledge of," and the noun "witness" in a correspondingly broad sense. In this sense of "witness" a person is a witness to his own actions.

As we shall see, the point just made about the notion of memory has been taken by some philosophers as proof that the notion of personal identity can be defined, wholly or in part, in terms of the notion of memory, and that memory facts (e.g., the fact that I remember playing chess yesterday) provide a criterion, or even the criterion, of personal identity. I shall consider later on the question whether there is any sense in which memory is (memory facts are) a criterion we can use in mak-

---

such a way that one can truly be said to remember that P when it is not the ease that P, or can truly be said to remember X occurring when in fact X did not occur. But I shall always use the word "remember" in what is sometimes called its "entailing sense," i.e., in such a way that "A remembers that P" entails "P," and "A remembers X occurring" entails "X occurred." This is, I think, by far the most common use of the word. In this sense of "remember," if "P" is false, or X did not occur, then the most that anyone can do is *seem* to remember that P, or *seem* to remember X occurring.

ing third-person identity judgments. But some philosophers have apparently taken this necessary truth about memory, that if a person remembers an event he must have been a witness to it, as lending support to the view that memory facts constitute the criteria (criterial evidence) we use in making past-tense statements about ourselves on the basis of memory. I shall argue that this necessary truth, or rather the fact that it is a necessary truth, leads to a very different conclusion, namely that in making such statements there is nothing we use as a criterion of personal identity. My basic argument will be stated in this section, and in the remainder of this chapter I shall apply it in criticizing some of the traditional theories concerning the nature of personal identity and the "longitudinal unity of the mind."

Suppose that I make the statement "I broke the front window yesterday," and suppose that in making this statement I have no knowledge concerning the past event reported (the breaking of the front window yesterday) other than what is provided by my own memory. Clearly I use no physical criteria of identity in making this statement, and it is in this sort of case, if in any, that it can plausibly be argued that first-person past-tense statements are grounded on criteria of identity that are nonphysical and psychological. Let us suppose, then, that my statement is grounded on a criterion of personal identity, presumably a psychological criterion. As we saw in the preceding section, if this statement is grounded on a criterion of identity it cannot be a memory statement; it must be based on memory in the sense of being a conclusion from what is remembered, not in the sense of being a report of what is directly remembered. It cannot be the case that I remember that I broke the window. What I remember must be that someone of a certain description broke the front window yesterday, and my claim that I broke it, or that I am the person who broke it, must be a conclusion drawn from this fact, and from what I know about my "present self," in accordance with my criterion of identity (whatever it is). I can remember the breaking of the window and the breaking of the window by a person of a certain description, but not, if such statements must always be grounded on criteria, *my* breaking the window.

It is a logical truth, as I have said, that if a person remembers a past event then he, that same person, must have been in a position to have direct knowledge of the event when it occurred. So if I remember the breaking of the window yesterday, or remember someone breaking the front window yesterday, it follows that I was present yesterday when the window was broken. And since, if I remember this, I am clearly entitled to assert the proposition "I remember someone breaking the front window yesterday," I am also entitled to assert what follows from this, namely "I was present yesterday when the front window was broken." But this last statement is a first-person past-tense statement, so on the view being considered it must contain an identity judgment and, if it is known to be true, must be grounded on a criterion of personal identity. In the case at hand, however, it clearly is not so grounded. It is not, as it would have to be if based on a criterion of identity, a conclusion from what I know about someone who existed in the past. What I know about the past, in the case we are considering, is what I remember, but this statement is not a conclusion *from* what I remember at all. It is entailed by the proposition that I remember a certain past event, but it is not itself a conclusion from any of the facts that I remember about the event.

What I have established so far is that if we can remember past events at all there are some first-person past-tense statements that can be known without being grounded on criteria of identity, namely statements to the effect that the speaker was present when certain past events occurred. This is sufficient to refute the claim that all first-person past-tense statements must be grounded on criteria of identity if they are known to be true, and refuting this claim, I think, undermines the plausibility of the view that what appear be first-person memory statements, e.g., my original statement "I broke the front window yesterday," must really be conclusions drawn from remembered facts in accordance with criteria of personal identity. And we are now in a position, I believe, to see that this view is false.

If I can know that I was present when an action was done without using criteria of identity, why cannot I know without using criteria that I did the action? Is it that I must employ a criterion in order to know *which* of the persons present was myself? In that case, presumably, I would not have to employ my criterion if I remembered that only one person was present, for that person, obviously, would have to be myself. But he would have to be myself *no matter what* I remembered about him, i.e., even if the remembered facts were such that I would have to conclude from them, in accordance with my criterion, that he was *not* myself. If I had a criterion that I could use in such cases, it should be possible for me to remember someone doing a certain action, discover by the use of my criterion that he was not myself, and then find, by consulting my memory of the incident, that he was the only person present when the action was done. And clearly this is not possible. A similar difficulty arises if we suppose that several persons were present. For why could I not find, by applying my criterion to my memories of these persons, that *none* of them was myself?

What is impossible is that I should be entitled to say, on the basis of what I remember, that I do remember a certain event and that I was not a witness to that event. This should not be confused with something that is quite possible, namely that I should have what is ostensibly a memory of a certain event and be entitled to conclude, from the nature of this memory, that I was not a witness to any such event. It might be that the event I seem to remember is of such a fantastic nature that I realize that no such event could have occurred. Or it might be that, while the ostensibly remembered event is one that quite conceivably might have occurred, what I seem to remember about it (the time, place, and circumstances of its occurrence) is such that I realize that I could not have been a witness to such an event. A case of the latter would be my seeming to remember a conversation with Premier Khrushchev, occurring in the Kremlin yesterday morning. Here I would conclude, not simply that I was not a witness to such an event, but that I do not really remember such an event at all, and that (unless I have independent evidence of its occurrence) there is no reason for thinking that such an event occurred. In asserting it to be impossible that I could have been a witness to such an event I would be making an implicit appeal to criteria of personal identity. But these criteria would be physical criteria; given other things I know, it is physically impossible that my body should have been in the Kremlin yesterday morning. What I would *not* have done, in this case, is to conclude on the basis of criteria of identity that each of the witnesses of a remembered event was someone other than myself. And what I am contending is that where I do remember an event, and know of it on the basis of memory alone, it is not possible for me to conclude on the basis of criteria of identity that a certain witness of the event *was* myself.

What I wish to conclude from this is that first-person past-tense statements can be, and frequently are, memory statements, i.e., statements that simply report what the speaker remembers, and are not conclusions from what he remembers. When this is so the speaker is not, in making his statement, identifying a remembered self as himself, and therefore the question of how he makes such an identification does not arise. I do not remember that someone broke the front window yesterday and then identify that person as myself; I simply remember that I broke the front window. To put this in another way, what I remember is not "the breaking of the window by someone," but is simply "breaking the window." And for me to remember breaking the window is the same as for me to remember *my* breaking the window.

Memories can, of course, be incomplete and fragmentary, and it is possible to remember that something was done without having a full memory of the doing of it. When this is so, one can remember that a certain action (or an action of a certain description) was done without realizing, at least at first, that it was oneself who did it. For example, I might say "I remember that someone told that story last week, but I don't recall who it was," and then be informed that it was I who told it. And I might remember that something was done and then come to realize that I did it without being informed of this by others. Two kinds of cases are possible here. I might remember that something was done and then conclude, from what I remember, that it *must* have been myself that did it. For example, I might say "It must have been I who was talking about that editorial, for no one else who was present reads the *Times*." Here my memory of the incident would still be incomplete. This would not be a case of my remembering someone doing something and then identifying that person as myself; it would be a case of my remembering that something was done, but not the doing of it, and using other information to make an extrapolation from the remembered facts. But the following can also happen: I might say "*Now* I remember! How could I have forgotten? It was I who was talking about that." Here an incomplete memory is surplanted by a more complete one, and the fragmentary recollection that something was done is surplanted by a memory of the doing of it, which in this case is a memory of *my* doing it. And again there is no question of my identifying a remembered past self as myself; in this case my coming to realize that I did something is not a matter of my drawing a conclusion at all, but is simply a matter of my coming to remember what I previously had not remembered.

6. In Section 9 of Chapter Two I stated, and attributed to Locke, an argument that has the appearance of showing that the identity of a person cannot consist in the identity of a substance. In the form in which I stated it, this argument is clearly unsound, for it has the absurd conclusion that the subject of some of a person's thoughts and experiences may not be the subject of all of that person's thoughts and experiences. When slightly modified, however, this argument can be seen to lead to a rather different conclusion, and to be, in fact, a special case of the argument of the preceding section.

Briefly stated, the original form of the argument goes like this. Because my consciousness is interrupted, i.e., because there are gaps in my memory, I am generally not in a position to know whether a given substance existing in the past is the same as one existing now, and therefore whether the subject of the thoughts, experiences, and actions that I remember is the same as the subject of my present thoughts, experiences, and actions. But any thought or experience that I remember must have been my thought or experience, and if I remember a thought or experience I cannot doubt that it was mine (Locke seems to say this of actions as well, but let us ignore this). Since I can doubt whether the subject of a remembered thought or experience is the subject of my present experiences, but cannot doubt that the remembered thought or experience was my thought or experience, it follows that the identity of a person cannot consist in the identity of a subject or substance, and that the persistence of a person does not require the persistence of a substance.

The first thing to be noted about this argument is that it invokes the principle invoked in the argument of the preceding section, namely the principle that if a person remembers a past event he must have been a witness to that event. Or at any rate, it invokes a principle very much like it. Let us restrict ourselves to a consideration of memories that are memories of past mental events, or in Locke's terminology, memories of past "ideas." In a sense this is no restriction at all, since for Locke all memories are, in the first instance, memories of ideas. Now according to Locke, if I am "conscious" of a past idea, i.e., if I remember it, then it must have been my idea. This is, in fact, a consequence of Locke's theory of memory. For someone to remember something, on that theory, is for him to "revive," or to have an idea that is a "copy" of, an idea he had had previously. But this claim can also be seen as a special case of the necessary truth stated in the preceding section. On the traditional conception, a person witnesses his own ideas, i.e., his own thoughts and experiences, in a way in which no other person can witness them. But if I remember an idea, I must have witnessed it (this is an application of the general principle), and since no one could have witnessed it except the person who had it, it must have been my idea.

As I suggested in Chapter Two, Locke apparently takes a certain sort of case as his paradigm, or model, of what it would be like to know with certainty that a substance existing at one time is the same as one existing at another time. His paradigm is the sort of case in which one knows that something existing at t_2 is the same as something that existed at t_1 because one has watched that thing, without interruption, throughout the interval between t_1 and t_2. Sometimes, certainly, we do know statements of identity in this way, and this seems to be the most certain way of knowing the identity of a material object. A detective who had been "tailing" a suspect might be asked whether he is sure that it was that person, and not an identical twin, whom he saw pawning a stolen watch, and his answer might be "I'm absolutely sure, for I didn't let him out of my sight from the time I started following him to the time he pawned the watch." Locke apparently thought that unless our knowledge of the identity of a mental substance can be grounded in a way analogous to this we can never be sure that one substance has not been replaced by another just like it, and can never be sure, therefore, that a mental substance existing at one time is numerically the same as one existing at another time. It is perhaps on similar grounds that H. P. Grice once held that if we accept the pure ego theory we cannot give a satisfactory answer to the question of how one knows that it was one self, and "not two similar selves," that had two successive experiences.[10] Given a certain picture, a picture of mental substances as things which ought to be in some sense observable and capable of being watched over a period of time, this view is a very natural one.

Now it seems to me that Locke's argument can be taken, not (as he took it) as an argument proving that the identity of a person does not involve the identity of a substance, but as a *reductio ad absurdum* argument showing that the statements one makes about one's own past on the basis of memory cannot be grounded as are the statements we make about the identity of other things. It shows, first of all, that they cannot be grounded in the way in which Locke apparently thought identity statements about substances must be grounded if they are to be known with certainty, i.e., on the basis of an uninterrupted observation of something over a period of time (the way

---

[10] "Personal Identity," p. 340.

in which, in my example, the detective's statement about the identity of the suspect was grounded). But from this it does not follow that a person (or self) is not a substance, or that the identity of a self does not involve the identity of a substance. This follows only if one accepts Locke's view as to how the identity of substances would have to be known. Since we can give no sense to Locke's conclusion, we must take the argument as showing, not that selves are not substances, but that if selves are substances then these substances can have knowledge concerning their own pasts that is not grounded in the way in which Locke thinks identity knowledge concerning substances must be grounded. But the argument can also be used to show that first-person past-tense statements based on memory cannot, in normal circumstances, be grounded on criteria of identity.

I shall now restate the argument so as to bring out what I think to be its real force. Suppose that I have an *un*interrupted memory of the interval between a certain time yesterday and the present moment. Suppose that now I remember a certain "idea," say an image, that occurred yesterday, remember also the substance or subject that had, or perceived, that idea, remember as well that I have not "lost sight" of that substance since the time at which it had that idea, and can therefore be sure that nothing has been substituted for it, and that it is identical with the substance that perceives my present ideas. If I could remember this then surely I *could* remember that at some point another substance *was* substituted for it, and know that it was *not* the same as the substance that perceives my present ideas. Given that I can perceive a thing of a certain sort, if my memory of what I observed (perceived, was aware of, was conscious of) between yesterday and the present could inform me that a thing of that sort that I observe now *is* the same as one that I remember existing yesterday, then it could inform me that a thing of that sort that I observe now is *not* the same as one that I remember existing yesterday. As I said in Chapter Two, by appealing to the fact that we constantly "lose sight" of our past selves as grounds for doubt as to whether we always remain the same substance, Locke implies that one substance could be replaced by another, and that if our consciousness were not interrupted we would detect such changes were they to occur. For it is only because our consciousness is interrupted that he thinks that such substitutions might occur without being detected. But if we know what it would be like to detect such a substitution, surely it is conceivable that someday we might detect one. Suppose, however, that I were to remember that the substance which had the idea (saw the image) yesterday had been replaced by another substance and was not the same as the substance that has my present ideas. If the identity of a person consists in, or essentially involves, the identity of a substance, then in this case I would have to say that the remembered idea belonged to someone other than myself. And this, as Locke saw, is absurd; if I remember the image then it must have been I that had it. So we must either draw Locke's conclusion, and say that the identity of a person does not involve the identity of a substance (a view that I have argued to be unintelligible or self-contradictory), or we must say that in the sense in which one can observe, and remember, that a material object, or another person, has or has not remained the same (has or has not been replaced by something else) during a certain interval of time, one cannot observe or remember that a mental substance, or oneself, has or has not remained the same.

7. Arguments similar to Locke's have often been taken to support the bundle theory of the self (or the logical construction theory). They have been taken to show that the identity

of a person does not consist in the identity of a substance, and that it must therefore consist in something else, in the holding of some relationship between noncontemporary experiences or mental events, this relationship being empirically accessible in a way in which the identity of a substance, it is thought, cannot be. In "The Philosophy of Logical Atomism" Russell said that "you can collect a whole set of experiences into one string as all belonging to you, and similarly other people's experiences can be collected together as all belonging to them by relations that actually are observable and without assuming the existence of a persistent ego." [11] Although Russell does not profess to know just what these relations are, he thinks it obvious that there must be such relations:

It does not matter in the least to what we are concerned with, what exactly is the given empirical relation between two experiences that makes us say, "These are two experiences of the same person." It does not matter precisely what that relation is, because the logical formula for the construction of the person is the same whatever that relation may be, and because the mere fact that you can know that two experiences belong to the same person proves that there is such an empirical relationship to be ascertained by analysis. Let us call the relation R. We shall say that when two experiences have to each other the relation R, then they are said to be experiences of the same person.[12]

The very fact that I can know that an experience occurring now and one that occurred yesterday are experiences of the same person (namely myself) shows, on Russell's view, that there is an empirical, observable, relationship of "co-personality," and that a person is a "certain series of experiences" related to one another by this relationship.

Far from supporting this sort of view, Locke's argument

---

[11] In *Logic and Knowledge*, pp. 276–277.

[12] *Ibid.*, p. 277. Reprinted with permission of George Allen & Unwin, Ltd.

can be used to show that it is mistaken. Let us suppose that there is an empirical, observable relationship of co-personality, and let us, following Russell, call this relationship R. We are to suppose that when I assert, on the basis of memory, that I had an experience, say a headache, yesterday morning, I am asserting this on the grounds that the past experience stands in the relation R to some present experience that I know to be mine. This leads to self-contradiction. For if I could set out to establish empirically, on the basis of what I remember and what I observe now, whether a remembered experience stands in the relation R to my present experience, it must be possible that I could find that it does not stand in R to my present experience. But if R were the relation of co-personality, and I could find that an experience I remember does not stand in R to my present experience, then I could find that an experience I remember was not my experience. And this is not possible.

An analogy may help to bring out more clearly the force of this argument. The persistence of a hurricane could be said to consist in the occurrence of a series of events related to one another in certain ways, and the bundle theory can be thought of as modeling the identity of selves upon the identity of such things as hurricanes. Now let us suppose, what may or may not be the case, that meteorologists have precise criteria for determining whether or not two successive events, say a rainstorm occurring in one locality and a hailstorm occurring in another, are parts (phases, manifestations) of one and the same hurricane. Given such criteria, a meteorologist who remembers a past weather phenomenon and is observing a present one could sensibly raise the question whether these phenomena belong to the same hurricane, and by considering what he knows about them (what he remembers about the one and observes about the other) and perhaps about intervening events, and by applying his criteria to these data, he could settle this question in one way or the other. And notice that I say "in one way or the other." The important point is that his investigation might come out either way; he might find that the two phenomena belonged to the same hurricane, but he might find that they did not. The reason why criteria are needed here, if such questions are to be answerable, is that one *can* observe, at different times, weather phenomena that do *not* belong to the same hurricane; the point of having criteria is precisely to enable us to distinguish these cases from cases in which the successive events do belong to the same hurricane.

It should be clear from what I have said that what is true of a presently observed weather phenomenon and a remembered one, with respect to the notion of "same hurricane," is not true of a presently "observed" experience and a remembered one, with respect to the notion of "same person." As a model to explain the nature of knowledge of self-identity, the case of the meteorologist who observes a series of different events, and sees that they are so related as to satisfy the criteria for being parts of a single hurricane, is no better than the case of the detective who watches a suspect without ever losing sight of him and is thus in a position to testify concerning his identity. But this, taken together with the arguments in Chapter Three, seems to me to show that the bundle theory of the self is no more successful than the pure ego theory in making selves empirically knowable. Yet, as we have seen, the *raison d'être* of the bundle theory is, precisely, to explain how the self can be empirically knowable. If it fails in this it has nothing to recommend it.

8. The argument I have been using rests on the principle that any experience that I remember must have been my experience, which I have regarded as a special case of the more general principle that if one remembers an event one must have been

a witness to that event. It will perhaps be thought that in using that principle I have unwittingly conceded that there is a
first-person criterion of identity, namely memory itself, and
that what I have said, far from refuting the bundle theory,
supports the most common version of it.

It is, indeed, a common view among bundle theorists that,
as H. P. Grice expressed it, "the self is a logical construction,
and is to be defined in terms of memory," [13] or as Russell once
said, "a total group of my experiences throughout time may be
defined in terms of memory." [14] In "The Philosophy of Logical
Atomism" Russell did not commit himself as to what the relationship of "co-personality" might be, but he suggests that it
might be memory: "What we know is this string of experiences
that makes up a person, and that is put together by means of
certain relations, such, e.g., as memory." [15] Locke is perhaps
the originator of this view, for he says, apparently intending
to define personal identity, that "whatever has the consciousness of present and past actions is the same person to whom
they both belong." [16] Hume held that the successive "perceptions" of a person are united by the relations of resemblance and cause and effect, but it was apparently his theory
of memory that led him to hold this. A memory, on Hume's
view, is a perception that resembles and is caused by the past
perception of which it is the memory. And according to Hume,
"the memory not only discovers the identity [of a person], but
also contributes to its production, by producing the relation of
resemblance among the perceptions." [17] To mention one more
philosopher who has held a view of this sort, A. J. Ayer, in his
book *The Foundations of Empirical Knowledge*, held that
there are "two different sorts of criteria for determining the

---

[13] "Personal Identity," p. 340.
[14] "On the Nature of Acquaintance," p. 138.
[15] Page 277.   [16] *Essay*, I, 458.   [17] *Treatise*, p. 261.

ownership of experiences." [18] One of these sets of criteria includes bodily identity, or "bodily continuity," as a criterion of personal identity. But there are also, says Ayer,

what may be called the psychological criteria of continuity of disposition and memory. We may say that a series of experiences constitutes the history of a single person if similar mental states recur throughout the series in similar conditions, and if, as the series is prolonged, its later sections always contain some experiences that are memories of the earlier.[19]

From the fact that there is a logical relationship between the notions of memory and personal identity, the relationship I have expressed by saying that if a person remembers an event he must have been a witness to the event, it is natural to conclude that one of these notions must be in some way definable or analyzable in terms of the other. But when one says that one remembers a past event, it surely is not the case that one has first established that one is the same as someone who witnessed the event and then concluded, from this fact and others, that one remembers the event. That one remembers a past event seems, from one's own point of view, a brute, unanalyzable fact. Thus it is plausible to suppose that the notion of memory is logically prior to the notion of personal identity, and that the latter must be definable or analyzable in terms of the former, rather than vice versa. Nevertheless, it is clearly a mistake, as I shall now try to show, to think that we have in memory a first-person criterion of identity that we use in making past-tense statements about ourselves, and that "being the memory of" constitutes the relationship of "co-personality" required by the bundle theory.

9. Let us begin by considering some revealing remarks of Hume's. He asks us to suppose that we could "see clearly into

---

[18] London, 1951, p. 142.   [19] *Ibid.*

the breast of another, and observe that succession of perceptions, which constitutes his mind or thinking principle." [20]
Some of the perceptions in this succession would be memories,
and hence resemblances, of earlier ones, and this resemblance
would "convey the imagination more easily from one link
to another, and make the whole seem like the continuance of
one object." Hume then goes on to say: "The case is the
same whether we consider ourselves or others." [21]

Now of course we cannot "see into the breast of another" in
the sense Hume has in mind, i.e., in the sense of perceiving,
or being directly aware of, another person's "perceptions" (feelings, sensations, and so on). Nor, I am sure, does Hume believe
that we can do this. But it is revealing that he begins by describing what we would see in the mind of another, and then
says that we observe the same in our own minds. What he
would like to do, I think, is to explain the knowledge one has
of one's own identity on the model of the knowledge one has
of the identity of other things. Hume has a picture of what
goes on in the mind of a person, a picture derived in part from
his view that remembering a past experience consists in having
a present experience, or perceiving a present image, that *resembles* the past experience. This picture therefore represents
what occurs in the mind of a person over a period of time as
analogous to what one perceives when, over a period of time,
one perceives the successive (and resembling) states of one and
the same object, and is entitled to assert, on the basis of these
perceptions (and one's memories of them), that the object experienced at the beginning of the series is identical with the
object experienced at the end of it. Thus it seems that if one
could observe what this picture represents one would be in a
position to make an assertion about the identity of a mind. The
cases in which one unquestionably does perceive a series of
resembling states analogous to the series represented in Hume's

---

[20] *Treatise*, p. 260.   [21] *Ibid.*, pp. 260–261.

picture are cases in which one is observing an object other than oneself. So it is natural that in presenting his picture as a representation of something observed Hume first presents it as representing what we would observe if we could see in the mind of *another* person. But from this he moves, again quite naturally, to the claim that this picture represents what one can observe occurring in one's own mind.

I shall argue that what Hume's picture represents is not something that one can observe in one's own mind. We might say, somewhat paradoxically, that the way in which Hume thinks that one can observe the contents of one's own mind is a way in which only another person could observe them. Or, since one person cannot observe the contents of another's mind at all, it is a way in which only God could observe them. The situation here is rather like one we discussed earlier. Figure 1 in Chapter Two, which represented a mental subject perceiving a mental object, was patterned after what we observe when we observe another person perceiving something. It seemed that if we could observe something corresponding to this picture we would be in a position to ascribe mental objects (images and the like) to mental subjects on the basis of observation. But it turned out that one cannot observe what this picture represents when the subject is oneself. And since the subject represented is a mental subject, and the object a mental object, it is equally impossible (though for different reasons) for one to observe what it represents when the subject is someone other than oneself. What that picture represents cannot be observed by anyone. And the same is true of Hume's picture.

Let us suppose, for the moment, that Hume's account of memory is correct, and that remembering something is having an "idea," or perceiving an image, that resembles some past "impression," which is what is remembered. Now of course identity judgments are often based on resemblance. So if my memories are resemblances of past experiences of mine, why can I not make identity judgments about myself on the basis of this resemblance? Why, that is, can I not ascribe a past experience to myself, or judge that the "past self" that had it is identical with my "present self," on the basis of its resemblance to a present memory of mine? But is this resemblance something that I can observe? Can I compare the past experience with the memory and see that they are similar? The fact that the past experience no longer exists does not, of course, prevent me from knowing what it was like. But *how* do I know what it was like? I *remember* what it was like. So can I compare what I remember it to have been like with my memory of it, and see that they are similar? But this would be to compare my memory of it with my memory of it, i.e., to compare my memory of it with itself. And surely it makes no sense to speak of comparing something with itself, to see whether there is a resemblance.

This argument can be generalized. For whether the relationship of "being the memory of" consists in resemblance or something else, it is not a relationship that one could observe to hold between a present memory and the past experience of which it is the memory. That is, one cannot know this relationship to hold on the basis of observation and memory in a way analogous to that in which I know that the typewriter I see now resembles the one I remember seeing on my desk yesterday. If I know of a past event solely on the basis of my memory of it (and this is the sort of case that concerns us), then in inquiring whether it is related in a certain way (in *any* given way) to another event I must be relying on my memory of it. And in that case I obviously cannot be raising any question as to whether I do remember it, or whether one of my present experiences is a memory of it. When I know on the basis of memory and observation that the typewriter on my desk yesterday exactly resembled, and is almost certainly identical with, the typewriter there now, my knowledge is based on memory in the sense of being a conclusion from remembered facts, namely what I remember about the typewriter that was on my desk yesterday. But my judgment that I remember a past experience, if based solely on my memory, cannot be a conclusion from any of the facts I remember about the past experience. For if it is solely on the basis of my memory of the experience that I know these facts, then in regarding them *as* facts I presuppose that I do remember the event, and hence there is no conclusion to be drawn. Clearly I could never conclude from what I remember about a past experience that I *do not* remember it. Neither, therefore, can I conclude from what I remember about a past experience that I do remember it. Of course, it is possible for me to conclude from the character of an apparent memory of a past experience that I really remember no such thing. But here I would also conclude that, in all probability, no such experience occurred. And my conclusion would not be from what I remember, but would be from the fact that I *seem* to remember something of a certain kind (something that could not have happened, or could not have happened to me). Certainly I would not be concluding on the basis of my memory of a past experience that it and my present memory are not related by the relationship "being the memory of." And there is no case in which I can conclude from what I remember about an experience that it and my present memory of it do stand in this relationship. Hence this relationship cannot be the observable relationship of co-personality that Russell and others were looking for.

If I could "see clearly into the breast of another," of course, there would not be this difficulty about my observing a resemblance, or the holding of the relationship "being the memory of," between a present memory and a past experience. If I could remember a past experience and at the same time observe a memory of it that is not my own memory of it (i.e., is someone else's), then in comparing that memory with the experience I would not be comparing it with itself. I would, in effect, be comparing one memory of the experience (someone else's) with another memory of it (my own), and here there would be two things to compare. It is not necessary for me to argue here that it is impossible for us to see into the minds of others in this way. It is sufficient to point out that the supposition that this is possible is inconsistent with the principle that any experience one remembers must have been one's own experience, and therefore with any attempt to define personal identity in terms of memory. For if I observed a resemblance between a memory belonging to another person and one of his past experiences, then I, along with the other person, would remember the past experience (and on Hume's theory would have a memory that resembles it).

Of course, it sometimes happens that one remembers something and also knows of it on grounds other than memory. And when this happens one can compare one's memory of what something was like with what one knows on other grounds to have been its nature. But it can hardly have been this sort of case that Hume was thinking of in suggesting that it is on the basis of an *observed* resemblance between past experiences and our memories of them that we make identity judgments about ourselves. The nonmemory knowledge we have of our own past experiences can only be based on knowledge (gained from photographic records, the testimony of other persons, and other such evidence) of past behavior, namely the past behavior (verbal or nonverbal) in which the experiences expressed themselves at the time of their occurrence. It is quite possible to find that what one knows in this way about a past experience resembles what one remembers about it. And if I have such knowledge of a past experience I can sensibly inquire whether the experience that I know in this way is one that I remember. For example, if Jones, who has a way of remembering trivial facts, tells me that exactly one year ago I had a severe headache (I told him about it at the time), I might wonder, and try to find out, whether the headache he is referring to is the same as one I now remember. Here I would be trying to find out whether a past experience (the one Jones is referring to) is one I remember. And I might even be trying to find out whether a past experience was mine, e.g., if I suspect that Jones has mistaken me for someone else. But suppose that I do conclude, from a comparison of what Jones describes with what I remember, that I remember the experience he is referring to, or that it was mine. Here I will not be concluding from what I remember about an experience that I remember it, or that it was mine; rather I will be concluding from what I remember about an experience that it is the experience Jones is referring to. It is only of an experience as known independently of my memory that I can ask whether I remember it, or whether it was mine. And in any case, in comparing what one remembers about a past experience with what one knows of it on other grounds, one can hardly be said to be observing a resemblance (or any other relationship) between earlier and later members of an observed succession of events.

Returning once more to Hume, it will perhaps be suggested that the resemblance I "observe" among my experiences is not between my present memories and the past experiences of which they are memories, but is rather between my *past* memories and the earlier experiences of which they were memories, and also between the numerically different memories that I have had, at different times, of the same past experiences. If we think of memories as resemblances of what is remembered, and as experiences that can themselves come to be remembered, it will seem plausible to suppose that every person does "observe" resemblances of this sort in what he remembers. And now it might seem that my observation of such resemblances can be the grounds of the judgments I make about my own identity. But, first, in observing such similarities I would *at best* be in a position to identify *past* selves with one another (e.g., a self of yesterday and a self of the day before); this would not explain how I can identify a past self with a present self, and therefore would not explain how I am entitled to make past statements about my present self, i.e., past-tense statements having the word "I" as subject. And, second, it would seem to follow from this account that if I "observed" a total lack of resemblance among the experiences I remember I should have to conclude that those experiences were not co-personal. But this is absurd. No matter what relation I observe holding between the experiences I now remember, if I remember them then they must have been my experiences. Hence it cannot be any relation that I observe (or remember) holding among them, neither the relation of resemblance, the relation "being the memory of," nor any other, that entitles me to say that they are mine, or that they all belong to the same person. This is simply a special application of the argument of Section 7.

10. In his article "Personal Identity" H. P. Grice gives the following as a reason for preferring a logical construction theory of the self to a pure ego theory:

Suppose the P. E. [pure ego] theory to be true and suppose I know that I had a headache yesterday, and that I had a toothache this morning. Now suppose that I am asked how I know that it is one self which had both experiences, and not two exactly similar selves. On the P. E. theory plus the P. N. [proper name] theory, I don't see how I could give any true answer, except "I just do know." This is, I think, rather unsatisfactory. But on a L. C. T. [logical construction theory], on the other hand, if I am asked this question I can answer truly "Because the experiences have to one another the relation R which constitutes 'belonging to the same self as.'" For instance, I should answer "Because I remember (or know to have occurred) both experiences, and any experiences I remember (or know to have occurred) must be co-personal." This answer would imply, I think, that the self is a logical construction, and is to be defined in terms of memory.[22]

Here, it would appear, the relation of co-personality, or "belonging to the same self as," is held to be, not the relation of "being the memory of," but the relation "being remembered by the same self as." Now I would not want to deny, of course, that the experiences a person remembers all belong to one and the same person. But I do not see how it follows from this that "the self is a logical construction, and is to be defined in terms of memory," *unless* it is supposed that one *uses* the fact that two experiences are remembered by the same person as the *criterion* for saying that they belong to the same person.

Grice asks, supposing that I had a headache yesterday and a toothache this morning, how do I know that it was one self that had both experiences? Why cannot one answer this by saying "Well, since both of them were *my* experiences, it follows logically that they were experiences of the same self"? To say this, of course, is not to commit oneself to any particular theory of personal identity, since on any theory it must be the case that all my experiences are experiences of a single person. But it is hardly likely that Grice was asking the absurd question "Given that I know that I had a headache yesterday and that I had a toothache this morning, how do I know that

---

[22] *Mind,* L (1941), 340.

these experiences belonged to one and the same person?" What question, then, was he raising? Was it the question "How do I know that I had a headache yesterday and a toothache this morning?" But suppose that I answer this by saying "I remember having a headache yesterday (or that I had a headache yesterday) and having a toothache this morning (or that I had a toothache this morning)." This answer, certainly, would not commit me to the view that personal identity is to be defined in terms of memory. But perhaps Grice's question is: "Given that I remember (not: remember having) a headache that occurred yesterday, and remember (not: remember having) a toothache that occurred this morning, how do I know that both these experiences belong to one and the same person?"

This last question sounds like the meteorologist's question "Given that I remember a weather phenomenon that occurred yesterday and a weather phenomenon that occurred this morning, how do I know that these two phenomena belong to one and the same hurricane?" And what Grice gives as the general form of the logical construction theory's answer to his question—"Because the experiences have to one another the relation R which constitutes 'belonging to the same self as' "—is, if "weather phenomena" is substituted for "experiences" and "hurricane" is substituted for "self," the form of the answer the meteorologist would give. And Grice thinks that the answer "Because I remember (or know to have occurred) both experiences, and any experiences I remember (or know to have occurred) must be co-personal" is a satisfactory answer of this form.

But notice the differences. The meteorologist can say "I *remember* that the phenomena have to each other the relation R which constitutes 'belonging to the same hurricane as,' " whereas Grice obviously cannot say "I remember that I remember both experiences, and any two experiences I remember must be co-personal." It would surely seem that if one can use the fact that a certain relation holds between two experiences as a criterion for saying that they are co-personal, it must be possible to know of the occurrence of two experiences, find them standing in that relation, and conclude on this basis that they are co-personal. But what sense could it make to say that I know of the occurrence of two experiences and know (have found) it to be a fact about them that I remember them both? *How* would I know this fact about them? Can I remember it? Surely it cannot be said that I know that I remember something by remembering that I remember it. And if I could remember two experiences and remember, as a fact about them, that they are remembered by me, then surely I *could* remember two experiences and remember, as a fact about them, that they are *not* remembered by me. And this is clearly impossible. But how else could I know this fact? We are concerned here only with cases in which one knows of events in one's past solely on the basis of one's memory. But the fact we are considering here, the fact that two experiences are remembered by me, is supposed to be a fact that I know about two *past* experiences, so if I know it at all I must, if the case is of the sort that concerns us, know it on the basis of memory. And this I cannot do.

It seems to me, in fact, that when I remember an experience I normally *cannot* be said to know, as a fact about that experience, that I remember it. Nor, for that matter, can I be said to know, as a fact about the experience, that it was mine. It makes sense to speak of knowing of a past experience that one remembers it, or that it was one's own, only where it would also make sense to speak of knowing of that past experience that one does not remember it, or that it was not one's own. And the latter makes sense only if one has nonmemory knowledge of the experience in question. I can be said to know that I remember a headache. But this is not to know of a particular headache that I remember it. And when I say I had a headache yesterday, and assert this solely on the basis of memory, I am not saying of a particular headache occurring yesterday that it was mine. Normally I can identify a past experience only as one I remember. And when this is so, there cannot arise any question whether I remember the experience or any question as to the ownership of the experience. In such cases, where one's knowledge of a past experience is based solely on one's memory, there is no room for the employment of criteria of personal identity. No question of identity arises, and hence there is none to be settled by reference to criteria of identity.

All this is related to the fact that, when I say on the basis of memory that I had an experience in the past, my statement is based on memory in the sense of being a memory statement, not in the sense of being a conclusion from what I remember. It is not a conclusion from what I remember about a particular past experience, and it is not a conclusion from the fact that I remember a particular past experience. There is, indeed, a certain artificiality about the locution "remember a past experience" that I have been using in this chapter. We do not normally speak of someone as remembering a headache; we say that he remembers having a headache, or that he remembers that he had a headache, or that he remembers that such and such a person had a headache. The reason why I have employed the artificial expression "remember an experience" is that without using some such expression one cannot formulate, in such a way as to make them even initially plausible, the sort of theories about personal identity that I have been attacking. It would be patently absurd to say that I can remember that I had a headache and then set about to discover, by applying criteria of identity to what I remember, whether it was I who had the experience. And it would be no less absurd to say that I can remember having a headache and then set about in this way to find out whether it was my experience. For a somewhat different reason it would be absurd to say that I can remember that such and such a person had an experience, and then set about to discover whether it was I who had it. For if one says "I remember that such and such a person (Jones, a tall stranger, the man sitting on the couch, or the like) had a headache yesterday," one implies, if one is speaking in an ordinary way, that the person referred to is someone *other* than oneself. So here again it is not an open question whether the "remembered experience" is one's own. To speak simply of "remembering an experience" makes it look as if it is an open question, and one that can be settled by use of criteria, whether the remembered experience belongs to the rememberer. But given the picture that lies behind the philosophical use of this expression, and the notion that remembering an experience is a special case of remembering an event to which the rememberer was a witness in the past, it turns out that this cannot be an open question. Remembering that Jones had a headache will not count as remembering a headache, for here it will not be Jones's headache, but at best only his pain behavior, that the rememberer witnessed in the past and can now be said to remember. So "I remember a headache" turns out to mean what would ordinarily be expressed by "I remember having a headache." The very picture that makes it plausible to say that one uses memory as a criterion in ascribing past experiences to oneself turns out to have the consequence that one uses no criterion at all.

Five

Mind, Body, and
Personal Identity

1. Although the nature of our knowledge of "other minds" has for some time been recognized as a philosophical problem, philosophical theories about the nature of "the Self" generally have little to say about the nature of the knowledge one has of selves other than one's *own* self. It tends to be assumed that one's knowledge of oneself, as expressed in first-person psychological statements, is the only *direct* knowledge of a person that one can have, and that it is by considering the nature of this knowledge that the nature of persons is to be discovered. The question "What is a person?" is to be answered by answering the question "What am I?" and the latter question is to be approached by asking questions like "What am I acquainted with (or: what *must* I be acquainted with) when I know that I have a toothache (an image, a thought)?" In Chapter Six I shall try to show that this approach to the "problem of the

self" rests on an idea that is fundamentally mistaken—though perhaps it is mainly because of the attractiveness of this approach and the plausibility of that mistaken idea that there is a philosophical problem about the nature of persons. What I want to discuss now is one of the more disastrous consequences of this approach.

It seems to me to be a consequence of most of the theories of the self that I have been considering, not simply that one cannot have *direct* knowledge of other persons (or at any rate of "other minds"), but that it is logically impossible for one to have any knowledge at all, or even any reasonable beliefs, about another person (or the "mind" of another person). In trying to make persons knowable to themselves these theories make them unknowable to persons other than themselves. That a theory has this consequence is, I think, sufficient proof that it is mistaken. Yet there is a very plausible view, implicit in most of the theories I have considered, from which this consequence follows. This is the view, developed in Chapter One, that persons are essentially nonphysical entities. More precisely, it is the view that psychological facts are logically independent of facts about human bodies (including facts about their behavior), and that personal identity is logically independent of bodily identity. In still other terms, it is the view that all relationships between psychological facts and physical (bodily and behavioral) facts are contingent relationships, and that bodily and behavioral facts can never be criterial evidence for the truth of psychological statements or statements of personal identity. This chapter will be, in the main, an attack on an argument which gives this view considerable plausibility. As we shall see in the next chapter, the plausibility of this argument has much the same source as the view that we can discover the nature of persons only by considering what persons are "acquainted with" when they make first-person psychological statements.

2. There is nothing novel about my claim that the view that all relationships between psychological facts and bodily facts are contingent has the consequence that it is logically impossible for one person to know a psychological fact about another person. But I must try to show, very briefly, why this is so and why this consequence is logically absurd.

If we know psychological facts about other persons at all, we know them on the basis of their behavior (including, of course, their verbal behavior). Sometimes we make psychological statements about other persons on the basis of bodily or behavioral facts that are only contingently related to the psychological facts for which we accept them as evidence. But we do this only because we have discovered, or think we have discovered, empirical correlations between physical (bodily and behavioral) facts of a certain kind and psychological facts of a certain kind. And if *all* relations between physical and psychological facts were contingent, it would be impossible for us to discover such correlations. Once one contingent relationship has been discovered, we can use our knowledge of it to discover others; having discovered that physical state *A* is correlated with psychological state *B*, we can find that another physical state, *C*, is correlated with *A* and therefore with *B*. But clearly the *first* such correlation that we discovered, concerning any given kind of psychological state, could not have been discovered in this way; in order to discover it we must have had knowledge of the existence of psychological states of the sort in question, and this knowledge cannot have been inferred from facts that we knew empirically to be correlated with the existence of such states, for as yet no such correlations had been discovered. Unless some relationships between physical and psychological states are not contingent, and can be known prior to the discovery of empirical correlations, we cannot have even indirect inductive evidence for the truth of psychological statements about other persons, and cannot know such statements to be true or even probably true.

It has often been suggested, of course, that one can discover empirical correlations between *one's own* psychological states and facts about one's own body and behavior, and that one's knowledge of these correlations can provide a basis for inductive inferences from the bodily and behavioral states of others to assertions about their psychological states. Later on I shall argue that if all such correlations were contingent it would not even be possible for a person to discover that such correlations hold in his own case. But even if one could discover this, one could have no grounds for supposing that the correlations that hold in one's own case hold in the case of other persons as well. For if all such relationships were contingent, one clearly could not have any a priori grounds for supposing that these relationships do not vary from person to person. And neither, for reasons already given, could one have any empirical grounds for supposing this.

A paradigm "psychological state" is the state of being in pain. If we can show that it is absurd to maintain that it is impossible for one person to know of another person that he is in pain, we will have shown that it is absurd to maintain that it is impossible for one person to know of another that he has a certain psychological state, and therefore, by the argument above, that it is absurd to maintain that all relationships between psychological states and physical states are contingent.

I take it to be a necessary truth that a person who understands the meaning of the words "I am in pain" cannot utter these words with the intention of making a true assertion unless he *is* in pain (or unless his utterance is a slip of the tongue —a complication that can here be ignored). This is just the point that is sometimes expressed by saying that a person cannot be mistaken in thinking that he is in pain, and is in fact one of the main sources of the idea that psychological states like being in pain are logically independent of bodily states (I cannot be mistaken in thinking that I am in pain, but it seems that I can be mistaken in thinking that my body is in any given state). But it follows from this that it is essential to having a correct understanding of the word "pain" that one says "I am in pain," intending to make a true assertion, only when one is in pain, from which in turn it follows that if it is possible to know whether another person understands the word "pain" it must sometimes be possible to know that, or whether, another person is in pain. But the word "pain" could not have an established meaning in our language if it were not possible for people to be taught its meaning and possible for us to determine whether a person is using it correctly, i.e., has correctly learned its meaning. But now consider the sentence (call it S) "It is logically impossible for one person to know of another that he is in pain." Only if the words in it are used with their established meanings does S express a statement that we can understand. It should now be clear, however, that if S expresses any statement at all it expresses a statement that implies that the word "pain" does not have an established meaning, since if it did have an established meaning it would be possible to establish whether another person understands it, which would not be possible if it were logically impossible for one person to know of another whether he is in pain. If "pain" is without an established meaning, so also is any sentence in which this word is used (and not simply mentioned). And S is such a sentence. So there is a logical absurdity involved in uttering S with the intention of making a true statement. The same difficulty will arise in the case of any sentence (whether in English or in some other language) that can plausibly be regarded as synonymous with S; what the sentence apparently asserts will imply that some word or phrase occurring in it is without an established meaning, and therefore that the sentence itself is without meaning. Of any sentence that appears to say that it is logically impossible to know that another person is in pain we must say either that it actually expresses no statement at all or that it expresses a statement that is necessarily false.

Having tried to show that it cannot be the case that all relationships between psychological states and physical states are contingent, I must now try to deal with the considerations that incline us to think that all such relationships *must* be contingent.

3. There is what I have called a "logical correspondence" between first-person and third-person statements. The statement "A sees a tree," said about A, is true if and only if the statement "I see a tree," said by A, is true. More generally, if S is a sentence in the third person that expresses a statement about a person A, and if S' is a sentence obtained from S by replacing the expressions in S that refer to A with first-person pronouns of the grammatically appropriate cases, and by making whatever changes are grammatically required by the insertion of these pronouns (e.g., replacing "is" by "am," "sees" by "see," and so on), then S' will make a true statement when asserted by A if and only if the statement expressed by S is true. This point can seem obvious and not very interesting, for we might express it by saying that the assertion that such and such is true of a certain person has the same truth value whether it is made by that person or by someone else. Looked at in another way, however, this can seem a remarkable and puzzling fact. For in many cases (though by no means in all) the grounds on which a third-person statement is made are not, and could not be, the grounds on which the corresponding first-person statement is made. If I say "A sees a tree," and have the best possible grounds for making this statement, I

will make it because I observe that A's eyes are open and directed toward a tree and because I have just heard A make the corresponding first-person statement. But it obviously cannot be on such grounds as these that A says "I see a tree." A cannot observe that *his own* eyes are open and directed toward a tree. And if we were to ask him how he knows that his eyes are open and directed toward a tree, he would probably reply that since he sees a tree his eyes *must* be open and directed toward one. For him, the assertion about his eyes would be a conclusion from the assertion that he sees a tree, and not vice versa. And of course, it cannot be the case that he says "I see a tree" because he has just heard himself saying "I see a tree." Again, if I say "A is in pain" my grounds will consist, in a typical case, of facts like the following: A's face is contorted, he is moaning, whimpering or screaming, he is "nursing" some part of his body, he has just said something like "I have a pain" or "My God, it hurts!" and so on. But it is obviously not on the basis of such facts as these that A says "I am in pain." It is not simply that as a matter of fact we make first-person psychological statements without using as evidence the behavioral facts that others use in making the corresponding third-person statements. For it would be absurd to suppose that one could use these facts as evidence for such statements, and equally absurd to suppose that first-person psychological statements are ill-grounded because they are not made on the basis of such evidence.

But while one does not *use* facts about one's own body and behavior as evidence in making psychological statements about oneself, it is certainly possible for one to know these facts. And one's knowledge of such physical facts can be independent of one's knowledge of the psychological facts for which other persons would regard the physical facts as evidence. For example, I might have a headache, this being something that

I know independently of knowing anything about my behavior, and then be told by someone else, or find by looking in a mirror, that my face is contorted. Again, it seems that I can discover empirically that when I see an object my face and eyes are turned toward that object. When I look in a mirror it is my face and eyes that I see. If I locate my finger in the middle of my field of vision, then move it "inward" until it touches my body, I will find by touch that it is with my face, not some other part of my body, that I have made contact. And if, while keeping an object in the center of my visual field, I use a measuring tape to determine the distance between that object and various points of my body, I will find that the object is closer to my eyes than to other points on my head.

But now it appears that the correlations between my psychological states and the bodily and behavioral states that others use as evidence of them (and which I use as evidence of the existence of those psychological states in other persons) must be contingent correlations, for it appears that I can discover these correlations empirically. And it seems conceivable that I might discover these correlations had *ceased* to hold, and that others had come to hold in their place, or that there had ceased to be any regular correlations at all between my psychological states and the states of my body. It seems that I might learn, from looking in mirrors, from overhearing what others say about my behavior, and from my own tactile and kinesthetic sensations, that when I am in pain it is never the case that I am displaying what are normally regarded as the outward expressions of pain, but on the contrary am generally smiling contentedly (to all appearances). And it seems that I might, by experiments of the sort described above, find that when I see an object in the middle of my field of vision it is generally the back of my head, not the front of it, that is nearest the object. Since it is not on the basis of bodily and behavioral facts that I know psychological facts about myself, it seems that any relationship that I can discover to hold between my psychological states and facts about my body and behavior must be a contingent relationship, one that could change and could be discovered to have changed (by me if not by anyone else).

In at least one case, that of seeing, it seems conceivable that one might discover in the case of other persons, and not simply in one's own case, that the relationship between a psychological state and bodily facts had changed. One can imagine, first of all, hearing someone claim that he sees things from the back of his head; perhaps he claims to have discovered that this is so by experiments of the sort described above. Of course, someone's claiming this would not by itself be sufficient to show that what he claims is true. But it is also imaginable that someone might regularly make true statements about things situated, or events happening, behind his back, and that we might find, on investigation, that he does not know the truth of these statements in any of the ways in which a normal person might know them (he is not using a mirror, is not receiving signals from a confederate, and so on). If this happened, and if the person expressed his statements as perceptual statements, we would certainly be inclined to say that he is able to see things behind his back. And if it would be correct to say this, it would seem that there is no logical connection, but only a causal (and hence contingent) one, between the fact that someone sees something and the fact that his eyes are open and directed toward that thing. The argument here is analogous to what I called in Chapter One the "third-person version" of the change-of-body argument.

The next few sections will be devoted to an examination of the view that the relationships between psychological states and bodily and behavioral states are relationships that one can discover empirically to hold, at least in one's own case, and could conceivably discover not to hold. I shall begin with the idea that it is possible (logically) for a person to see objects when his eyes are not directed toward them, and shall consider first the suggestion that one could discover this to happen in the case of persons other than oneself.

4. However accurately a man is able to describe events occurring behind his back, it is clear that he could not be said to see those events *with his eyes* (unless he were seeing them in a mirror). And if we found a person possessing an exceptional ability to make true statements about what is happening behind his back, what we would be inclined to say is not that he sees those events with his eyes, but that he sees them with, or from, some point on his back. Now as the word "see" is commonly used and defined, it is self-contradictory to say that someone literally sees things without using his eyes. The interesting question, however, is whether there could be a form of perception which, whether or not the current use of the word "see" would permit us to call it seeing, is exactly like seeing except that it does not involve the use of the eyes. It seems to me that there could be, and for the sake of brevity I shall sometimes express this by saying that it is conceivable that someone might see things without using his eyes; I shall use the word "see," in a slight departure from its ordinary meaning, so that it is not analytically true that we see with our eyes. What I want to argue, however, is that to admit that it is possible to see without the use of the eyes is not to admit that a person's seeing something (a material object, or a publicly observable state of affairs) is logically independent of facts about his body (and of his having a body). I shall try to show that it is senseless to suppose that there could be a kind of seeing, or a kind of perception like seeing, that does not involve the perceiver's hav-

ing a body *some* part of which plays the role that in ordinary vision is played by the eyes.

It is conceivable that a man in America might prove to be capable of making true statements about what is happening in Russia without knowing the truth of these statements in any ordinary way (he is not in radio contact with anyone in Russia, is not making informed inferences from newspaper reports, and so on). Here it would clearly be incorrect to say that the man sees the events reported in his statements. We might say that he is clairvoyant (which would simply be to give a name to his ability, not to explain it), but there is an important conceptual distinction between perception, strictly so called, and clairvoyance. So in the case of the man who is able to make true statements about events occurring behind his back, we must ask what would have to be true of the case, in addition to his making these statements and their being true, in order for it to be correct to say that he *sees* those events, or at least *perceives* them in a way analogous to seeing, as opposed to knowing of them "by clairvoyance," i.e., simply being able to make true statements about them. What is required, I think, is that he should speak and behave in such a way as to enable us to pick out some point on his body as the point of view *from* which he sees. For one thing, there would have to be a point on his body such that he is normally able to give true descriptions of events occurring "in front of" that point, but is not able to do this if there is an opaque object between that point and the place at which the event is occurring. For another, he would have to be able to make what I shall call "egocentric" statements, statements in which words like "this," "here," "there," "near," "far," "left," and "right" are used to identify or locate objects or events in relation to the speaker, and statements whose truth or falsity depends, in part, on the way in which the objects or events referred to are spatially related to a certain point on the speaker's body, this being the "point of view" from which he sees.

The last point is of special importance. Involved in the ability to see is the ability to locate objects in relation to oneself without observing one's own body. Anyone who can see and has learned to speak a language must be able to use sentences like "It is directly in front of me," "It is slightly to my right," and "It is coming directly toward me" (or synonymous sentences in another language) to make true statements about objects he sees. This is part of what is meant by saying that seeing involves having a *visual field*; if a person sees an object he must be able to say *where* in his visual field the object is. Now if someone says "It is directly in front of me," or "It is in the middle of my visual field," and the "it" referred to is a physical object, how are we to determine whether his statement is true? What does "in front of" mean here? The human head is a roughly ellipsoid object; why is one side of it the "front" rather than any of the others? The main reason, surely, is that we see from one side of the head and not from the others. The side from which we see we call the front of the head. And if a person says of an object "It is directly in front of me," what we must do in order to determine whether his statement is true is to see how the object referred to is related to the point on the speaker's body from which he sees. For his statement to be true that point on his body must be "turned toward" the object, i.e. (roughly speaking), must be on the side of his body that is nearest the object. Of course, there will always be *some* side of a person's body that is turned toward (nearest) a given object; what is necessary, if we are to be able to determine the truth-value of statements of the sort being considered, is that there should be some *identifiable* side such that only if *that* side of a person's body is turned toward an object will his assertion that the object is directly in front of him be true. On that side of his body will lie the "point of view" from which he sees, and it is by reference to that point that we would check on the truth of such statements as "It is directly in front of me," "It is slightly to my right," "It is in the left side of my visual field," and "It is moving directly toward me."

It hardly needs to be explained how we know that in normal vision the point of view from which a person sees is the place where his eyes are, for this is part of what is meant by "normal vision." A difficulty arises, however, when we suppose that someone might see from some point on his body other than his eyes. In order to check up on the person's perceptual statements, we would have to know what part of his body is the point of view from which he sees. It seems that we would have to locate this point empirically. But how could we do this? Suppose that for some reason we are led to entertain the hypothesis that Jones is able to perceive things occurring behind his back. This hypothesis excludes the possibility that Jones perceives these things from his eyes or any other point on what we would normally call the front of his body, but it leaves open a number of possibilities; perhaps he sees from the base of his skull, perhaps from his left shoulder blade, perhaps from his right ear, and so on. But before we can ask from which point on his back or sides he sees we must know that he does see from *some point or other* on his back or sides. In order to know this, however, we must know that he is able to make true perceptual statements about things behind his back, and this would involve knowing that he is able to make true egocentric statements about those things. But as we have seen, in order to determine whether egocentric statements are true we must know the point of view from which the speaker sees. In order to discover this point of view we would already have to know it, so it seems that we could never get started.

These considerations do not show that we could never conclude that a person sees things behind his back, but they do show, I think, what sort of "conclusion" this would have to be. The following could certainly occur. We might observe, first of all, that a person is able to make true statements about what is happening behind his back, statements that are not egocentric and can be determined to be true without reference to the speaker's point of view, and we might discover that he does not know these statements in any of the ways in which a normal person might know them. So far we would not have sufficient grounds for saying that he sees or perceives things behind his back; if *just* this occurred, we might say that the person is clairvoyant. But then we might discover, perhaps by accident, that if we place a bandage over a certain spot on the person's body, say the base of his skull, he is no longer able to make true statements about what is happening behind his back. We might then ask him to locate various objects in his visual field, and find (for example) that he says that an object is in the center of his visual field when and only when the base of his skull is turned toward the object. As yet, of course, we would not be in a position to say of any of his egocentric statements that it is true (for we would not yet know the point of view by reference to which his statements are to be judged true or false), and so would not be in a position to say that since a certain egocentric statement is true it must be the case that the person sees from a certain point on his body. What we would know concerning any particular egocentric statement made by this person would not be the categorical fact that it *is* true, but the hypothetical fact that *if* it is a true perceptual statement then the person sees from a certain point on his body (e.g., that if his statement "It is in the middle of my visual field" is true, when the "it" referred to is an object toward which the base of his skull is turned, then he sees from the base of his skull). But if, over a period of time, the person made a large number of egocentric statements, and we noticed that of all or most of these statements it would be true to say "If this is a true perceptual statement, he sees from point A," we would probably be strongly inclined, though we would not be logically compelled, to say that he does see from point A. In saying this, I think, we would not so much be drawing a *conclusion* from the observed facts as making a *decision* in the light of them. The decision would be to alter our criteria for the truth of perceptual statements. If we adhered to our original criterion, which involves using the eyes as the point of view by reference to which the truth of perceptual statements is to be judged, we should have to say in this case that the person's egocentric statements are generally false, or else that they are unintelligible and not really egocentric statements at all. In saying that the person sees from point A (e.g., the base of his skull) we would be adopting a new criterion for the truth of his perceptual statements, one that would make them generally true rather than generally false or unintelligible and would be adopted for just this reason.

It should be noticed that, in trying to give sense to the idea that a person might see from a point of view other than his eyes, I had to imagine the person seeing from this point of view for some period of time, a period long enough for him to make a number of different egocentric statements. This is important. While there are imaginable phenomena that might naturally lead us to say that someone sees from a point other than his eyes, e.g., that he has ceased seeing from his eyes and now sees from the base of his skull, there are no imaginable phenomena that could lead us to say, with any intelligibility, that the point of view from which a person sees is *constantly* shifting its position, e.g., that he sees at one instant from his eyes, at the next from the base of his skull, at the next from his right index finger, and so on. It is, if anything, even less imaginable that a person's point of view might shift to a point not located on his body (meaning by "his body" the body from whose mouth his perceptual statements are uttered). To say that a person sees from a constantly shifting point of view would be as much as to say that he sees from no point of view at all, and that he therefore does not see at all. I shall try to bring out more clearly why this is so.

Supposing for the moment that it is possible for the point of view from which a person sees to be constantly shifting position (from one point on his body to another, or from one body to another), what could possibly show us from what point a person sees *now*? It will be useless for us to consider what perceptual statements the person made in what circumstances in the past, or to wait and see what perceptual statements he makes in what circumstances in the future, since for all we know (on this supposition) the point of view from which he sees now was not his point of view in the immediate past and will not be his point of view in the immediate future. Given the limitations inherent in our supposition, the following seems to be the only possible criterion of what a person's point of view is: If a person makes an egocentric perceptual statement at *t*, we are to ascertain the location of his point of view at *t* by determining what his point of view would have to be in order for his statement to be true; e.g., if a person says of a certain object "It is in the center of my visual field," his point of view will be whatever part of his body is turned toward that object. But this criterion fails to take account of the fact that perceptual statements can be *false*. It is just because egocentric perceptual statements can be false, and can be discovered to be false by reference to the speaker's point of view, that they are informative in the way they are. If a person says "There is a chair directly in front of me," we know where, if his statement is true, we can find a chair, and we know this just because we know his point of view independently of knowing whether that particular statement is in fact true (and so could conceivably find, by reference to that point of view, that his statement is false). For the same reason the statement "I see a chair on my right" gives us different information from that given by the statement "I see a chair on my left." If the criterion suggested above were adopted, then the only thing that would falsify any of these statements would be the state of affairs in which there are no chairs at all anywhere in the vicinity of the speaker. In that case nothing could falsify one of these statements without falsifying the others; they would convey the same information, and the occurrence in them of the egocentric terms "right," "left," and "in front of" would serve no function. And if we interpret the supposition that points of view can be constantly shifting as allowing the possibility that a person's point of view need not be located on his body at all, then on the suggested criterion there would be no way at all in which egocentric perceptual statements could be falsified. If there is a chair anywhere, then there is a point, indeed an infinite number of points, such that if that point (or one of those points) were someone's perceptual point of view his statement "There is a chair directly in front of me" would be true. The same is true if the statement is "There is a chair on my right" or "There is a chair on my left." And the pure existential statement "There is a chair somewhere" is unfalsifiable in principle. To adopt the suggested criterion and suppose that points of view can be constantly shifting in an unrestricted way is to make the cash value of the statements "There is a chair directly in front of me," "I see a chair on my right," and so forth the same as that of the pure existential statement "There is at least one chair (somewhere in the universe)." And to do this is to obliterate the distinction between egocentric statements and other kinds of statements, and with it the distinction between perceptual knowledge and clairvoyance.

If the relationship between seeing and the body were a purely contingent one, it ought to be possible for a person's point of view to be constantly shifting its position on his body; it ought to be possible, indeed, for one's point of view not to be located on one's body at all. But it should be apparent from what I have said that nothing could show that a person's point of view is constantly shifting in this way and that this is not even a logical possibility. I think that we can conclude that it is a necessary truth about seeing that if a person sees (or perceives in a way analogous to seeing), he must see (or perceive) from some point on his body, and that the point from which he sees (or perceives) must retain the same position on his body for a considerable length of time, and can sensibly be said to have changed only in very special circumstances. Having argued this I shall revert to the ordinary use of the word "see," on which (I believe) it is analytically true that people see with their eyes. But if anyone is inclined to question the analyticity of this, or to feel that it expresses an inessential feature of the concept of seeing, he may regard the statement "People see with their eyes," whenever I assert or imply it in subsequent discussions, as an abbreviated formulation of the necessary truth stated above.

5. I have argued that nothing could show that the point of view from which a person sees is constantly shifting its position on his body. But it might be argued that while I could never discover that someone *else's* point of view is constantly changing in this way, I might conceivably discover that *my own* point of view is constantly shifting. When I say of a material object that it is in the middle of my visual field,

other persons can establish the truth or falsity of my statement only if they already know the location of my perceptual point of view. But *my* knowledge of the truth of my statement seems to be of quite a different kind. It seems that I can know, simply from what I see, that a certain object is in the center of my visual field, and *then* set about to determine (by making measurements, using the sense of touch, and so on) which part of my body is "turned toward" the object and is the point of view from which I see it. And it seems that I might do this on a number of occasions and locate each time a different part of my body as the point of view from which I see.

Let us grant, for the moment, that it is conceivable that I could *seem* (to myself) to be seeing things from a constantly shifting point of view, and that I can imagine what it would be like for this to seem to me to be happening. But what I seem to see, or think I see, is not the criterion of what I *do* see. No one denies that our perceptual statements about material objects can be mistaken and are subject to correction by other persons. So the question arises, can I imagine that I might see things from a constantly shifting point of view, and not merely that I might seem (to myself) to do so? We can give what appears at first sight to be a description of what it would be like to seem (to oneself) to be seeing things in this way. It does appear that I can imagine that the contents of my visual field, described in "sense-datum language," i.e. (roughly), in statements like "I seem to see a red book in the middle of my visual field," might be constantly and abruptly changing, and that while this happens my body might seem to remain stationary. It also seems that I can imagine that whenever I try to touch the point of view from which I see (by placing my finger in the center of my visual field, and then moving it "inward") I might on each different occasion seem to touch a different part of my body. But supposing I can imagine such things, can I imagine anything further that would show (show *me*) that what would seem to me to be happening, if these imagined events occurred, was actually happening?

When a question arises as to whether things really are as they appear to be, there are normally things one can appeal to in an attempt to settle the question. One can appeal to experiences other than those whose veridicality is in question (e.g., if one suspects that one is having a visual hallucination, one can appeal to one's tactile experiences), and one can appeal to the testimony of other persons. But suppose that I have a set of experiences, call it A, which makes it appear that my point of view is constantly shifting; suppose that the experiences in A are such that *if* they are veridical then I must be seeing from a constantly shifting point of view. And let us consider first whether any publicly observable facts, i.e., facts I could know on the basis of the testimony of other persons, could confirm for me the veridicality of the experiences in A. If so, then anyone who knew these facts and also had reason to think that I have the experiences in A would *ipso facto* have reason to think that my perceptual point of view is constantly shifting. But I have already shown that it is impossible for anyone to have reason to think that another person sees from a constantly shifting point of view. It follows that either (1) there are no publicly observable facts that could confirm the veridicality of the experiences in A, or (2) it is not possible that another person could have reason to think that I have the experiences in A. And in fact we must accept (1), for (2) is contrary to our original supposition. For we are supposing, to begin with, that it is conceivable that someone might have the experiences in A. And we must be supposing further that a person could not be mistaken in thinking that he has the experiences in A; unless we suppose this we will be faced, not simply with the question of how a person having the experiences in A could know that these experiences were veridical (that what seems to him to be happening is really happening), but also with the presumably absurd question of how a person could know that he really has these experiences (that it really does seem to him that certain things are happening). But it follows from the first supposition that if I were to report having the experiences in A then anyone who understood my language would find my report intelligible. And it follows from this together with the second supposition that any such hearer, unless he had reason to think I was lying, would have reason to think that my report was true, i.e., that I really did have those experiences. But if it is conceivable that someone might have certain experiences, surely it cannot be an a priori truth that anyone who reports having them must be suspected of lying; in other words, if such a report would be intelligible it must be possible that it could be reasonably believed. But this is to say that on our suppositions another person *could* have reason to believe that I have the experiences in A, namely my telling him that I have them. And from this it follows that (2) is false and (1) true, i.e., that no publicly observable facts could confirm the veridicality of the experiences in A.

But while I could not appeal to the testimony of other persons, or to any publicly observable facts, to confirm the veridicality of the experiences in A, could I not perhaps appeal to private experiences other than those in A? Let us suppose that I have a second set of experiences, call it B, which seems to confirm the veridicality of the experiences in A; let us suppose that if the experiences in B are veridical then the experiences in A are also veridical. But if the experiences in B are to be used to confirm the veridicality of the experiences in A, clearly they must themselves be experiences whose veridicality I have no reason to question. Now the veridicality of the experiences in A is questionable because, among other things, no publicly observable facts could tend to confirm it. And the veridicality of the experiences in B will be questionable for exactly the same reason. If publicly observable facts could confirm the veridicality of the experiences in B they would *ipso facto* confirm the veridicality of the experiences in A, which is not possible. Hence there is nothing I could legitimately accept as confirming the veridicality of such a set of experiences, and therefore nothing I could accept as confirming the impression (supposing that I could have such an impression) that I see from a constantly shifting point of view.

6. But it might be argued that if I will admit that one could *seem* to see things from a constantly shifting point of view I will have admitted all that is claimed by the view that psychological facts are only contingently related to facts about human bodies. What is distinctively mental about seeing, it might be said, is the having of visual experiences, or the sensing of sense-data, and this is something that can happen whether one sees a material object or not. Whenever I see something *or seem* to see something I have a visual experience. And while I can be mistaken in thinking that I see something of a certain kind, I cannot be mistaken in thinking that I have a certain visual experience, i.e., at least seem to see something of a certain sort. A person who is having a visual experience can be said to be seeing a material object only if his eyes are open and directed toward an object of the kind he seems to see. But one can have a visual experience when this condition is not satisfied, e.g., when one is seeing an afterimage or having a hallucination. Since this can happen, it might seem that one can imagine its happening as a matter of course. And if this is imaginable, it would appear to follow that there is only a contingent relationship between the having of visual experiences (the element in seeing that is mental) and facts about the body.

Mind, Body, and Identity

The same, as we have noted, might be said of other sorts of experiences. Nobody denies that pain is sometimes not expressed in behavior. And as we have seen, that I generally behave in certain ways when in pain appears to be a fact that I can discover empirically, and it seems conceivable that a person might discover empirically that he *does not* behave in these ways when in pain. So again the relationship to behavior seems to be contingent. Of course, I could never discover in the case of another person that all of the relationships between psychological facts (e.g., private experiences) and bodily and behavioral facts had changed, or that these relationships were constantly changing. But I could, so the argument goes, establish that this is so in my own case.

If it is true throughout a period of time that when a person's body is in a certain state (or is behaving in a certain way) he generally has a certain psychological state, or that when he has a certain psychological state his body is normally in a certain state, let us say that during that period of time a certain "psychophysical relationship" holds in the case of that person. I have not denied that some psychophysical relationships are contingent, so I do not wish to deny that it is sometimes possible for a person to find that a psychophysical relationship that is generally believed to hold in the case of all persons does not hold, or has ceased to hold, in his own case. Wherever another person could find that a certain psychophysical relationship had ceased to hold in my case, I could discover this too. And of course, the way in which I would discover this would be different in one respect from the way in which another person would discover it. What another person would find is that one sort of behavior or bodily state, which he accepts as showing the existence of a certain psychological state, has ceased to be correlated (in my case) with another sort of behavior or bodily state, the occurrence of which he had previously regarded as good inductive evidence for the existence of the psychological state in question. Whereas I would simply find that when I am in a certain psychological state my body is generally not in a certain state, and vice versa; my knowledge of my psychological state, unlike the other person's knowledge of it, would not be grounded on knowledge of my body or behavior. It is just this difference that makes it plausible to suppose, concerning *any* psychophysical relationship that is normally believed to hold in the case of everyone, that I can imagine finding that it has ceased to hold in my case. What I shall now try to show, however, is that where nothing that another person could observe (concerning my body and behavior) could show that a certain psychophysical relationship had ceased to hold in my case, nothing that *I* could observe, or can imagine happening, could show this either.

Let us grant that I can imagine what it would be like to have, at any given time, a set of experiences that are not related in the normal way to facts about my body. By "the normal way" I mean the way in which we suppose other persons' experiences to be related to facts about their bodies and behavior when we make statements about their experiences on the basis of bodily and behavioral facts. What we have to consider is whether this imaginable state of affairs, which I admit might occur occasionally, could become the usual state of affairs, i.e., might become the rule rather than the exception. Can I imagine what it would be like for this to happen in my case? Well, I can imagine this state of affairs existing five minutes from now, I can imagine it existing six minutes from now, I can imagine it existing seven minutes from now, and so on. But does it follow from this that I can imagine that it might exist five minutes from now, *and* six minutes from now, *and* seven minutes from now, and so on, i.e., that it might exist five minutes from now and continue to exist for some extended period of time? Certainly this does not follow.

To avoid unnecessary verbiage, let us call this state of affairs S. If at a given time I have a set of experiences that are not related in the normal way to facts about my body, then at that time the state of affairs S exists in me. The existence in me of S at a given time might consist, for example, in my seeming to see a chair while having the tactile and kinesthetic sensations that a normal person has when his eyes are closed and his hand is covering his eyes, in my feeling a pain while having the muscular sensations that normally accompany smiling, and so on. Let us suppose that from the nature of my experiences at a given time I can know whether S occurred at that time. Then, supposing that S occurs at t_1, there will be no problem about how I could know at t_1 whether S was occurring, for we can suppose that while a person is having certain experiences he cannot fail to know that he is having them. But supposing that S could occur at t_1 *and* at t_2 *and* at t_3, how would I know that this had occurred? Obviously I could not know this till t_3, at which time my beliefs about what had occurred at t_1 and t_2 would be memory beliefs. And while I cannot be mistaken about the nature of my present experiences, I *can* be mistaken about the nature of my past experiences. While the statement "I seem to see something red" may entail that I am having an experience of a certain sort (i.e., in traditional terminology, that I now see a red sense-datum), neither the statement "I seem to remember seeing something red yesterday" nor the statement "I seem to remember *seeming* to see something red yesterday" entails that I had an experience of that sort yesterday (that I saw a red sense-datum yesterday).

The claim that one can imagine what it would be like for the state of affairs S to become, in one's own case, the rule rather than the exception is, I think, equivalent to the claim that one could *establish* that this had occurred in one's own case; one could express this claim by saying that there is something one can imagine occurring that would *show* one that this had happened in one's own case. But of course, to say that something has become the rule rather than the exception is to say something about what has happened over a period of time. So consider the statement "During the interval between t_1 and t_2 (suppose this to be a fairly long period of time) the existence of S in me was the usual state of affairs." Clearly I could not be said to have verified this statement prior to t_2. But what can I imagine occurring at t_2 or afterward that would show me that this statement was true? Surely it is not enough that I can imagine having at t_2 memories which testify that S existed throughout most of the interval between t_1 and t_2. For the memories, as I have said, might be mistaken. Surely, then, if I know what it would be like to verify the assertion that between t_1 and t_2 the state of affairs S was the usual state of affairs, I ought to be able to imagine something that would show that these memories were *correct*, i.e., that I actually remembered having a certain series of experiences and did not merely seem to remember this. But this, by the nature of the case, is impossible. If I seemed to remember having certain experiences in the past and wanted to check up on my memory, I could do so only by examining evidence that other persons could also examine, i.e., diaries, reports of my past behavior, and so on. But of course there is nothing that another person could take as showing that S had become, in my case, the usual state of affairs. So the public evidence, to which I would have to appeal if I wished to check up on my memories of my past experiences, could never support my memory that S had been the usual state of affairs between t_1 and t_2. If I were to report this memory to another person, he would have to conclude that my memory was mistaken (he might conclude that I had *dreamt* this queer series of experiences). And this, it seems to me, is just what I would have to conclude if I had such a memory.

If someone claims that he can imagine finding that the normal psychophysical relationships have ceased to hold in his case, we can reply that the most he can claim to imagine is that it might at some time *seem* to him that this had happened. And from this claim it in no way follows that any psychophysical relationship might cease to hold, or that all psychophysical relationships are contingent.

7. Those who have held that all psychophysical relationships are contingent have usually tried to account for our knowledge of other minds by holding that all inferences from bodily and behavioral facts to psychological assertions are inductive inferences grounded on psychophysical correlations which each person can discover to hold in his own case. This account assumes (1) that a person can empirically discover the required psychophysical relationships in his own case, and (2) that, having discovered such correlations to hold in one's own case, one is entitled to assume that they hold in the case of other persons as well. The traditional objections to this account have been objections to (2); it is argued, I think rightly, that unless we can have noninductive knowledge of the psychological states of other persons we cannot be entitled to suppose, and it is not even meaningful to suppose, that the psychophysical relationships that hold in the case of one person hold in the case of all persons. But assumption (1), I think, has received insufficient attention. For if (1) were true, all psychophysical relationships would be contingent, and in that case knowledge of other minds would be impossible, unless (2) is true after all. If (1) can be shown to be false, however, it is unnecessary

to refute (2) in order to refute this account of how we have knowledge of other minds.

I think that the argument of Section 6 shows that (1) is false. For if it is not conceivable, but is logically impossible, that one could discover that the "normal" psychophysical relationships do not hold, or have ceased to hold, in one's own case, one's knowledge that they do hold in one's own case cannot be purely empirical. But it can be seen in another way that (1) is false. If my knowledge of the psychophysical relationships that hold in my case is entirely empirical, how did I begin discovering these relationships, i.e., how did I discover the first one? In particular, how did I obtain the knowledge of my bodily states that I would need to have in order to discover any correlations between bodily states and psychological states? I cannot have known my bodily states from kinesthetic sensations and the like, for in order to do this I would already have to have knowledge of a psychophysical relationship; I would have to know that the occurrence of certain sensations indicates, and therefore is correlated with, the existence of certain bodily states. Can I have known my body by observation, e.g., by seeing that it was in a certain state? Surely I cannot have done this if it is a contingent fact, which I did not as yet know, that visual experiences "correspond" to objective physical facts in the way they do, i.e., that in general one seems to see (has the experience of seeing) an object of a certain kind only when one's eyes are directed toward an object of that kind. It will perhaps be said that we can have knowledge of our bodies that is neither based on observation nor inferred from sensations; for example, we seem to have such knowledge of our own voluntary bodily movements. But if it is the case (as I think it is) that sometimes I just know, and not *from* anything (not on the basis of evidence or observation), that my body is in a certain state, then there exists a psychophysical correlation between my having beliefs of a certain kind (what we might call "evidenceless bodily beliefs") and facts about my body, i.e., between my having such beliefs and their being true. So we must ask whether *this* relationship is contingent. If it is contingent, then it is conceivable that it might not have held, i.e., that such beliefs might have been generally false. But if such beliefs could be generally false, then either I have empirical grounds for thinking that my beliefs of this sort are in fact generally true, in which case they are not "evidenceless" after all, or else I do not have such empirical grounds, in which case my beliefs may, for all I know, be generally false, and therefore do not constitute knowledge even if they happen to be true. It seems clear that if *all* psychophysical relationships were contingent there would be no way in which one could discover, even in one's own case, that any such relationship holds.

8. Let us turn now to the problem of personal identity and the view that there is only a contingent relationship between personal identity and bodily identity. In Chapter One I tried to make plausible, by my "brain transfer" example, the idea that one and the same person might "inhabit" different bodies at different times. I shall have more to say about this argument later on. But let us suppose, for the sake of discussion, that the "change-of-body argument," as presented in Chapter One, does show that in cases like my brain transfer example it would be correct to say that a person had changed bodies. It is clear that more than this is involved in the claim that there is a purely contingent relationship between personal identity and bodily identity and that bodily identity is not a criterion of personal identity. Earlier in this chapter I said that if certain things occurred we might say, without absurdity, that a person is able to see from some part of his body other than his eyes. But we

saw that to admit this is not to admit that there is only a contingent relationship between seeing and the body, since if the latter were the case it ought to be possible for the "point of view" from which a person sees to be *constantly* shifting its position on his body. Likewise, to say that under certain circumstances we might say that someone had changed bodies is not to say that there is only a contingent relationship between personal identity and bodily identity, since if the latter were the case it should make sense to suppose that someone might be constantly changing bodies, i.e., that he might have one body at one time, another body an instant later, still another an instant after that, and so on. It can be shown, I think, that this does not make sense.

The contrast is made, in discussions of personal identity, between "bodily" (or "physical") and "psychological" criteria of identity. And when it is denied that bodily identity is essential to personal identity, and that the criteria of personal identity include the criteria of bodily identity (e.g., spatiotemporal continuity), it is generally held that the criteria of personal identity must be psychological criteria. If, as I have argued, there are bodily criteria for psychological facts, then the distinction between bodily criteria and psychological criteria is not as clear as it initially appears to be. But it might be contended that while bodily facts do enter into the making of third-person statements of identity, and enter in as criterial evidence, considerations of bodily identity do not enter in. To determine whether a person existing at t_1 is the same as a person existing at t_2 I must make use of facts about the body of the person existing at t_1 and facts about the body of the person existing at t_2, for only so can I discover the psychological facts that would settle the question whether these are one and the same person. Nevertheless, it might be said, the answer to this question, while not independent of all facts about these bodies, is logically independent of the answer to the question of whether they are identical. I shall try to show that this is false.

Two sorts of "psychological criteria" of personal identity have been proposed, and it is sometimes said that both are included in our criteria of personal identity. We sometimes conclude that A is the same person as B from the fact that A's character, personality, and interests are closely similar to B's. And similarity in these respects has been held to be a criterion of personal identity. Again, we sometimes conclude that A is the same person as B on the grounds that A remembers events to which B was a witness, or actions which B performed. And memory is frequently claimed to provide a criterion of personal identity. I will show, however, that we could not know the truth of statements of personal identity in either of these ways if we could not generally use bodily identity as a criterion of personal identity.

9. To begin with similarity of personality, character, and the like, clearly this is neither a logically necessary nor a logically sufficient condition of personal identity. It is not a logically necessary condition, for the character and personality traits of a person can change. It is not a logically sufficient condition, for there is no contradiction involved in supposing that two persons, existing at the same time, might have exactly the same set of personality and character traits. From the fact that the personality and character of a person can change it follows that we have criteria of personal identity other than similarity of personality and so on, for only by reference to such criteria could we conclude, as we frequently do, that a person's personality has changed. And from the fact that personality and character traits can be shared by more than one person it follows that these are not "individuating characteristics" in the sense in which spatial location is. From all of this, I think, it

follows that similarity with respect to personality and so on can be a criterion of personal identity only in a very attenuated sense, if at all, and could not possibly be our sole criterion of personal identity.

This can be seen in another way. In order to find out anything about a person's character, personality, interests, and so on, one must observe him over a period of time. You cannot tell at a glance what a person's personality and character traits are, or what his interests are. But of course, to observe a person over a period of time in order to find out about his personality traits one must observe *one and the same* person over a period of time. If I want to find out about the personality of A, it is the actions of A, not those of B or C, that I must observe. But how am I to know that I am observing the same person? Clearly I cannot use similarity of personality, character, interests, and so on as my criterion of identity here, for as yet I know nothing about anyone's personality or interests; that is just what I am trying to discover. Here, where I know no psychological facts that I could use as my criteria of personal identity, it is difficult to see how "observing the same person" could signify anything different from "observing the same body." So the use of similarity of personality and so on as evidence of personal identity seems clearly to presuppose that bodily identity is a criterion of personal identity.

The argument above goes against *any* view according to which personal identity is logically independent of bodily identity, and according to which some kind of psychological fact is, to the exclusion of bodily identity, the sole criterion of personal identity. It will perhaps be said that in some cases it is possible to know that a person has a certain psychological trait without observing his body over a period of time. Though we cannot tell at a glance that a person is generous, or interested in astrophysics, we can sometimes tell at a glance that a person is in pain. But it would be a mistake to suppose that there is any piece of behavior, occurring in an instant, that is an expression of pain, or of any other psychological state, independently of how the agent behaves before and after its occurrence. Consider a case in which a person winces, grabs his arm, and moans. If immediately before doing this he had said "Now I am going to pretend that I am in extreme pain," and if immediately after exhibiting this "pain behavior" he had smiled, his behavior would not be evidence that he was in pain. But if we suppose that there is no essential connection between personal identity and bodily identity, and that a person might inhabit a given body for only an instant, then how, when we observe someone who is behaving as if in extreme pain, could we be sure, or even have any reason to suppose, that just this sort of thing had not happened? We could know, of course, that the *body* whose (apparent) pain behavior we were observing had not just uttered the words "Now I am going to pretend that I am in extreme pain," or done something else that shows the behavior not to be genuine pain behavior. But this would not help us, for on this view we would have, as yet, no reason to suppose that the *person* who now inhabits that body is the *person* who previously inhabited it, and no reason, therefore, to suppose that the *person* who is now exhibiting pain behavior did not previously do something, e.g., announce an intention to pretend that he was in pain, which shows (or would show if we knew of it) that the behavior is not genuine pain behavior. The same point holds no matter what psychological state we consider.

This point comes out still more clearly if we consider that our knowledge of the psychological states of a person must often be based on what he says. In the first place, the possibility of our knowing a person's psychological state on the basis of his testimony requires that personal identity and bodily identity must coincide for at least the amount of time it takes to utter a sentence. For if we hear the words "I want to go home" come from a certain mouth, we clearly cannot conclude that someone wants to go home and at the same time question whether all of these words were uttered by one and the same person. If Jones says "I want to lie down" while Smith is saying "He will not go home," and both are talking at the same speed, the words "I," "want," "to," "go," and "home" will have been uttered in that order, but neither Jones nor Smith will have expressed a wish to go home. In the second place, supposing that we hear the words "I want to go home" uttered, and know that they were uttered by a single person, how do we know that the speaker understands the use of these words, and means by them what we would mean by them? It would be possible, certainly, for a person to utter that series of words without understanding their meaning. And there could be a language in which that set of words, or at any rate the series of sounds by which we express them, would have a meaning totally different from what they have in English. Only if a person is speaking English, and understands the meanings of certain expressions in English, is his uttering of the sounds "I want to go home" evidence that he wants to go home. Clearly we could never regard anything that anyone says as testimony of anything if it were not possible in principle to establish what a person means by what he says, i.e., whether he is speaking a certain language (one that we understand) and has a correct grasp of the use of the expressions in the language that he is trying to speak. But how could we establish this except by observing how he, *that same person*, uses those expressions and others in a variety of circumstances? So again the question arises, what is our criterion of identity here?

The upshot of my discussion thus far is that if we can use any psychological fact at all as grounds for a statement of personal identity we must be able to have knowledge of personal identity that is not based on any psychological facts. It seems clear that what we in fact do is to accept bodily identity as showing personal identity, and that, for example, to observe how a person uses certain words in different circumstances is to observe the verbal behavior of one and the same *body* at different times and under varied circumstances. Where we cannot rely on someone's testimony, because we are trying to establish whether it is testimony, or of what it is testimony, and where we cannot use any psychological facts about a person as evidence, because we are still in the process of discovering such facts, there is nothing except bodily identity that we could use as our criterion of personal identity.

10. Let us turn now to the idea that memory provides the sole criterion of personal identity, or at least a criterion that is independent of bodily identity. Since it is true of any linguistic expression that establishing whether a person understands its use would involve observing the person's behavior over a period of time, this is of course true of the word "remember" and the expressions used in memory statements. Our reliance upon the memory testimony of other persons presupposes bodily identity as a criterion of personal identity at least as much as does our reliance on the testimony of other persons concerning their present experiences and other psychological states.

But there is a more direct way in which our reliance on memory testimony presupposes criteria of personal identity that do not involve the use of memory facts as evidence of personal identity. We saw in Chapter Four that it is involved in the meaning of the word "remember" that if a person remembers a past event then he, the same person, must have been a witness to the event (in the broad sense of "witness" introduced in Chapter Four). And of course it is tautologically true that a person can remember doing a past action only if he himself did that action. Clearly, moreover, what a person says he remembers is not the criterion, or the sole criterion, of what he actually does remember, for a person can be mistaken in claiming, and in believing, that he remembers something. How, then, can we establish whether a person does in fact remember something? Surely we can do this only by establishing whether what a person claims to remember having done in the past is something he, the same person, actually did do, or whether an event he claims to remember is an event to which he, the same person, was a witness. But to establish this we must have criteria of identity. And since we are trying to find out whether a person remembers something, we cannot use the fact that he remembers something, or rather that he claims to remember it (for this, until we have established the truth of his memory claim, is all that we know), as our criterion of personal identity. We cannot say "He remembers doing X, so he is the person who did X," for what we are trying to find out is whether, in fact, he does remember doing X. So what can we use as our criterion of personal identity? Suppose someone says "I remember breaking the front window yesterday," and we wish to establish whether in fact he does remember this. It would not be sufficient for us to establish that the window was broken yesterday; we must establish that the person who broke it is the very person who now claims to remember breaking it. If we are not relying on the person's memory claim, but are trying to check up on it, we cannot use memory as our criterion of personal identity. It does not follow from this, of course, that we cannot use other psychological facts (e.g., similarity of personality) as evidence that he is the person who broke the window. But we can use such facts as evidence, I have already argued, only if bodily identity is a criterion of personal identity.

Normally, of course, we accept the memory claims of other persons at face value. But the question of how we would check up on the truth of a memory claim is nevertheless important. If we can justifiably accept memory claims at face value, at least in certain circumstances, it must be the case that memory claims, or at least memory claims made under certain circumstances, are generally true. And if this is the case, it is either contingently the case or necessarily the case. If the former, then in accepting a memory claim at face value, i.e., in accepting it as true when one has no independent evidence of its truth, one must be making an inductive inference; it must be that one has discovered empirically that memory claims (or memory claims made under certain circumstances) are generally true, and takes this general truth as justifying one in accepting the given memory claim as true. But in order to establish such an inductive generalization one would have to be able to check up on the truth of memory claims and, as argued above, would have to be able to use bodily identity as a criterion of personal identity. If, however, it is a necessary (or logical) truth, rather than a contingent one, that memory claims are generally true, then of course this truth is not known empirically, and in that case inferences of the form "He claims to remember doing X, so (probably) he did do X" are not inductive.[1] But even if it is not possible for memory claims to be generally false, it must be possible for individual memory claims to be false. It is essential to the notion of remembering as knowledge of an objective past that there be a distinction between remembering something and merely seeming to remember it. And since we allow it to make sense to speak of a memory claim as being mistaken, there must be something that we would accept as

---

[1] Later on, in Chapter Six, Section 5, I argue that it is a necessary truth, not a contingent one, that sincere and confident memory claims are generally true.

showing that a given memory claim is false, i.e., there must be ways of checking up on the truth of memory claims. It cannot be a necessary truth that *all* memory claims are true, or even that all sincere memory claims (all memory beliefs) are true. Moreover, even if it is a necessary truth that memory claims, or sincere memory claims, are generally true, we can be in a position to accept memory claims at face value, or to use the making of a memory claim as evidence for a statement of personal identity, only if we have a way of identifying particular utterances as memory claims. We must have ways of determining whether a person understands the use of the word "remember," whether what sounds like a memory claim in English is really one, and whether an expression in another language can be translated as expressing a given memory claim. I have already argued that in order to determine whether a person understands a certain expression (*any* expression), or how he is using it, we must be able to use bodily identity as a criterion of personal identity. But this will be especially true of the expressions used in memory statements if it is a necessary truth that memory claims are generally true. For if this is a necessary truth, the crucial test of whether a person understands the use of the word "remember" and its cognates will be whether in general he utters what appears to be a certain memory claim only when that memory claim would be true. But in order to apply this test we would have to have a way of determining whether a certain memory claim would be true if asserted by a particular person at a particular time, and thus, as was shown above, would have to be able to use bodily identity as a criterion of personal identity.

11. Assuming, as I do, that spatiotemporal continuity is a logically necessary condition of identity in the case of material objects, it is self-contradictory to suppose that a material object

might undergo discontinuous change of place, i.e., might change its location without preserving spatiotemporal continuity. But the notion of discontinuous change of place is not in itself incoherent; the "move" of the Dodgers from Brooklyn to Los Angeles might be said to have occurred instantaneously upon the signing of certain contracts and documents. And if the identity of persons were logically independent of bodily identity, there would apparently be no logical reason why persons, as opposed to human bodies, should not undergo discontinuous change of place. Indeed, anyone who holds that persons (souls, minds) can change bodies, but holds that persons cannot exist in a disembodied state, or that persons cannot sensibly be said to have spatial positions except when they are embodied, presumably does hold that persons are capable of discontinuous change of place. In this section I shall present an argument, independent of the arguments given earlier, to show that in general the persistence of persons must preserve spatiotemporal continuity, i.e., that it is impossible that persons could constantly be changing place in a discontinuous manner.

It is a striking fact that motion, though it involves the persistence through time of the moving object, is often directly observed rather than inferred. I must infer the motion of the hour hand of a clock, e.g., from the fact that its position relative to the face of the clock is different from what it was a while ago, but that the second hand is moving is as much a fact of direct experience as that it is a certain color. I can of course be mistaken in thinking that I see that something is moving, but so can I be mistaken in thinking that I see that something is black or red. When said of a "sense-datum," e.g., an afterimage, the statement "It is moving" is as "incorrigible," and as incapable of being reduced to a more primitive description of what is experienced, as the statement "It is red."

Obviously instantaneous or discontinuous motion, e.g., the "move" of a baseball team from one city to another, cannot be directly observed in the sense in which the motion of the second hand of a clock can be directly observed. Only continuous motion, i.e., motion in which spatiotemporal continuity is preserved, can be observed in this sense. If I observe something at place p_1 and then later on observe that same thing at place p_2, my knowledge that something has moved from p_1 to p_2 will be inferential knowledge (having among its grounds an assertion of the identity of the observed objects) unless I observed something moving along some continuous line joining p_1 and p_2. And I think that it is partly because there is an experience of motion that spatiotemporal continuity occupies the central role it does as a criterion of identity. It is not as if spatiotemporal continuity just happens to be the criterion we have adopted, out of many possible criteria of identity, to be the criterion for the identity of material things. It does not seem to be just a matter of convention that we use spatiotemporal continuity as a criterion of identity. On the contrary, when I see motion (as opposed to inferring it) there seems to be no way in which I can describe what I see except by saying "It (or: something) is moving," and in saying this I imply the persistence of something through time, and therefore the identity of something existing at one time with something existing at another time.

But let us suppose (*per impossibile*) that persons, regarded as distinct from human bodies, are capable of undergoing discontinuous changes of place, that such changes can occur instantaneously, and that there is no limit to the frequency or rapidity with which such changes can occur. And let us imagine that I am now watching a mouse move from right to left across a smooth surface of uniform color extending as far as I can see, and that the mouse is the only object that I see apart from

the surface on which it is moving. On the supposition just
made it should be possible that just when the mouse reaches
the center of my field of vision I might be moved, instantaneously, to another place on that surface (or a surface just like
it) where another mouse, exactly like the first one, is at the
center of my field of vision and is just beginning to move toward the left. So let us suppose that this happens. From t_1 to
t_2 I am at a place p_1, watching a certain process, and from t_2
to t_3 I am at a different place p_2, watching a process that is
different from, but apparently continuous with, the process I
was watching at p_1. Surely I would not detect the change. I
would think that I had watched a mouse move from the right-
hand side of my field of vision to the left-hand side, but I
would be mistaken. To vary the case, suppose that when the
mouse reaches the center of the left-hand side of my field of
vision I am moved, again instantaneously, several yards to my
left, so that now I see the mouse (the same one this time) in
the middle of the right-hand side of my field of vision. Now
it will appear to me that a mouse has just vanished into thin
air and that another mouse has materialized several yards to
its right. But again the appearance will be illusory, for it will be
one and the same mouse that I see. Finally, suppose that at
intervals of a hundredth of a second apart I occupy a number
of different positions on the surface, moving instantaneously
from one to another, that in each of these positions I see a
different mouse, which in each case remains stationary during
the brief instant in which I see it, and that the position of each
mouse in my field of vision is slightly to the left of that occupied by the mouse seen in the previous instant. Now it will
appear to me that a single mouse has moved across my field
of vision from right to left, whereas I will have seen a number
of different mice, none of which was moving at all.

My purpose in describing this fantasy is to show that in

ascribing identity on the basis of observed spatiotemporal continuity, in denying identity on the basis of observed discontinuity, and in ascribing motion to things on the basis of direct observation, we must assume that we ourselves are not changing position in a discontinuous manner. But it is not quite right to call this an assumption. We can perhaps allow that a person might occasionally change bodies, and thereby undergo discontinuous change of place. But there is nothing that I or anyone else could accept as showing that I am constantly changing place in this way, and the same goes for every other person. For if (*per impossibile*) a person's position were constantly changing in this way, he could never discover this, no matter what he experienced and no matter how reliably he remembered his experiences. He could not, of course, correctly assign positions to objects by reference to his own position, regarding the latter as a fixed point of reference. And he could not use any other object as a "landmark," or point of reference, by relation to which the positions of other things (including himself) could be identified, for he would have no way of identifying any object as "numerically the same thing again." In short, he would have no way of applying the concepts "same place," "different place," "same thing," and "different thing." So we might say that for each of us it is an a priori requirement, not a contingent fact, that our successive positions during any interval of time form a continuous line, or at least that they do so normally. Roughly speaking, each of us regards his own successive positions during any interval of time (or at least any interval of time of which he has an uninterrupted memory) as a paradigm, or standard, of a spatiotemporally continuous set of points—a standard by reference to which observed phenomena can be judged to be continuous or discontinuous. To put this in still another way, the legitimacy of ascribing motion to things on the basis of direct observation, the use of spatio-

temporal continuity as a criterion of identity, and the very ap-
plicability of the concept of spatiotemporal continuity to experience, require that persons be entities whose persistence
through time preserves spatiotemporal continuity, or at least
does so normally. And given the central status of spatiotemporal
continuity as a criterion of the identity of material things, it is
a necessary condition of our having the notion of "one and the
same material thing" that we (who have this notion) generally
preserve spatiotemporal continuity in our persistence through
time. For we could hardly be said to have this notion if we
had no way of applying it to our experience.

12. It should be evident from the arguments of Sections 9
and 10 that nothing that one can imagine could show, or have
any tendency to show, that other persons were constantly
changing bodies. But it may still seem that each of us can
imagine what it would be like for himself to be constantly
changing bodies. As we saw in Chapter One, what makes it
plausible to suppose that personal identity is logically independent of bodily identity is not so much the fact that we
use "psychological" facts as evidence for the truth of identity
statements about other persons as it is the way in which we
make memory statements about our own past histories. Now
I have already shown, in Chapter Four, that while one does
not use bodily identity as a criterion of personal identity in
making memory statements about one's own past, this is not
because one uses something else as a criterion but is rather
because one uses no criterion at all. So it cannot be held that
each of us has a nonbodily criterion of identity by means of
which he can determine that he is, or is not, constantly changing bodies. Nevertheless, it can easily seem imaginable that
one's memory might testify that one has constantly been changing bodies. My actual memories seem to support the assertion

that what is now my body has always been my body. But it seems that I can imagine what it would be like to remember a very different past, one in which, for example, I was in Paris at one instant, in New York a split second later, in Moscow a split second after that, and so on, and in which I did not "inhabit" any given body for more than a fraction of a second. If this is imaginable, however, the relationship between personal identity and bodily identity must be a contingent one.

I shall presently argue that no one can imagine remembering, or knows "what it would be like" to remember, such a migratory past. But I am doubtful whether it makes sense to say even that one can imagine *seeming* to remember, or having *apparent* memories of, such a past. I know what it would be like to have projected in front of me, in rapid succession, realistic (colored and stereoscopic) pictures of scenes in Paris, New York, and Moscow, and there is a sense in which I can imagine remembering (or seeming to remember) seeing such a series of pictures. If one thinks that one can imagine remembering (or seeming to remember) having actually been in Paris, New York, and Moscow in rapid succession, one is perhaps thinking that remembering this would be something like remembering such a series of pictures. But a memory of a glimpse of what looked like the Kremlin cannot be called a memory, not even an apparent memory, of seeing the Kremlin unless the other memories associated with it, e.g., the memories of what happened before and after the glimpse, are compatible with the proposition that one was in Moscow at the time at which the remembered glimpse occurred or is remembered as occurring. Moreover, unless we suppose that a person can have a spatial position that is not the position of any human body at all, we cannot suppose that a person is constantly changing bodies without also supposing that the person is constantly undergoing discontinuous change of place, i.e., that his identity does not preserve spatiotemporal continuity. But I have already argued, in Section 11, that no matter what a person experiences, and no matter how reliably he remembers his past experiences, there is nothing he could intelligibly accept as showing that he has constantly been changing location in a discontinuous manner. And I think that it follows from this that it cannot be a correct description of any set of memories to say that they are memories, or even apparent memories, of a personal history in which spatiotemporal continuity was not generally preserved.

Nothing I have said so far shows that it is impossible to seem to remember, to have apparent memories of, a past in which one was constantly changing bodies but nevertheless preserved spatiotemporal continuity, i.e., a past in which one (one's "soul") was constantly, but not instantaneously, moving from body to body, and in which one frequently inhabited no body at all (whenever one was "between bodies"). Whether this is possible turns in part on whether it is possible to imagine what it would be like to have no body, for one could hardly imagine remembering (or seeming to remember) being without a body unless one could imagine being without one. It is plausible to say that one can imagine what it would be like to seem to be looking in the direction in which one's body should be and not to see any body. But imagining this is not equivalent to imagining what it would be like to have no body, for if the imagined experiences did occur the reasonable conclusion to draw would be that one was having a peculiar sort of hallucination, not that one had no body.

But the main point I want to make is an application of the argument developed at length in Section 6. The *most* that anyone can imagine is that he might *seem* to remember a past that is incompatible with his having "inhabited" any body for any appreciable period of time, and the imaginability of this does not show that one could actually remember such a past, for if anyone did seem to remember this there would be nothing that he or anyone else could accept as showing that his memories were correct. He could not confirm his apparent memories by checking them against the memories (or apparent memories) of other persons, for we have already seen that nothing that anyone else could observe (or remember observing) could be evidence that he had such a past.

Six

How Is Self-Knowledge

Possible?

1. Underlying the theories about persons and personal identity that I have been criticizing is the idea that the criteria for the truth of statements about persons, and therefore the criteria that reveal the nature of persons and personal identity, must be criteria that we use in making these statements in the first person. If there are criteria for the truth of these statements, according to this idea, it must be directly on the basis of these criteria, i.e., because we have observed that they are satisfied, that we make the statements in the first person, and it must be because we are in a position to observe that the criteria are satisfied that we are entitled to make them or justified in making them. In at least some cases, it is supposed, the fact in which the truth of a psychological statement about a person consists must be one that the person making the statement can directly observe to hold. For statements like "I see an image"

and "I have a toothache" are not inferred from anything (not even from "criterial evidence"), yet these statements are made with certainty and it seems unquestionable that we are justified in making them. Here, it seems, the fact in which the truth of the statement consists must be its *own* criterion, and must be observable by the person (and only the person) the statement is about.[1] In the case of first-person memory statements there is less inclination to say that one can literally observe the fact in which the truth of the statement consists. For such statements imply the persistence of a person (the speaker) through time, and there is, as we have seen, a tendency to think that no statement implying the persistence or continuance of something can be either an observation report or a memory report.[2] Such statements, one is inclined to say, can only be known inferentially. Yet, just because they do imply the persistence of a person through time, it seems that such statements cannot be true unless criteria of identity are satisfied. But when one makes such statements about oneself one seems to know their truth in the most direct way possible; it certainly does not seem that in making a first-person memory statement one is drawing an inductive inference (e.g., is inferring that bodily

---

[1] Normally we would not say that someone who simply observes that P knows that P on the basis of criteria. Nor can we say this if knowing that P on the basis of criteria is equated with believing that P on the basis of adequate noninductive evidence that P, for a person who directly observes that P cannot naturally be said to know that P on the basis of *any* sort of *evidence*. But if we want to contrast knowing something on the basis of criteria with knowing something on the basis of inductive evidence, we might allow simply observing something to be the case as a special and limiting case of knowing something to be the case on the basis of criteria. Here the observed state of affairs might be said to be its own criterion. There is, of course, no sharp distinction between (1) observing that something is Φ and (2) observing that something has properties X, Y, and Z, and thereby knowing that it satisfies the criteria for being Φ.

[2] See Chapter Four, Section 3.

criteria of identity are satisfied). So it seems that one must, in making them, have direct access to (must observe or remember observing) facts that are criterial evidence for their truth.

It is not difficult to see how this idea underlies the demand that the subject of awareness, if there is one, be an object of awareness, the denial that the persistence of a self implies the persistence of a subject, and the view that psychological facts about a person must be "analyzable" into facts that are directly observable by that person himself. But it also underlies the view that psychological facts are logically independent of bodily and behavioral facts, and that personal identity is logically distinct from bodily identity. For whatever one has to observe in order to be entitled to make present-tense psychological statements about oneself, one does not have to observe facts about one's body or behavior.[3] And whatever one has to observe in order to be entitled to make a past-tense statement about oneself on the basis of memory, one does not have to observe facts that are evidence for the truth of statements about the identity of one's body. But if there are facts that one must observe in order to make such statements, and if these facts are the criteria for the truth of the statements, then the criteria are not physical (bodily and behavioral) criteria. And if this is so, the relationships between physical and psychological facts, and between bodily identity and personal identity, can only be contingent relationships.

In my arguments in the last three chapters I have been attacking, for the most part indirectly, the idea expressed above, i.e., the idea that the criteria for the truth of first-person psychological statements must be criteria that we use in making first-

---

[3] In the case of some psychological states, e.g., being in love, angry, etc., it is possible for one to say "I am (have been) behaving in these ways, so I must be such and such (in love, angry, etc.)." But this is not possible in the case of the sorts of psychological states we have been concerned with.

person psychological statements. I now want to attack what seems to me the main source of this idea. One wants to say that we *know* such statements to be true when we assert them, or at least that we often or generally know them to be true; that we are *justified* in asserting them, or *entitled* to assert them; and that this can be explained only on the supposition that we make such statements because we observe, or know directly, that the criteria for their truth are satisfied—for it is clear that we do not make such statements on the basis of indirect inductive evidence. That we normally make such statements, believing them to be true, when in fact they *are* true seems inexplicable unless we make this supposition. When I say I am having a certain experience, I generally *am* having that experience, so apparently there must be something that *tells* me that I am entitled to say that I have it. And what tells me that I am entitled to make a first-person psychological statement cannot be a mere inductive indicator of the truth of the statement, for such statements are not inferred. Since we do not make first-person psychological statements on the basis of bodily and behavioral facts, and do not make first-person memory statements on the basis of criteria of bodily identity, it would seem that either we are not justified in making such statements at all, which seems absurd, or else that the criteria for the truth of such statements must consist in nonphysical facts.

Against the view just described I shall argue that our ability to know first-person psychological statements to be true, or the fact that we make them (for the most part) only when they are true, cannot possibly be explained on the supposition that we make them on the basis of criteria. A qualification must be made here. My contention is not that we never use criteria in making first-person psychological statements, but is rather that the criteria we do use (when we use any) are not

214

criteria for saying that something is true of ourselves. Often a first-person statement contains or entails a statement that is not itself about the speaker. For example, the perceptual statement "I see that there is a eucalyptus tree on the hill" contains or entails the statement "There is a eucalyptus tree on the hill," and the memory statement "I remember that there was a hurricane here last October." contains or entails the statement "There was a hurricane here last October." Now such statements may well be based on criteria, for instance (in the examples given), on the criteria for something's being a eucalyptus tree, or the criteria for something's being a hurricane. In such cases I shall say that the first-person statement is based on the criteria for the truth of a "nonpersonal component" of it. What I wish to attack is the view that a first-person statement, if known to be true or asserted with justification, must be based on the criteria for the truth of the *whole* statement, and not simply on the criteria for the truth of its nonpersonal components. It is the view that, for example, my statement "I see a eucalyptus tree on the hill" must be based on the criteria for its being true of *me* that *I see* a eucalyptus tree on the hill, and not simply on the criteria for its being true that there is a eucalyptus tree on the hill.

2. What I am here calling first-person psychological statements can be divided into two groups, those that are "corrigible" and those that are "incorrigible." Among the corrigible statements are perceptual statements of the ordinary sort—i.e., statements in which the reported object of perception is a material object or a publicly observable state of affairs—and memory statements. It is characteristic of these that a person can make such a statement sincerely, i.e., believing it to be true, when in fact the statement is false and could in principle be discovered to be false by other persons. Among the incor-

rigible statements are statements about "private" experiences and mental events, e.g., pain statements, statements about mental images, reports of thoughts, and so on. These are incorrigible in the sense that if a person sincerely asserts such a statement it does not make sense to suppose, and nothing could be accepted as showing, that he is mistaken, i.e., that what he says is false. While sincere first-person statements of the first sort can be discovered to be false by reference to the criteria for the truth of the statements, this is not so of statements of the second sort. That a statement of the second sort is a sincere assertion is itself a logically sufficient condition of its being true, and that such a statement has been asserted with apparent sincerity is itself criterial evidence that it is true. But our other criteria (our "nonverbal criteria") can show, or indicate, that such a statement is false and therefore not a sincere assertion (e.g., if someone says "No, it doesn't hurt a bit," but is biting his lip and grimacing); and they can show that a person does not understand the meanings of the words he is uttering, and that what sounds like an incorrigible psychological statement is not really one (if, for example, a person characteristically utters the words "I am in pain" when anyone observing him would conclude from his behavior that he is exceptionally contented, and refuses to utter them when exhibiting what others would take to be manifestations of pain).

I suggested in Chapter Three that it is characteristic of a certain kind of statements, what I there called "first-person experience statements," that being entitled to assert such a statement does not consist in having established that the statement is true, i.e., in having good evidence that it is true or having observed that it is true, but consists *simply* in the statement's *being* true.[4] This can be said of both kinds of statements distinguished above. Corrigible first-person statements com-

---

[4] See Chapter Three, Section 9.

monly have nonpersonal components, and if it is asked how a person is justified in asserting a nonpersonal component of such a statement the answer may be that he has established, that he observes or remembers observing, that the criteria for the truth of the component statement are satisfied. But if someone asks how a person is justified in saying, or what entitles him to say, that he perceives or remembers something, and is not asking how the person knows the truth of a nonpersonal component of his perceptual or memory statement, we can answer only that the person does perceive what he claims to perceive, or does remember what he claims to remember. We establish whether the person is justified in making such a statement by establishing whether the statement as a whole is true (i.e., if "P" is a nonpersonal component of his statement, whether he perceives, or remembers, that P, and not simply whether it is the case that P), and to establish this we must have bodily and behavioral criteria for the truth of the whole statement. But the person himself does not establish this at all; he establishes, perhaps, that the nonpersonal components of his statement are true, but he does not establish, and does not have to establish, that it is by observation, or by memory, that he knows them to be true. Likewise, turning to incorrigible statements, if anything can be said to justify a person in saying on a particular occasion that he is in pain, it is simply his being in pain, not his having evidence of this or his observing it to be so, that justifies him.

I think that there is a strong philosophical inclination to say that one cannot be justified in saying something in the way in which I have said that we are justified in making first-person psychological statements. One feels that if one simply utters certain statements when in fact they are true, but without having established that they are true, then it can only be an accident, a coincidence, that the statements are true when one asserts them, and that one cannot be said to *know* their truth. There is perhaps a sense of "justified" in which a person can be said to be justified in making a statement only if he has observed or has good evidence that the statement is true. If the word "justified" is used in this sense then, on my view, we cannot be said to be justified in making first-person psychological statements (which is not to say that we are unjustified in making them[5]), though we can sometimes be justified in asserting the nonpersonal components of such statements. But there is a tendency to think that unless we are justified in this sense in making such statements, and make them because we observe the criteria for their truth to be satisfied, we cannot be in any sense entitled to make them. And what this mainly comes to, I think, is the idea that it is only by supposing that we are justified in this way in making such statements that it can be explained how it is that we commonly make them when they are true and seldom make them when they are false.

We must now consider the fact that is supposed to be explained by the supposition that we have criteria on the basis of which we make first-person psychological statements, namely the fact that these statements, or the beliefs expressed in them, are generally true. We shall see, first in the case of the incorrigible statements and then in the case of the corrigible ones, that this fact cannot possibly be explained in this way. But we must also consider what sort of explanation can be given of this fact; we must consider how it is that the making of a first-person psychological statement, unlike the making of other empirical statements, can be justified simply by the fact that the statement is true (instead of by the fact that the speaker observes or has evidence that it is true), or, using the term

---

[5] See Wittgenstein, *Investigations*, p. 99: "To use a word without justification does not mean to use it without right."

"justified" in a narrower sense, how it is that such statements can be made without justification and nevertheless be generally true.

3. Concerning first-person statements of the kind that I have called "incorrigible," e.g., pain reports, we can say, not simply that such statements are *generally* true when asserted, but that they are *always* true when sincerely asserted. It is just the mark of an incorrigible statement that its being honestly asserted is a logically sufficient condition of its being true. Once we are clear about this, however, we should no longer be inclined to conclude from the "fact" that such statements are generally true that there is something, our observing that criteria of some kind are satisfied, that justifies us in asserting them. There is no difference between believing that one is in pain and being in pain, so there can be no question of explaining how it "happens" that one believes that one is in pain only when in fact one is in pain.

But this matter needs to be pursued further, for there is a strong philosophical inclination to say the following: "I of course make no inference when I say 'I am in pain.' There would be an inference only if the fact with which I am acquainted when I say this, the fact on the basis of which I say it, were some fact other than the fact that I am in pain. But when I say 'I am in pain,' what I am acquainted with, or directly aware of, is just the pain itself, or just the fact of my being in pain. It is this direct awareness that justifies me in saying 'I am in pain.' If by 'criterion for saying that I am in pain' is meant something from which it can be inferred that I am in pain, then of course I use no criterion. But if by this is meant something that shows that I am in pain, then I do have a criterion; the pain, or the fact of my being in pain, is itself the criterion, for it shows me that I am in pain. It is just by being aware of the pain that I know I am in pain. And no one else can be shown that I am in pain in this way, for no one else can be directly aware of my pain in the way in which I can. My criterion, therefore, is a private one."

These remarks rest on a mistake. The mistake lies in the view that I know I am in pain *by* being "acquainted with" or "aware of" some entity or fact. This view is not so much false as senseless. We *seem* to explain my ability to know (or correctly assert) that I am in pain by saying that I have direct awareness of my pains, but we do not really do so. The illusion that we have an explanation here derives from the fact that our so-called awareness or consciousness of mental objects is regarded, illicitly, as a kind of perception or observation,[6] and from the fact that when words like "see," "perceive," and "observe" are used in their literal senses it is explanatory (sometimes) to say that one knows something to be the case *because* one sees, perceives, or observes it to be the case, or because one sees, perceives, or observes a certain entity. But if we consider how it is that statements like "I know there is a tree on the hill because I see one there" can be informative and explanatory, it becomes clear that the statement "I know I am in pain because I am aware of a pain" cannot be informative or explanatory in anything like the same way.

In the ordinary sense of "observe," what one knows to be the case because one observes it to be the case must be such that it would be possible for one to know it in other ways, i.e., on the basis of something other than direct observation; it must be something that one could believe to be the case even if one were not observing it to be the case; and it must be something that could be the case even if one were not observing it to be the case. In general, the question "How do you know that *P*?"

---

[6] See Chapter Two, Section 8, where the sources of this idea are discussed.

and the expression "I know that P because . . ." have application only if there is more than one way in which one could know that P. If I say "I know that P because I observe that P (or because I observe X, of which 'P' is a description)" I am, in effect, identifying one of the possible ways of knowing that P as the way in which I do in fact know it. An explanation of how one knows something, moreover, is always an attempt to justify one's knowledge claim. When I say "I know that P because . . . ," I do not present my knowledge that P as an accepted fact for which I am offering something like a causal explanation; I am trying to show *how* (not *why*) I know that P, and this involves trying to show *that* I know it (as opposed to merely believing it). The truth of my knowledge claim is something I am trying to show, not something I am taking for granted. Now, what sort of justification is one offering when one says "I know that P because I observe that P"? One is not citing one's knowledge of facts that are evidence that P. Rather, one is indicating that one is in a position to know that P without evidence. In so doing one indicates to others the appropriate way of appraising the validity of one's knowledge claim; one indicates that one's claim to know is not based, as it might have been, on knowledge of facts that are evidence that P, and hence that checking up on the validity of one's claim will consist, not in evaluating the evidence one offers in support of it (for one offers no evidence), but in determining whether one is in fact in a position to know the thing in question without evidence, i.e., whether one is in a position to observe that it is the case.

Being in a position to know that P without evidence is not simply believing that P without evidence when P is in fact the case. The fact that knowing something on the basis of observation involves being in a "position" to know it without evidence is closely related to the fact, emphasized in Chapter

Five, that perception is always from a "point of view." Roughly speaking, to say that there is such a thing as knowing facts about an object Y without evidence is to say that there is a contingent relationship R such that for any normal person X, if we know that X stands in R to Y we are normally justified in concluding, on the basis of this knowledge, that X has true beliefs of a certain kind about Y. An example of the relationship R would be the relationship that holds between a person and an object when, in normal lighting conditions, there is no opaque object standing between the person and the object and the person is within a certain distance of the object and has his eyes open and turned in its direction. If we know that a person is so related to an object we can normally conclude that he has true beliefs concerning the visual properties of the object (its color, shape, and so on). By expanding on this account we can explain what it means to say that a person is in a position to know without evidence what is happening in a certain locality, in a position to know how one object is related spatially to another, and so on. In general, being in a position to know something without evidence can be said to consist in having a property, normally a relational property (standing in R to something), that one might not have had. Given that we know of the existence of such properties, there is an obvious sense in which we explain someone's ability to make true statements of a certain kind by saying that he has a property of the appropriate sort, for we know that *any* normal person who had that property would have that ability. There is an equally obvious sense in which the having of such a property can justify a person in making a statement, for it gives the statement, if it is of an appropriate kind, a high likelihood of being true. But such explanations and justifications can be given only where it is possible in principle to establish empirically whether a person does have the appropriate property, i.e., is in the appropriate position. For in giving such a justification for a statement of one's own one is not simply claiming that one's statement is justified, but is trying to show that it is, so it must be possible for others to see that it is (or that it is not). And we can find that a person is, or is not, in a position to know something without evidence; we can determine, for example, whether a person's eyes are open and directed toward a certain object, whether his fingers are touching a given thing, and so on.

It should now be evident that there is no such thing as being in a position to know without evidence (in the sense just explained) that one is in pain, and that "being aware of a pain" is not being in such a position. If being aware of a pain were observing a pain, and therefore involved being in such a position, it would have to be the case that it can be an open question, to be settled empirically, whether a person who is in pain and thinks that he is in pain is in fact aware of a pain; that it is possible for a person to be in pain without being aware of a pain; and that being aware of a pain is one of several possible ways of knowing that one is in pain. But none of these things is the case. More generally, if anything at all is to count as observing a pain (or observing that one is in pain), and therefore as being in a position to know without evidence that one is in pain, it must be possible for it to be an open question, to be settled empirically, whether a person who is in pain and thinks that he is in pain is entitled to say without evidence that he is in pain, and it must be possible for a person to think that he is in pain without being entitled to say without evidence that he is in pain. And neither of these things is the case. We can say "It was raining, but Jones was not in a position to say that it was, for he had no evidence and was not in a position to observe that it was raining," but it would be absurd to say "Jones had a headache, but he was not entitled to say that he did, for he had no evidence and was not in a position to be aware (or to know without evidence) that he had a headache." Just because there is no such thing as my knowing *from* evidence that I am in pain there can be no such thing as my being in a special position to know *without* evidence that I am in pain. One can say "I know that Jones has a mustache now, but I've not seen it (Smith told me about it)," but it would be absurd to say "I know that I have a pain, but I am not aware of any pain (Smith tells me that I have one, and his information is usually reliable)." It is nonsense to speak of my knowing on inductive grounds, or on the basis of the testimony of others, that I am in pain. So if "I am aware of a pain (or that I have a pain)" were an answer to the question "How do you know that you have a pain?" it would be the *only possible* answer to that question. But if the question has only one possible answer, which must always be correct, it is at best a pointless question. And of course it is not a question that people (other than philosophers) ever raise. But it is not simply that we do not raise this question because we know in advance what the answer must be. There is no logical possibility of my being unjustified in thinking that I am in pain, so it is senseless to suppose that there is something other than (logically independent of) my thinking this that justifies me, and senseless (and not merely pointless) to ask what this justification is.

It may be objected that there is obviously such a thing as being in a special position to know that a certain person is in pain, namely, being that person. Certainly the following dialogue might occur. A: "Is the new patient still in pain?" B: "Yes he is." A: "How do you know?" B: "I am the new patient." But would this be a case of a person justifying his claim to know that he is in pain by saying, or indicating, that he is in a position to know this without evidence? What B is explaining is not his knowledge that he is in pain but rather his knowledge that the new patient is in pain. And he could be mistaken in claiming to know the latter (for he could be mistaken in thinking that he is the new patient), which he could not be in claiming to know the former. It makes sense to say that B might not have been the new patient, whereas it does not make sense to say that B might not have been himself, so the "fact" that B is himself provides no explanation of his knowledge that he is in pain. An explanation of how one knows something must assert that something that might not have been the case is in fact the case. If we explain someone's knowledge that P in terms of his having evidence that P, we explain it by saying that he has knowledge (of the evidence) that he might not have had. If we explain his knowledge by saying he observed that P we are saying he is (or was) in a position that he might not have been in. But where P is the statement "I am in pain," or any other incorrigible first-person statement, no such explanation can be given and none can sensibly be demanded.

4. Since sincere perceptual and memory statements, unlike sincere pain statements, can be false, it seems legitimate to ask how it happens that such statements are generally true. It is prima facie plausible to suppose that such statements are usually true because they are made on the basis of the criteria for their truth, and this of course implies that the criteria are nonphysical. I have already argued, in Chapter Three, that it is absurd to suppose that a person says he perceives something because he perceives himself perceiving it, or because he perceives some fact that is evidence that he perceives it, and, in Chapter Four, that it is absurd to suppose that first-person memory statements are made on the basis of criteria of personal identity. From this it seems to me to follow that first-person perceptual and memory statements are *not* based on the criteria for their truth. Those arguments aside, however,

what I shall now try to show is that it follows from the corrigibility of first-person perceptual and memory statements that the supposition that such statements are based on the criteria for their truth does not explain, but on the contrary makes utterly mysterious, the fact that such statements are generally true when sincerely asserted.

What distinguishes corrigible first-person psychological statements from incorrigible ones is just that sincere corrigible statements can be false and can in principle be discovered to be false by persons other than the speaker. If this were not true of first-person perceptual and memory statements, then these would be incorrigible rather than corrigible, and the argument of the preceding section would apply to them. There would in that case be no difference between perceiving something and merely seeming (to oneself) to perceive it, and no difference between remembering something and merely seeming (to oneself) to remember it—just as in fact there is no difference between being in pain and merely seeming (to oneself) to be in pain.[7] And in that case, paradoxically, perceptual statements could not in any sense be said to be based on observation; if it were impossible for sincere perceptual statements to be false, it would be impossible for the "nonpersonal components" of such statements to be false, and there would be no such thing as being in a position to know a nonpersonal component of such a statement to be true. Certainly there could then be no question of explaining, either by the supposition that such statements are based on the criteria for their truth or in some other way, how it "happens" that such statements are generally true when sincerely asserted. But I think that it will be universally agreed that such statements

[7] For this reason the sentence "I seem to be in pain" is, if not senseless, without a role to play in our language.

are corrigible rather than incorrigible. So let us see what follows from this.

If first-person perceptual and memory statements are corrigible, then, as I have said, it must be possible for a sincere statement of this sort to be discovered to be false by persons other than the speaker. How is it that such statements would be discovered to be false? If a person says "I see a tree," we will know that his statement is false if we know that his eyes are not open and directed toward a tree. If a person says "I played tennis yesterday," we will know that his statement is false if we know that the body which utters this statement was not involved in a game of tennis on the previous day. If there were not bodily facts of this sort that would show such statements to be false, no sense could be given to the assertion that such statements can be false when sincerely asserted, and such statements would be incorrigible rather than corrigible. But what, given that such statements can be shown to be false in this way, is the cash value of saying that in fact such statements are generally true when sincerely asserted? Surely it is this, that in general such a statement is sincerely asserted when the facts about the speaker's body are not such that if others knew these facts they would have to conclude that the statement is false. That is, it is generally the case that when a person claims to see an object of a certain kind his eyes are open and directed toward an object of that kind, and it is generally the case that when a person claims to remember a past event of a certain description he is identical, in accordance with physical criteria of identity, with someone who witnessed an event of that description in the past. This is not to say that the fact that a person's eyes are open and directed toward an object is sufficient to make it true that he sees that object, or that a fact of bodily identity can be sufficient to make it true that a certain person remembers a particular past event. But if a person's eyes are open and directed toward a certain object, and if *in addition* he sincerely claims to see that object, or an object of that kind, then there can be no doubt that he does see that object. Likewise, if a person was (is identical with in accordance with physical criteria of identity) a witness to a past event, and if *in addition* he sincerely claims to remember that event, or an event whose description is uniquely satisfied by that event, then there can be no doubt that he does remember that event.[8]

If this is correct, it follows from the corrigibility of first-person perceptual and memory statements that the fact that such statements are generally true when sincerely asserted consists in the fact that in general such statements are sincerely asserted (or believed) only when certain things are true of the body of the speaker. But how could *this* fact be explained by the supposition that such statements are asserted on the basis of the criteria for their truth? It might be explained in this way if it were true (1) that the bodily facts in question are (or are among) the criteria for the truth of the statements, and (2) that the statements are made on the basis of these bodily facts, i.e., because the speaker observes, or has established, that these facts hold. But (2) is clearly not the case, as everyone acknowledges. To suppose that the criteria for the truth of these first-person statements consist of facts that are

---

[8] This must be qualified. If we know that a person witnessed an event which he sincerely claims to remember, but know also that he has read about the event or heard it described by other persons, there can be a question whether he really does remember it. In such a case various considerations are relevant to the question whether he does remember the event; for example, whether in his description of the event he is able to go beyond what he read or was told, whether his confidence in the correctness of his description would be affected if we raised doubts about the reliability of those who told him about it, and so on. However, I do not believe that this qualification affects the point I am making.

logically independent of bodily facts, and that these statements are made on the basis of these nonphysical criteria, is to leave totally unexplained the fact that these statements are generally made only when certain bodily facts hold. This supposition therefore leaves totally unexplained the fact that sincere statements of this sort are generally true.

5. It would seem, offhand, to be a contingent fact that sincere perceptual and memory statements are generally true. That any particular sincere perceptual or memory statement is true is certainly a contingent matter, and it might seem to follow from this that it can only be a contingent fact that such statements are generally true. And if, as was argued in the preceding section, the fact that such statements are generally true comes down to the fact that such statements are generally uttered when certain things are true of the bodies of those who assert them, this would certainly seem to be a contingent fact, for it would seem that the existence of a correlation between a person's body being in a certain state and his making a certain kind of statement (a statement not *based on* facts about his body) can only be a contingent fact.

I wish to argue, however, that it is a necessary (logical, or conceptual) truth, not a contingent one, that when perceptual and memory statements are sincerely and confidently asserted, i.e., express confident beliefs, they are generally true. Here I am not restricting the application of the expression "perceptual and memory statements," as I did in the preceding section, to statements that actually *say* that the speaker perceives or remembers something (statements of the form "*I see* that *P*" and "*I remember* that *P*"), but shall use this expression to refer as well to statements that are not in the first person but are directly based on observation or memory, i.e., are putative reports of what the speaker perceives or remembers; if a person says simply "*P*," but is prepared to say "I see that *P*," then his statement is, in the present sense, a perceptual statement, and if a person says simply "*Q*," but is prepared to say "I remember that *Q*," then his statement is, in the present sense, a memory statement. However, it is still the former kind of perceptual and memory statements, what might be called explicit perceptual and memory statements, that I am mainly interested in, for these, unlike the others, are always first-person psychological statements, and it is only of these that it is normally plausible to say that they express *self*-knowledge.

The minimal claim that I wish to make is that the following is a necessary truth: Given any two contingent statements, "*P*" and "*Q*," if we know about "*P*" that someone has sincerely and confidently asserted it as a perceptual or memory statement, and know nothing about "*Q*" except what it asserts (what statements it is), then on the basis of this knowledge "*P*" is more likely to be true than "*Q*" is. It is a necessary truth, not an inductively discovered generalization, that the mere fact that a statement has been sincerely and confidently asserted by someone as a perceptual or memory statement gives *some* reason for believing it to be true. It may be that this minimal claim is all that I need to establish for the purposes of my later discussions. But I believe that I can establish the stronger claim that it is a necessary truth that such statements are generally true, i.e., are true more often than not.

That this is a necessary truth is suggested by things I have already said. In the last chapter I said that there are imaginable circumstances in which we would be strongly inclined to say that a person sees from a point of view other than his eyes. This would happen if a person made a number of statements, apparently perceptual statements, most of which could be counted as true perceptual statements if and only if we could regard some point other than the speaker's eyes as the point of view from which he sees. Likewise, we have seen that there are imaginable circumstances in which we would be strongly inclined to say that a person had "changed bodies." This would happen if a person consistently made statements, apparently memory statements, most of which could be counted as true memory statements if and only if the person had in the past "inhabited" a body other than his present one. In both cases, if we accept the supposition that the statements in question are perceptual statements or memory statements, we are inclined to modify the criteria for the truth of such statements (in the case of memory statements, the criteria of personal identity) in such a way as to make most of the statements true. This suggests that it is a necessary truth that such statements are generally true. I shall now try to show that this is the case.

My first argument is this. A primary criterion for determining whether a person understands the meanings of such terms as "see" and "remember" is whether under optimum conditions the confident claims that he makes by the use of these words are generally true. If most of a person's apparent perceptual and memory claims turned out to be false, this would show, not that the person had exceptionally poor eyesight or an exceptionally bad memory,[9] but that he did not understand, had not correctly grasped, the meanings of the words he was uttering, or was not using them with their established meanings, i.e., was not using them to express the perceptual and memory claims they appear to express. So to suppose that it is only a contingent fact, which could be otherwise, that confident perceptual and memory statements are generally true is to suppose

---

[9] The mark of poor eyesight is not a tendency to make confident perceptual claims that are false; rather, it is a tendency to make only cautious perceptual claims, or none at all, in circumstances in which persons with normal eyesight would make, or would be willing to make, confident perceptual claims. Similarly in the case of bad memory.

that we have no way of telling whether a person understands the use of words like "see" and "remember," or means by them what others mean by them, that we can never have any good reason for regarding any utterance made by another person as a perceptual or memory statement, and that we could therefore never discover the supposedly contingent fact that perceptual and memory statements are generally true. And this is a logically absurd supposition. To bring out this point more clearly, suppose that we have discovered a new people whose language we do not as yet know, and that someone has proposed a way of translating this language that involves regarding a certain class of statements (or utterances) as perceptual statements and another class as memory statements. Suppose further that we find these statements to be most commonly uttered, confidently and assertively,[10] in circumstances in which their proposed translations would be false. For example, the expression translated by the English sentence "I see a tree" is commonly uttered, confidently and assertively, when the speaker's eyes are not open or not directed toward a tree, and the expression translated by the English sentence "I ate meat last night" is frequently uttered by vegetarians but seldom by anyone who did eat meat on the previous evening. If this happened, surely there could be no reason for regarding the proposed way of translating their language as correct, and there would be every reason for regarding it as mistaken. Anything that might seem to show that the confident and sincere perceptual and memory statements that people make are generally false would in fact

---

[10] To say that a sentence is uttered "assertively," as I use that term, is to say that it is uttered in the manner of a person making an honest assertion, as contrasted with the manner of a person who is simply mentioning a sentence, e.g., with the purpose of discussing its meaning or syntax. Not all assertive utterances are assertions; e.g., those made by actors in plays are not.

show that we are mistaken in regarding certain utterances as expressing certain perceptual and memory claims.

It can be seen in another way that it cannot be a mere contingent truth that confident and sincere perceptual and memory statements are generally true. If one maintains that this is a contingent truth, one must also hold that it is only a contingent truth, which could be otherwise, that *one's own* sincere and confident perceptual and memory statements, i.e., one's own confident perceptual and memory beliefs, are generally true. For if I could rightly claim that it is a necessary truth, not a contingent one, that *my* confident perceptual and memory beliefs are generally true, then surely every other person would have an equal right to claim that it is a necessary truth that *his* confident perceptual and memory beliefs are generally true; any argument I could give for my claim about myself would presumably be stated in the first person, i.e., by use of the first-person pronouns, so any other person could use the same argument, word for word, to establish a corresponding claim about himself. And if it were necessarily true of each and every person that his confident perceptual and memory beliefs are generally true, it would be necessarily true of confident perceptual and memory beliefs in general that they are generally true. Supposing, then, that it is only a contingent fact, which could be otherwise, that my confident perceptual and memory beliefs are generally true, how do I *know* this to be a fact? If it could have been the case that these beliefs are generally false, how do I know that this is not actually the case? If I were to say "I confidently believe each of these things to be true, yet it could be the case, *and for all I know is the case,* that all or most of them are false," surely I would be confessing that the beliefs in question are completely irrational, and that none of them can legitimately be said to constitute knowledge. Yet of course it is precisely one's confident beliefs, and especially one's confident perceptual and memory beliefs, that one expresses by saying "I know . . ."; it is not a psychological fact, but rather a logical fact, that one cannot help regarding one's confident perpetual and memory beliefs as constituting knowledge. So there seems to be a kind of inconsistency involved in saying that for all one knows to the contrary all or most of one's confident perceptual and memory beliefs may be false. But again, if one does know, as a matter of contingent fact, that most of one's confident perceptual and memory beliefs are true, *how* does one know this?

It is plausible, though I think a mistake, to suppose that one's knowledge that the confident perceptual and memory claims of other persons are generally true is simply knowledge of an empirical generalization, and that one's reliance on individual perceptual and memory claims made by other persons (for instance, when I believe that it was raining outside a few minutes ago because my wife says that she looked outside and saw that it was raining) is always inductively based. But it is plainly absurd to maintain that I have established empirically that my own confident perceptual and memory beliefs are generally true and that I rely on my individual perceptual and memory beliefs because I have established this generalization. In the first place, I cannot be said to *rely* on my *beliefs* at all. It is absurd to speak of my believing that P on the basis of the fact that I believe that P.[11] In the second place, it is impossible that I could ever establish, as a contingent fact, that my confident perceptual and memory beliefs are generally true. For how could I establish this? Could I establish it on the basis of observation and memory? But if I am trying to find out whether my perceptual and memory beliefs are generally true, and hence am not already taking it for granted that they are,

---

[11] Cf. Wittgenstein, *Investigations*, p. 190: "One can mistrust one's own senses, but not one's own belief."

then in beginning my investigation I must allow that for all I *as yet* know it may be that my perceptual and memory beliefs are generally false. I must, as it were, disqualify anything that I believe on the basis of observation or memory as evidence that I can appeal to in trying to determine whether my beliefs are generally true. Perhaps I can start off with the knowledge that I *seem* to perceive certain things and *seem* to remember certain other things. But this knowledge will be of no use to me unless I know that in general, at least in certain circumstances, I do perceive what I seem to perceive, and do remember what I seem to remember. But clearly I could not know this if I did not already know the very thing in question, namely that my confident memory and perceptual beliefs are generally true. And if it is a contingent fact, which could be otherwise, that my confident perceptual and memory beliefs are generally true, and if I cannot establish this fact on the basis of observation and memory, then surely there is *no* way in which I could establish it.

It seems to me, then, that the view that it is only a contingent fact that my confident perceptual and memory beliefs are generally true, and that it is possible that they are generally false, has the absurd consequence that I can never be justified in asserting anything on the basis of observation and memory. Conversely, if I am justified in regarding my confident memory and perceptual beliefs as constituting knowledge (which, as I have said, I logically cannot help doing), then it is a necessary truth, not a contingent one, that my confident perceptual and memory beliefs are generally true. But if this is true of me, it must be true of others; anyone else can give the same argument about himself. It seems to me, therefore, that it follows from the logical possibility of anyone's knowing anything about the world that perceptual and memory beliefs are generally true. I cannot intelligibly make perceptual and memory statements, confidently claiming them to be true, without acknowledging that the confident memory and perceptual statements made by others are generally true. And certainly I cannot reasonably expect others to accept my perceptual and memory statements as true on my testimony, i.e., because I have sincerely and confidently asserted them, without being willing, normally, to accept their sincere and confident perceptual and memory beliefs as true on their testimony.

6. One reason why it is plausible to think it is a contingent fact, not a necessary one, that sincere and confident perceptual and memory statements are generally true is that there is a contingent fact, or a class of contingent facts, that is easily confused with it. It seems clear that it is only contingently true of me that I generally utter the words "I see a tree," in a confident and assertive manner, only when my eyes are open and directed toward a tree. And of any person it can only be contingently true, if it is true at all, that he generally utters that sentence under those conditions. Likewise, of any given person it can only be contingently true, if it is true at all, that after having eggs for breakfast he will respond to certain questions by uttering the sentence "I remember having eggs for breakfast this morning," and that in general he utters this sentence, confidently and assertively, only when he has had eggs for breakfast. Much more generally, it is true, but is only contingently true, that sentences which in fact express perceptual and memory statements are most commonly uttered, confidently and assertively, in circumstances in which the statements expressed by them would be true.

It is not easy to state this contingent fact (or contingent facts of this kind) in a way that clearly distinguishes it (or them) from the necessary truth discussed in the preceding section, and the formulation above is not altogether satisfactory.

To speak of a *person* is already to speak of a being that can be presumed to have the capability of remembering and perceiving, and to speak of a *sentence* is already to speak of something having an established meaning. Because of this, it is not altogether clear that even the facts stated above are purely contingent; it is not clear that an aboriginal in Borneo who happens to have uttered a set of sounds just like those I utter when I say "I see a tree" can be said to have uttered the *sentence* "I see a tree," and it is not clear that it makes sense to suppose that people might commonly utter that *sentence* in a confident and assertive manner without asserting the *statement* "I see a tree," i.e., without the speaker's saying that he sees a tree. But the contingent fact that I am interested in is about the making of certain sounds and gestures, not about the asserting of certain sentences. In the preceding paragraph I should have spoken, not of the *sentence* "I see a tree," but of the *sounds* "I see a tree," meaning by this the characteristic pattern of sounds made by English-speaking people when they utter the sentence "I see a tree." And it is better not to describe this as a fact about *persons*. I shall therefore state it as a fact about *human beings*, using the term "human being," in a technical sense, to mean "something that looks like, and has the physical characteristics (anatomical structure, chemical composition, and so forth) of a person." What might be regarded as essential attributes of persons, e.g., being able to remember some of their past actions, being capable of learning the use of language, and so forth, I shall regard as only contingent properties of human beings. My distinction between persons and human beings is similar to Locke's distinction between a person and a man. On Locke's use of the term "man," the identity of a man, as distinguished (possibly) from the identity of a person, is simply the identity of a human body. And I shall use the term "human being" in such a way that the identity of a human being is just the identity of a human body, something about which we can judge in exactly the way in which we judge concerning the identity of any material object.

I can now bring out more clearly the nature of the contingent truths stated above and their relation to the necessary truth that sincere and confident perceptual and memory statements are generally true. It is a *necessary* truth that *if* a group of human beings are persons, and do make perceptual and memory statements, there will exist correlations of a certain kind in their behavior—correlations between the uttering of certain sounds (or the making of certain gestures) and its being the case that the speaker's eyes are open and directed toward an object of a certain kind, and correlations between the uttering of certain other sounds (or the making of certain other gestures) and certain things having happened to the speaker in the past. But that such correlations do exist in the behavior of any group of human beings will be a *contingent* fact. If we should come across such a group of human beings for the first time, it would be just the existence of such contingent correlations that would show us that they do make perceptual and memory statements, and it would be this, among other things, that would show us that they are in fact persons. And of course there could be a group of human beings in whose behavior no such correlations could be found; such a group of human beings could not be said to speak a language in which perceptual and memory statements are made, even if they commonly uttered the sounds by which such statements are expressed in languages like English and Russian. It is just because the sounds "see" and "remember" are uttered by certain human beings (English-speaking people) in the circumstances in which they are uttered, i.e., because certain contingent generalizations are true of them, that they express the meanings they do.[12] If a group

---

[12] These generalizations are of course very complicated, more so than I have indicated, for the words 'see" and "remember" are often mentioned

of human beings could not be taught, or trained, to utter some sounds (or to make some gestures) in such a way that correlations of the kind I have described would come to exist in their behavior, they could not be said to perceive or remember at all in the sense in which persons do, and could hardly be said to be persons at all.

Two points of importance can now be made. First, the necessary truth that perceptual and memory statements are generally true is best expressed in the conditional statement: "If perceptual and memory statements are made at all, most sincere and confident perceptual and memory statements are true." This conditional statement, because it is a conditional statement, does not describe anything that happens, and therefore does not report any happening or set of happenings for which an explanation can be demanded. On the other hand, the existence of contingent correlations of the sort discussed above *is* something for which an explanation can be demanded. But the explanation of the fact that these correlations exist is hardly to be found in any epistemological theory, e.g., in the supposition that first-person perceptual and memory statements are made on the basis of grounds or criteria. Strictly speaking, the fact to be explained is not the fact that statements of a certain kind are true, and is not a fact about the making of statements at all; what is to be explained is an empirical phenomenon, the fact that certain correlations exist in the behavior of human beings, and it is to the natural sciences (perhaps to physiology), not to epistemology, that we must turn if we want an explanation of it.

7. "What we have to mention in order to explain the significance, I mean the importance, of a concept, are often extremely general facts of nature: such facts as are hardly ever

---

rather than used, and are often used, by actors and others, in utterances that are not assertions.

mentioned because of their extreme generality." [13] This remark of Wittgenstein's can be applied to the problems I have been discussing.

One general fact of nature, which is clearly of the kind Wittgenstein had in mind, is that different human beings respond in the same ways to the same training in the use of language. It is just a fact of nature that the gestures used in the teaching of linguistic expressions elicit similar responses in different human beings; for example, human beings react in a fairly uniform way to the gesture of pointing, and unless there were *some* gesture, the gesture of pointing or some other one, to which human beings *naturally* respond in a uniform way, i.e., without being trained to do so, the gesture of pointing could not play the role it does in ostensive teaching, and no other gesture could play that role. And as the result of being given a certain training different human beings will make similar linguistic responses in similar situations; i.e., if one human being utters certain sounds in one kind of situation and not in others, the same will generally be true of other human beings who have received the same training in the uttering of those sounds. If this were not so of at least some human beings, language would be impossible, and no sound could be said to express a meaning. What defines the *correct* response to the training in the use of a word (e.g., an ostensive definition together with the training which prepares human beings for being given ostensive definitions), and what also defines what is to count as the correct use of the word, is the *typical* response of those to whom the training is given. If the typical response of human beings to the ostensive teaching of the word "red" were different, both the correct response and the meaning of that word (or sound) would be different. And if there were no typical response at all, i.e., if every human being responded to the "training" in a different way, and it were impossible by

[13] Wittgenstein, *Investigations*, p. 56.

further training to get human beings to respond in a uniform way, the sound "red" would not express a meaningful word at all, and the "training," i.e., the making of certain gestures and saying "Red!" would not be training.

Another general fact of nature, and a special case of the one described above, is that the uniform effect of a certain kind of training is a tendency, on the part of the human beings so trained, to utter certain sounds while exhibiting the behavioral manifestations of pain and not to utter them while exhibiting the behavioral manifestations of well-being and contentedness. Following a remark of Wittgenstein's, we might express this by saying that human beings can be taught "new pain-behavior." [14] If this were not so there could be no pain-*language*, e.g., there could be no word meaning what we mean by "pain."

Still another general fact of nature is that human beings are capable of being so trained in the use of language, or in the making of sounds and gestures, that as the result of their being given a certain training there will exist in their behavior correlations of the sort discussed in the preceding section, correlations that make it possible for the uttering of certain sounds by members of a group of human beings to be regarded as the making of first-person perceptual and memory statements. If human beings did not have this capacity, the concepts of perception and memory would not apply to them, except in the way in which they apply to nonhuman animals. The point here is not simply that if human beings did not have this capacity they would not generally make *true* perceptual and memory statements, though this is of course the case. It is rather that if they did not have this capacity they would not make perceptual and memory statements at all, could not be taught to make them, and could not be said to have beliefs that are expressible in such statements.

What human beings are capable of being trained to do is to

---

[14] *Ibid.*, p. 89.

utter certain expressions, or to make certain sounds, when, or only when, certain conditions are satisfied. The test of whether a human being has been so trained (e.g., has been trained to utter the sounds "I see" in the circumstances in which it would be correct for him to use the English *words* "I see") is simply whether he utters the sounds when, or only when, the appropriate conditions are in fact satisfied; it is not essential that he should have *established* that those conditions are satisfied, and still less is it essential that he should utter the sounds because he has established this. Sometimes, to be sure, a human being can be taught to utter a sound in the following way: he is taught to determine whether certain conditions are satisfied and to utter the sound only if he finds that those conditions are satisfied. But it could not be the case that the use of linguistic expressions is always learned in this way. And, what is more important here, it *need* not be the case that the use of linguistic expressions is always learned in this way. Viewed simply as a natural phenomenon, the fact that as the result of a certain kind of training human beings utter certain sounds (e.g., the sounds "I see a tree") when certain conditions are satisfied (e.g., when the speaker's eyes are open and directed toward a tree), and utter them without establishing that the conditions are satisfied, is no more mysterious than the fact that a child who has been burnt in the past now shuns fire without first establishing that he has been burnt in the past. As a natural phenomenon this is simpler, and probably more easily explainable in causal terms, than the making of statements on the basis of grounds or criteria, i.e., the making of statements (and the uttering of the sounds which express statements) by a human being because he has established that certain conditions are satisfied. The former seems mysterious only when the existence of the conditions can be regarded as the criterion for the truth of a certain statement, and when the making of the sounds can be regarded as the asserting of that very statement. And then it seems mysterious because we have a faulty theory of knowledge, a faulty conception of how statements must be made if we are to be "entitled" to make them, and not because there is anything inexplicable about what actually happens.

I have already argued that first-person psychological statements of the sorts I have been concerned with cannot be made on the basis of the criteria for their truth, and that it is a necessary truth, not a contingent one, that such statements are generally true if they are made at all. If, after this has been shown, one is still inclined to ask how it is possible for us to make such statements on the right occasions without grounding them on the criteria for their truth, the only answer is that it is just a fact of nature that human beings can be so trained that they are able to make such statements; that the result of the training is precisely an ability to say certain things under certain conditions (these often being the conditions for the truth of what is said) without first ascertaining whether those conditions are satisfied; and that if human beings did not respond to training in this way there would be no such things as first-person psychological statements.

8. From some of my remarks, especially in Chapter Five, it may appear that I regard the identity of a person as simply the identity of a living human body, and that I have rejected as completely mistaken the idea that there is a philosophically important difference between the identity of persons and the identity of other things. I have argued that bodily identity must be a criterion of personal identity, and that if it were not a criterion nothing else could be evidence of personal identity. And I have attacked the view that the real criteria of personal identity must be nonphysical and psychological criteria that persons use in making identity judgments about themselves; I have

argued that first-person judgments of personal identity (and first-person judgments that imply the persistence of the speaker) are either based on the same criteria that are used in making third-person identity judgments, or, if grounded solely on memory, are not based on criteria of identity at all. It therefore may seem that I have been arguing that bodily identity is the *sole* criterion of personal identity, and that the view that there are other criteria rests on the mistaken view that first-person memory statements must be based on criteria of identity, and on the related and equally mistaken view that since we do not *use* bodily facts as criteria in making certain kinds of first-person statements it cannot be the case that there *are* bodily criteria for the truth of those statements.

Now it seems to me that the fact that persons can make identity judgments about themselves, or statements implying the persistence of themselves, without using criteria of personal identity, and that such statements are generally true and can be said to express knowledge, itself constitutes an important difference between the identity of persons and the identity of other things. Only about persons can identity judgments be made in this way. And the noncriterial knowledge that a person has of his own identity, or of his own past history, can be shared with, i.e., communicated to, other persons; if a person reports that he remembers doing a certain thing, other persons can accept his reporting this as evidence that he, the very person who reports this, did do the thing in question. And it can be seen from this that the view that bodily identity is the sole criterion of personal identity is inconsistent with what I have argued in the present chapter. If bodily identity were the sole criterion, then we would have to be making an inductive inference when we accept a person's claim to remember doing a certain thing as evidence that he did do that thing. It would then be the case that we have discovered empirically, using bodily identity as our criterion of personal identity, that the sincere and confident memory statements persons make are generally true (generally correspond to facts about the past histories of the bodies that utter them), and that having discovered this we are willing to make inductive inferences of the form "He claims to remember doing X, so he probably did do X." But I have maintained that it is a necessary truth, not a contingent one, that confident and sincere memory statements are generally true. If this is so, inferences of the form "He claims to remember doing X, so he probably did do X" cannot be merely inductive, for they are warranted by a generalization that is necessarily rather than contingently true.

Let us return briefly to the "change-of-body argument" discussed in Chapter One.[15] If one is inclined to accept the memory claims of Brownson as evidence that he is (has become) Brown, the inference one is inclined to make is not of the form "He claims to remember doing X, so he probably did X," but is of a more complex sort. Roughly, it has the form "He claims to remember doing X, Y, and Z under such and such circumstances and at such and such times and places, and it is true that X, Y, and Z were done by someone under precisely those circumstances and at those times and places, so there is reason to think that he is the person who did those actions." But it seems to me that if inferences of the first sort are not inductive, neither are inferences of the second sort. And to say that inferences of the second sort are legitimate (as they certainly are, at least under certain circumstances), and yet noninductive, is tantamount to saying that memory is a criterion of personal identity.

It should be noted that if such inferences were merely inductive and if bodily identity were the sole criterion of personal identity, it would be patently absurd to make such an inference

---

[15] Sections 8–10.

in a case in which the body of the person making a memory claim is known not to be identical with the body of the person who did the action that he claims to remember. The absurdity would be that of asserting something to be true, or probably true, on the basis of indirect evidence while having direct and conclusive evidence that it is false. But in my "brain-transfer case" the claim that Brownson is Brown does not, I think, strike us as having this sort of absurdity. That such cases so much as incline us to admit the possibility of bodily transfer, or leave us in doubt as to what to say, is itself prima facie evidence that memory is a criterion of personal identity. We can know this much without knowing how the conceivable conflicts between this criterion and the criterion of bodily identity, envisaged by philosophers in describing "puzzle cases" like my brain-transfer case, should or would be adjudicated.

As for the question of how the case I have described should be judged, I have little to add to what I have said already. We can each report what we find ourselves inclined to say about this case, but to do this is not to take sides on a philosophical question. The question of what most people *would* say if the imagined events occurred is of course a factual question, and not a question for philosophers to decide. But something can be said, of a philosophical nature, about what would be the case if such events were to happen and if nearly everyone were to agree that a change of body had taken place. First, it clearly cannot be said that in making this judgment people would be *mistaken*; at most it can be said that in making it they would show that they had adopted new criteria of personal identity, and that their judgment would not be in accord with our present criteria. Second, it cannot be said that they would be completely abandoning our present criteria of personal identity (for I have argued that memory is one of our criteria, and they would be using it as one), and it cannot even be said that their judgment would be *clearly* not in accord with our present criteria. It cannot be said that they would be abandoning bodily identity as a criterion of identity; all that can be said is that they would be refusing to regard this criterion as decisive in all cases, and would be allowing it to be overweighed by other criteria in some circumstances.

9. I have argued from its being a necessary truth that confident and sincere memory statements are generally true that we are not reasoning inductively when we accept the making of such a statement as evidence of its truth. But it might be objected that this is a faulty inference. As we saw in Section 6, if memory statements are made there must exist correlations in the behavior of those who make them, correlations between the making of certain sounds and facts about the past bodily histories of those who make them. And it might be said that it is our knowledge of the existence of such correlations, itself a contingent fact, that justifies us in relying on the memory testimony of other persons, and that our reliance on such testimony is inductively based after all. The inference "He says that he played tennis yesterday, so he probably did" is not itself an inductive inference. But it would seem that the inference "He uttered the sounds 'I played tennis yesterday,' so he probably played tennis yesterday" could only be justified on inductive grounds. And is it not really inferences of the latter sort that we are making when we "accept someone's testimony"? If it be insisted that in making such inferences it is what a person *says*, not what sounds he makes, that we use as evidence, we have to ask how we know what a person is saying when he utters certain sounds. And as we saw earlier, if a question arises whether a person understands the meanings of the expressions he uses in what seem to be memory statements, the question can be settled only by our establishing

whether what the person apparently claims to remember doing or witnessing in the past are normally things that he actually did do or witness. If in most cases it turns out that his apparent memory claims do correspond to facts about his past history, this shows that he understands the use of the word "remember" and the other words he utters, and that his apparent memory claims are really memory claims and so can generally be relied upon. Must it not be much the same sorts of considerations, i.e., our having observed certain correlations between what people say and what they have done in the past, that justifies our general reliance on people's testimony, or rather our general acceptance of what people say as testimony? If so, it would seem that our reliance on what people say, as evidence for statements about their past histories, is in the end inductively grounded.

In answer to this I must begin by pointing out how seldom we raise any question as to whether a person understands the meanings of the expressions he utters, e.g., whether a person who seems to have made a memory statement (uttered what *sounds like* a memory statement) has really done so. We often question the *truth* of what people say, though it would be nonsense to suppose that the sincere memory and perceptual statements might be generally false. We sometimes question the *honesty* of a person who is giving testimony, though again it would be nonsense to suppose that people might always or generally lie. But unless the terms being used are technical or recondite ones, or unless the speaker is a child or a foreigner, it simply does not occur to us to question whether the person understands the meanings of the expressions he utters. That there must be ways in which such a question could be settled if it were raised (i.e., that it must be possible in principle to determine whether a person understands the meaning of a given expression) is a point of considerable importance. That as a general rule such questions are not raised is also a fact of considerable importance.

It will perhaps be said that it so rarely happens that a person who does not understand a given language utters what sounds like a well-formed sentence in that language, and utters it in circumstances in which it would not be clearly inappropriate to use that sentence to make a statement, that we are quite justified on inductive grounds in not regarding the logical possibility of this happening as a real possibility. But I do not think that this can be the whole story. It is, I should like to say, part of our "form of life," to use Wittgenstein's expression, that we accept what other persons say at face value, without normally raising or even considering the question whether they understand the meanings of the expressions they utter, or whether their apparent testimony is really testimony. Normally there is no inference, and certainly not an inductive inference, from "He uttered the sounds 'I went for a walk yesterday'" to "He said that he went for a walk yesterday." We regard a person who is talking, not as making sounds from which, knowing the circumstances in which such sounds have been uttered in the past, we can make certain inductive inferences, but as *saying something*. We regard what he says as *having meaning*, not simply in the sense in which a barometer reading has meaning, i.e., as indicating that something has happened, is happening, or is about to happen, but as expressing what *he* means. It would be misleading to describe this as a *belief* on our part, the belief that people who use the words we use generally mean by them what we mean by them. It is rather a matter of attitude, of the way in which we respond to a person who is talking. (Here I am guided by Wittgenstein's remark: "My attitude towards him is an attitude towards a soul. I am not of the *opinion* that he has a soul.") [16] If this

---

[16] *Investigations*, p. 178.

attitude were one of belief, we could inquire into the grounds of the belief. But this is just what we do not do. It is part of the expression of this attitude that the question of what justifies us in regarding what others say as testimony does not arise. We say "I heard him say that he will come," not "I heard him utter the sounds 'I will come,' and gathered from this that he was saying that he would come."

In Section 6 I introduced a technical use of the term "human being" and insisted on a conceptual distinction between human beings, things that look like and have the physical character-istics of persons, and persons. The "attitude" referred to above can be further described by saying, this distinction notwith-standing, that we regard human beings as persons without hav-ing evidence that they are persons. Involved in being a person is having a memory, and this involves having the ability to make, without evidence, true statements about one's own past. It is part of our attitude that we normally do not demand evidence that particular human beings have this ability, though there could be human beings who do not have it. We regard others, not as things that behave in certain complicated ways and *so* (by definition) can be called persons, but as beings *like ourselves*. No one can believe that he himself always or gen-erally speaks without meaning, and it is nearly as difficult for one to believe that this could be true of another human being. In accepting the memory testimony of another person one thinks of oneself, not as inferring something about that person's past from his present behavior (though *in a sense* this is what one is doing), but as *sharing* the *uninferred* knowledge he has of his past; one accepts his memory statements almost as if they were one's own. Thus there is a certain artificiality about the distinction I drew in Chapter One between the "third-person version" and the "first-person version" of the change-of-body argument. When my brain-transfer example is described in the third person, it is only by an effort that we can bring ourselves to view the case in a purely "behavioristic" way. We find it natural to say, not that Brownson uttered certain sounds and made certain movements, but that he made certain statements, and expressed memories of Brown's past actions. And in doing this we are already to some extent putting ourselves in the place of Brownson, and are likely to feel the plausibility of the first-person version of the argument without actually expressing it in the first person.

The attitude I have been describing is certainly related to the contingent correlations discussed in Section 6 and the "general facts of nature" discussed in Section 7, but it is not related to them as a conclusion from inductive evidence. It is not that we have discovered that these correlations hold and concluded that the attitude is a reasonable one. It is rather that we simply do have this attitude, and because the facts are as they are it generally serves us well (the predictions we make about the behavior of others on the basis of their statements of intention generally turn out to be true; we generally do not go wrong in acting on what we take to be the memory and perceptual statements of other persons; and so on).

But perhaps it will be said that it is just an accidental fact about us that we have this attitude, and that there could be a race of human beings, more rational than we are, who do not take for granted what we take for granted and who demand grounds for what we accept on a sort of "animal faith." I do not think that this can be so. It not only *is not* the case, but, I think, *could not be* the case, that in general we regard certain of the utterances of other human beings as memory claims because we have established, inductively, that certain correlations exist in their behavior. Under special circumstances I might raise a question whether what sounds to me like a memory claim is really one, and such a question could be settled empirically, by observations of the behavior of the person who made the apparent memory claim. But except when we have definite grounds for supposing the contrary, we must, I believe, regard other human beings as speaking a language, our own if the words sound familiar, without having any general empirical justification for doing so.

Let us consider whether it would be possible for me to question whether there is anyone at all (other than myself) who speaks the language I speak, and then to discover empirically, by observing correlations between the uttering of sounds and the past histories of those who utter them, that those around me do speak the language I speak and that certain of their utterances are memory claims and can generally be relied upon. In carrying on such an investigation I would of course have to rely on my own memory. But one's memory can be mistaken. It is essential to the very notion of memory, as knowledge of an objective past, that there be a distinction between remembering something and merely seeming to remember something. And for there to be such a distinction there must be such a thing as checking up on one's memory and finding that one does, or does not, remember what one seems to remember. As Wittgenstein has pointed out, there are and must be circumstances in which we would accept other sorts of evidence concerning the past as more authoritative than our own memories.[17] An important way of checking up on one's own memory is by reference to the testimony of other persons. But this sort of check would not be available to me if I could not even regard the utterances of other human beings as testimony (e.g., as memory claims) until I had completed my investigation and established the required set of correlations. And the possibility of my checking up on my memories in any other way presupposes the possibility of checking upon them in this way.

---

[17] *Ibid.*, pp. 27–28, 93–94.

Perhaps it will be said that I can know that one of my memories is mistaken by seeing that it conflicts with the rest of my memories. But how is it that memories can "conflict"? If I seem to remember seeing that a certain lot was vacant the day before yesterday, and also seem to remember seeing a tall building on that lot yesterday, I shall conclude that one or the other of my memories must be mistaken. But it is not that these memories are in themselves inconsistent. They "conflict," but what this means is that the conjunction of them is incompatible with a general truth I know about the world, namely that tall buildings cannot be built in a day. But could *my own* past experience, or rather my present memory of it, be sufficient to give me the general knowledge of the world, of causal laws and so on, that I would need in order to be able to conclude from what I seem to remember that one of my memories is false? I think not. If I am trying to make generalizations on the basis of my past experience as I remember it, but am not trying to make these generalizations consistent with the experience of other persons as well as with my own, there is no reason why I cannot make these generalizations complicated enough to be consistent with all my memories. To be sure, if I try to make my generalizations fairly simple, I shall probably find it impossible to make them consistent with all my memories. But suppose that I have formulated a set of relatively simple generalizations that are consistent with a majority of my memories, but inconsistent with a small minority of them. Can I conclude that the recalcitrant memories are false? Is it not possible that I could formulate a different set of generalizations, equally simple, that would "save" an equally large but different set of my memories, so that memories that would be "false" according to the first set of generalizations would be "true" according to the second set, and vice versa? Just as the concept of a true account of reality, of how things are and have been, is different from the concept of how things seem *to me* to be and to have been, so also it is different from the concept of the simplest account consistent with most of *my* experiences, or with most of *my* memories. Yet the latter is just what my concept of reality would have to be if I could be entitled, without yet regarding what others say as relevant to the question of how things are and have been, to declare that certain of my memories are false because of other memories that I have, i.e., because they are incompatible with the simplest account that saves most of my memories. Unless I were willing in some circumstances to accept the utterances of other persons as memory claims, and as evidence concerning what has happened in the past (among other things, what has happened to *me* in the past), and were willing to do this without first having conducted an empirical investigation to determine whether I am ever entitled to do it, I would in effect be admitting no distinction between the way things are and the way they seem to me to be, and could therefore make no distinction between finding the appropriate correlations in the behavior of other persons and merely seeming to have found them.

10. In the beginning chapters of this book I tried to show how problems about self-knowledge have led philosophers to regard persons (or the minds of persons) as entities distinct from human bodies, and to question the apparent truism that selves are substances. Having discussed at some length the relation of the problem of self-knowledge to the mind-body problem, I shall now try to show how my conclusions bear on the traditional question of whether selves are substances.

As noted in Chapter One, some philosophers, notably Thomas Reid and Bishop Butler, have held that personal identity is "indefinable." [18] I have suggested that we might

_____
[18] Section 11.

express this as the view that there are no criteria of personal identity. And I think that I am now in a position to give an explanation of why philosophers have held this view. It has been commonly assumed that the criteria of personal identity, if there are any, must be criteria we use in making identity judgments about ourselves, and that the most important class of first-person identity judgments are the judgments we make about our own pasts on the basis of memory. But I have already argued at length, in Chapter Four, that judgments of the latter sort are not grounded on criteria of personal identity. I believe that Reid and Butler realized this fact, and that since they made the assumption just referred to it is quite understandable that they should have concluded that there are no criteria of personal identity and that personal identity is indefinable (or unanalyzable).

In Chapter Two I observed that one way in which we might attempt to make sense of the question whether selves are substances is by interpreting it in terms of the notion of analysis.[19] To hold that selves are substances on this interpretation is to hold that statements about selves are, at least in certain respects, *un*analyzable (or "fully analyzed"). And I think that foremost among the statements that any substance theorist would want to hold to be unanalyzable are statements of personal identity. As was pointed out in Chapter One, there is an inclination to say that if statements about the identity of Φ's are analyzable into statements that are not themselves identity statements (roughly, if the persistence of a Φ through time can be regarded as consisting in the occurrence of a succession of events or states, or in the successive existence of different momentarily existing things), then the identity of Φ's is not "real" or "genuine" identity. And I believe that anyone who says that selves are substances, and intends this to be more

---

[19] Section 7.

than a truism, will want to hold that the identity (persistence) of selves is "real" rather than "fictitious." Although hurricanes can be said to persist through time, and in a perfectly good sense are "subjects having properties," I doubt whether any traditional substance theorist would want to count hurricanes as persisting substances. There are doubtless many reasons for this, but surely one reason is that it is quite plausible to speak of the persistence of hurricanes (as it is not prima facie plausible to speak of the persistence of persons and ordinary material objects) as consisting simply in the successive occurrence of events related in certain ways. It is precisely in the case of such entities as hurricanes that it is natural to speak of identity (through time) as analyzable and fictitious, and this explains, at least in part, our disinclination to count such entities as substances. It is therefore not surprising that Reid and Butler, who insisted on the indefinability (or unanalyzability) of personal identity, also insisted that selves are substances. And a prima facie strong reason for claiming that selves are substances, where this claim is intended to assert more than the truism that selves can be said to persist and have properties, is what I take to have been Reid's and Butler's reason for holding that personal identity is indefinable, namely that we use no criteria of identity in making past-tense statements about ourselves on the basis of memory.

I have already argued, of course, that it does not follow from the fact that we *use* no criteria of identity in making memory statements that there *are* no criteria for the truth of such statements and the identity judgments implicit in them. And I have argued that in fact there are criteria. So Reid and Butler were mistaken if they reasoned along the lines indicated above.

What I have just said, however, can give no comfort to advocates of the logical construction theory of the self. In the first place, these theorists were apparently looking for an analysis of statements of personal identity in terms of the criteria which (they supposed) each person uses in making statements about his own identity on the basis of memory, and I have already argued that we use no criteria in making such statements. In the second place, I have not claimed, nor do I believe, that the criteria of personal identity we do use (in making other kinds of statements) are such as to enable us to give a reductive analysis of statements of personal identity, i.e., a translation of them into statements that are not identity statements and make no reference to persons.

But, in reference to the last point, it seems to me doubtful whether *any* of the entities of which we speak in ordinary life are such (or have concepts such) that it is possible to give a reductive analysis of identity statements about them. Possibly one could invent a concept such that there would be reductive criteria for the truth of identity statements involving that concept. But I believe that in the case of concepts actually in use, even such concepts as those of hurricanes and regiments (the identity of the latter being the favorite traditional example of "fictitious identity"), no such criteria in fact exist. It seems most unlikely that statements about hurricanes and regiments can be analyzed "without remainder" into, respectively, statements about individual weather phenomena (and their relations to one another) and statements about individual men (and their relations to one another). So if the claim that Φ's are substances is taken to mean simply (1) that Φ's can be said to have properties and persist through time, and (2) that there are no reductive criteria for the truth of statements (or at any rate identity statements) about Φ's, then even hurricanes will turn out to be substances.

This raises the question of whether there is, underlying the view that persons are substances while hurricanes are not (or that the identity of persons is "real" while that of hurricanes is "fictitious"), any important logical difference between the identity of persons and the identity of such things as hurricanes. If there is such a difference it is fairly unimportant whether we decide to mark it by the use of such terms as "substance," "real," and "fictitious"; all that matters is that the difference be such that we can see the naturalness of marking it in this way. I think that there is such a difference. I shall not attempt to *prove* this, for that a difference is "important," or that it is "natural" to mark a distinction in a certain way, is not something susceptible of proof. However, I shall attempt to indicate what I think this difference is, and how it is relevant to the traditional dispute as to whether selves are substances.

There is noncriterial knowledge of the identity (or persistence) of persons, namely that expressed in memory statements. So far as I can see, there is no noncriterial knowledge of the identity of such things as hurricanes. If all knowledge of personal identity were noncriterial, personal identity could be said to be indefinable in the sense that I believe was intended by Reid and Butler. This is of course not the case. However, it is not merely an accidental fact that there is noncriterial knowledge of personal identity; rather, it is essential and central to the notion of a person that there be such knowledge. For something to lack altogether the ability to have this kind of knowledge of itself would be for it to lack a kind of memory the possession of which seems essential to being a person, namely the ability to remember particular events and actions in the past. And if, for the idea (implicit in my interpretation of Reid and Butler) that Φ's are substances if and only if all "direct" knowledge of the identity of Φ's is noncriterial, we substitute the idea that Φ's are substances if and only if it is essential to the concept of a Φ that there be noncriterial knowledge of the identity of Φ's, then we can give sense to (and, using this as our criterion of substantiality, make true) the assertion that persons are substances while hurricanes are not.

As indicated in Chapter Five, there is a sense in which we have noncriterial knowledge of the identity of material objects.[20] For it can sometimes be directly observed, as opposed to being inferred, that a material object is, or is not, moving, and to say that a thing is, or is not, moving implies the persistence (the "continued identity") of that thing through time. And I think that the possibility of this kind of knowledge is essential to the concept we have of material objects. The ability to have this kind of knowledge seems clearly to be involved in the ability to know that a material object observed now is the same as one observed a while back on the basis of having watched it continuously between then and now. It is not clear whether the latter sort of knowledge should be classified as noncriterial or as based on criteria (spatiotemporal continuity); it seems to fall in between these classifications. But it seems clear that if we could not have this kind of knowledge of the identity of material objects our concept of material objects could not be what it is. So a case can be made, using the criterion of substantiality indicated above, for saying that persons and material objects are substances (that their identity is "real") and that entities like hurricanes are not substances (that their identity is "fictitious"). But a case can also be made for saying that the status of personal identity is different from, and in a sense more fundamental than, that of the identity of material objects. As I argued in Chapter Five, our ability to have noncriterial knowledge of the identity of material things, and the special status of spatiotemporal continuity as a criterion of the identity of material things, is dependent upon the fact that persons are spatiotemporally continuous entities that can know their own pasts without using spatiotemporal continuity (or anything else) as a criterion of identity. There is a sense,

[20] Section 11.

I have argued, in which each person regards his own successive positions as a standard or paradigm of a spatiotemporally continuous series of positions. And I am inclined to say that the identity (through time) of persons is the paradigm of genuine identity (through time). It would be perverse, after everything else I have written, for me to express this by saying that persons and only persons are substances, or that personal identity and only personal identity is genuine identity. But I hope that I have helped to make it understandable why some philosophers have wanted to say this.

Index

Index